GETTING A LIFE

To dear Arthur
Very best wishes
Tom
15/03/16

Published works:

The Boiled Frog Syndrome
A Sindrome do Sapo Cozido, published in Brazil
The Authentic Tarot
Health Hazards & EMFs, published Elsevier Ltd

getting a
life

an autobiography

thomas saunders

SilverWood

Published in 2014 by SilverWood Books

SilverWood Books Ltd
30 Queen Charlotte Street, Bristol, BS1 4HJ
www.silverwoodbooks.co.uk

ISBN 978-1-78132-277-2 (paperback)
ISBN 978-1-78132-278-9 (ebook)

British Library Cataloguing in Publication Data
A CIP catalogue record for this book is available from
the British Library

Set in Sabon by SilverWood Books
Printed on responsibly sourced paper

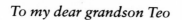

To my dear grandson Teo

Contents

Acknowledgements 9

Foreword 11

Introduction 13

Part I The Family 17

    1   The Early Years 19

    2   Mayfield School 39

    3   Student Days 47

    4   Marriage 58

Part II Thomas Saunders Chartered Architect 73

    5   Gainful Employment 75

    6   The Practice 87

    7   The Thomas Saunders Partnership 110

    8   'Retirement' 129

Part III Travel 135

    9   India 137

    10 The Amazon 152

    11 France 185

    12 Oceans of Pleasure 196

Part IV Metaphysics 211

    13 Occult Explorations 213

Part V The Return 249

    14 Janet 251

Epilogue 261

Appendices 265

    I   Moments of Music 267

    II   Random Writings 274

    III Blank Verse 294

    IV Additional Notes 308

    V   Relevant Dates 321

Acknowledgements

I have to thank my wife, Janet for her persistence that encouraged me to embark on the writing of these biographical recollections.

I must also thank all my family, friends, foes, detractors, cheats, acquaintances and the completely unknown strangers whom I have drawn into the orbit of my life: all these people, in some major or minor measure, have shaped the person I am today.

Foreword

Getting A Life

*Ordinary riches can be stolen, real riches cannot. In your soul
are infinitely precious things that cannot be taken from you.*

Oscar Wilde

There's a saying that I quite like: 'It's not how far you fall; it's how
high you bounce'. We are all going to take a fall at some stage in
our lives and rather than wallow in despair we could do no better
than to look more closely at the life of Thomas Saunders: a master
of reinvention who found the courage to pay attention to what his
intuition was telling him. He bounced back many times.

One wonders what would have happened had Thomas not realised
that he had 'reached the top of the ladder, but that the ladder was
leaning against the wrong wall'. Probably not very much. He would
have been financially and materially successful, possibly moderately
content.

Instead, he has found that it is possible to do what we all say
we want to do. He has spent a lifetime following his passions and,
importantly, earning a living by doing things that he loves. He has
rebuilt and reinvented himself several times along the way and made
time to be curious. How many architects do you meet that have
travelled 1500 miles into the Amazon; lived in the Arctic with the
Inuits; sailed the Atlantic; and followed a personal quest, taking in
healing, dowsing, the wisdom of the Tarot and myths, the study
of ancient symbolism, sacred geometry and the healing powers of
buildings? The simple answer is that you just don't meet many people
like that – architects or otherwise.

Thomas is an ordinary person who has led an extraordinary life.
He epitomised the 'classless society' and 'social mobility' even before

it was a glimmer in an Oxbridge-educated politician's eye.

His story gives us hope that, regardless of our origins or the disadvantages our early life may present us with, consistent hard work, focus and drive can take us anywhere we want to go. It also offers us a cautionary note that comes with the benefit of hindsight. If we fail to take care of our spirit and inner voice, our hard work, focus and drive can take us in the wrong direction.

There is much research now that says that curious people live longer, are happier, enjoy more meaningful relationships, find more opportunity, and find small pockets of meaning in their everyday lives. On all of those measures Thomas Saunders appears to be a very curious man indeed. I can pay him no greater compliment than that.

It's interesting that many of his adventures feature global corporate boardrooms, rainforests, oceans, and Arctic tundra. These are the kinds of things that we associate with adventurers. Yet some of his greatest adventures, his understanding of who he is and his study of the Tarot, have taken place largely inside his head. He gives us further hope that whoever we are, wherever we are, regardless of our resources, our minds can take us on the greatest of adventures.

At the time of writing, he is an octogenarian, brimming with vitality, awash with wonder and oozing his gentle wisdom. You only have to be in his presence for a short time to realise that this is a story that is by no means over. There is still time for many more adventures.

Malcolm McClean
Founder, The School of Curiosity

Introduction

On reflection, my life has been an eternal quest to answer the perennial questions: *Who am I? Why am I here? What is my destiny?*

This book is about that quest.

In 1961, aged twenty-eight, I set up a practice from my little back bedroom. Twenty-one years later it had become one of the most successful international firms of architects in London. The twenty-first anniversary of The Thomas Saunders Partnership (TTSP) was celebrated in the Plaisterers' Hall in the City of London.

The more the practice developed, the less I was a hands-on practising architect. Instead, my role had become that of a PR *'meeter and joiner'*, writing articles and giving interviews to the architectural media, and a general prospector for more business in the UK and abroad. Surely, I asked myself, there should be more purpose to my role than simply being the titular head, meeting and greeting clients and presenting the prizes on golf days.

After the ceremony, I gave the partners the required two years' notice that I would leave the practice and sever all financial and contractual ties.

Undoubtedly the work of the American philosopher Joseph Campbell was a major influence on my decision. He said: "The real killer in life is when you find yourself at the top of the ladder and realise it is leaning against the wrong wall". The 'wrong wall' represents a lifetime spent on acquiring material wealth to overcome our insecurities and the fear of our own mortality without taking care of our spiritual self.

As the founder and senior partner, the creation and development of the practice was undoubtedly an achievement, and yet I had begun to feel restless and unfulfilled. No one knew that for some time there had been a compulsion to respond to my quiet inner voice – gut feelings, intuition, whatever you want to call it – and embark once more on a journey to...wherever!

On the positive side, I had travelled extensively, both on TTSP business and on holidays. Visits to India, Brazil, North America, the Middle East, Europe, Japan and East Africa had transformed my outlook and opened my mind to the interrelatedness of all things in life and our common bond with nature, art and architecture. The buildings led me to discover the underlying, esoteric – *sacred*, if you will – design and structure based on the fundamental principles of harmonic ratios, musical intervals and proportional volumes. These principles determine the architectural geometry which resonate with the same harmonic ratios and proportions in our body. Sadly, my fellow partners resisted my attempts to incorporate this perennial philosophy and ancient teachings into our design concepts which were later included in my book, *The Boiled Frog Syndrome*.

The experiences and explorations of the outer world drew me to seek other, wider fields of the inner, esoteric world and to balance my material world with an endeavour and understanding of the occult (hidden) realms. With hindsight, it is clear to me that my travels to the Amazon and Arctic, my ocean sailing, and my excursions into the metaphysical world were the classic, archetypal journeys of the mythical hero. My diary notes show that for a fairly long period there were plans and ambitions formulating at the back of my mind to establish myself as a writer and explore the esoteric mysteries of architectural design.

My work and research flourished for the next seven years until I carried out a certain property development which failed when the market collapsed. I lost every penny, including my multi-million pound house in Cheyne Walk, Chelsea. Kind friends let me have a small flat and offered me 'street money' and the use of a telephone to start to rebuild my life.

At the same time that I lost a fortune, I found the love and greatest blessing of my life. I met Janet who, seven years later, became my wife. Eventually we moved from London to live in the South of France, and recently returned to our London roots.

Four years ago, in 2010, I was looking forward to gearing myself up for the fourth rewrite of a novel I had begun over thirty years earlier and had wrestled with ever since. (Even the great literary master Tolstoy rewrote *War and Peace* seven times!) It had not crossed my mind that 2011 would mark the anniversary of the practice I had founded fifty years before until Tim Jennings, who is now the current MD of The Thomas Saunders Partnership, telephoned me to say he intended to organise a big celebration. He asked if I could give him a few brief notes on the early period from 1961 until he joined the practice at about the time I was leaving in 1984.

These 'brief notes' interrupted my 'war' and not too much 'peace' with the novel rewrite and became an extended mini-history that included the turns of fate, events and meaningful coincidences that led to my setting up on my own.

When Janet read the fourteen pages, she encouraged me to write the full story that spanned the eighty years of my life. Further encouragement came from my friend and mentor John Baldock, an erudite man of wisdom and renowned author of books on traditions and mysticism. In the Foreword to my book *The Authentic Tarot* he wrote:

> We all have in us a book to write...[Yet] in reality we are already writing...the book of our life [and] have been writing it ever since we came into this world... But for these disparate elements to have meaning we need to string them together...until they form a coherent story...[when] we may begin to find certain recurring patterns [and] insights into hitherto unacknowledged aspects of ourselves... Once we realise that it is we who create these underlying patterns, we have a choice [to] either continue to live our lives just as before, or...use our increased understanding as a means of discarding those aspects of ourselves which impede our personal growth.

At first I resisted writing more than a few anecdotal pieces until, while rummaging through old personal papers, I rediscovered a number of box files filled with brochures, essays, diaries and copies of letters. There was also a notebook of early morning jottings referred to in the text as 'Dawn Notes'. Often, these writings, begun in about 1974, were contrived – in the sense that they were not addressed to anyone in particular. Many were written in foreign hotel bedrooms during some of my lone business trips that sometimes lasted four or five weeks.

The pieces helped me maintain contact with friends and family, and they also acted as a sort of diary, which through introspection helped to put my life into perspective. Unexpectedly, I found a letter, dated November 1976, where I had written that I had it in the back of my mind to write a book one day but that I soon realised I was far too young to write memoirs!

The encouragements to continue were reinforced by my own feeling that most of us would like to discover more about our family tree and the lives and times of those who have gone before us.[1]

---

1 In S.A. Nigosian's book, *The Zoroastrian Faith*: 'They say concerning the same Adurbad [The chief diety of Zoroastrianism, creator of the world, the source of light, also called Ohrmazd] that he said: Every person ought to know: "Where have I come from? For what purpose am I here? Where do I return?" I, for my part, know that I come from Ohrmazd the Lord, that I am here so as to make the demons powerless, and that I shall return to Ohrmazd.'

PART I

The Family

1

The Early Years

1932–1946

My Grandparents

The most serene memory of my early childhood is the faint image I have of being suckled at my mother's breast. Soon after my birth in May 1932 my family – mother Cissy (Frances), father Joe (Josiah), and sister June – moved from a flat in London's East End to a rented house in Windsor Road, Ilford, Essex. That way we could be near my grandparents and my father's siblings – two sisters and four brothers – who all lived within a mile or so of each other.

Granddad Tom and Grandma Charlotte lived in a narrow-fronted Victorian cottage in a long line of identical terraced houses in Uphall Road. On the right of the dark, pinched hallway and narrow staircase was the door to the front parlour. Until the 1950s, most front rooms in suburban houses were reserved for Sunday afternoons, special occasions such as Christmas, and the laying out of the dead before a funeral. My grandparents' parlour was crammed with a polished mahogany chiffonier with shelves and a mirror, a sofa, and two bulky armchairs in blue moquette, a low side table that took up most of the space and a black cast iron fire surround and brass fender.

The door at the end of the hall led to the all-purpose living room at the back. Here, the scrubbed pine dining table was usually covered with a soft brown velveteen cloth which was folded away at mealtimes; heavy varnish-backed chairs, wedged between the door from the hall and the green-ledged, braced and battened door to the scullery; and two armchairs, one each side of the fire. The fireplace had a glazed tile surround, iron fender, and a black iron kettle, permanently hissing on the fire, ready for tea-making at any time of day.

To get into the room you had to squeeze between the table on one side at the back of the room and the sideboard with drawers for cutlery, cupboards for plates, and Grandma's needlework box. A fruit bowl, a biscuit barrel, some faded sepia photos and other oddments were neatly lined up along a white lace runner. Through the tall sash window, the bulk of the gasometer on the other side of the River Roding dominated the view.

Two steps down from the living room was a flagged stone floor scullery where the gloss-painted creamy walls contrasted with the eau de Nil green colour of the walk-in larder door and the cupboards under a timber bench that housed a shallow stone butler sink, wooden drainer and black iron cooking stove. A latched, battened door opened out to the backyard where my grandparents kept a dozen hens. There was an all-pervasive acrid smell from the nearby gasworks and the droppings in the chicken run. Stout wood palings fenced off the row of backyards from the embankment to the River Roding, which marks the border between Essex and the County of London.

The only lavatory was outside in the backyard. Next to its green door the tin bath which hung on a nail in the wall was brought into the scullery every Friday and filled with kettles and saucepans of hot water for the household bath-night routine. The first users refilled the kettles to top up the hot water for those coming last.

Two of my father's aunts also lived in the house: Granddad's fragile sister Naomi, who came back to London in the 1930s after living forty years in Santa Barbara where she survived the great earthquake; and Grandma's spinster sister Annie, a devout member of the Salvation Army who always seemed to be dressed in black uniform and bonnet – even indoors. They had joined the household after the children had grown up and left.

It is difficult to contemplate how Tom and Charlotte ever managed in such a cramped cottage, to bring up their seven children plus one or two family orphans, two cats, and Bengie, their Alsatian dog. The house could never have been empty for more than an hour or so for several decades. They must have learned peace, tolerance and severity the hard way over the years.

I know little about Tom's family other than that he was from the poor side. Other Saunders included a brother, or it could have been a cousin, who was a high-ranking officer in charge of the Tower of London in the First World War, and a relative in the Indian Army who came back to London in the 1950s with his Indian wife and daughters so he could see out his last days in England.

Most Sundays, and certainly every Christmas, the whole Saunders family of uncles, aunts and cousins, would congregate and somehow cramp ourselves into the Uphall Road house. I have another serene image from those early days: walking hand-in-hand with Granddad to fetch a jug of porter at the Papermakers Arms while Sunday lunch was cooking. However many turned up for the family Sunday lunch ritual, we managed to squeeze round the table, all eyes watching Granddad sharpen his carving knife and slice up the roast rib of beef. While he did so one of the men eked out the jug of porter and another passed round the gravy. Grandma and my mother or one or two of my aunts served the roast potatoes and greens.

My only memories of Grandma are her dressed in black, sitting by the fireside with its steaming kettle, darning woollen socks and sewing on buttons. Her serene presence belied a formidable strength of will and the unstinting love and comfort she gave to her children and grandchildren. According to my mother, however, whenever Granddad reprimanded any one of them she would unfailingly offer him her loyalty and support – at least in front of others.

Granddad had the bulk, sinew and muscle of a man who had worked manually all his life but his soft, smiling face gave him the air of a tender, benign giant. There was a deep scar across his shiny bald head that marked a Boer War wound. I can only remember him wearing an off-white flannel shirt, its attachable collar discarded but the brass collar stud with its blackened ivory veins left loose in the top buttonhole. The cuffs of the rough shirt were rolled up just above his thick hairy wrists, and the sleeves tucked up above his elbows with elasticised arm bands. His khaki and leather braces were probably old army issue, as was his wide, well-worn leather belt with brass buckle, wrapped around his waist a few inches below the top of his trousers.

I felt completely secure and loved by Granddad, and can remember being jogged up and down on his knee to a rhyme that went something like "...little Tommy tittle mouse lived in a little house..." Granddad had insisted that I be called Tom, after himself and his eldest son, although my mother had wanted to call me Jack. But with the exception of one male cousin who was about ten years older, all my other cousins were girls, so she went with Tom.

Much later in her life my mother often talked with great love and affection about Granddad, his gift of fairness and his ability to settle family quarrels. She admitted he was the only person from whom she could accept being told that she was in the wrong. Other members of the family have confirmed that he did indeed have the judgement and rough wisdom that could calm my mother's frequent outbursts of paranoia over the most trivial of matters that could otherwise be exploded into a full scale persecution.

Granddad had to be strong and tough to keep his family together, especially his five tearaway sons. He had spent several years away serving in the Boer War, and most likely had served in the First World War also, alongside his sons Tom and Sid. As soon as my father reached sixteen, in 1916, he decided that he too would join his older brothers fighting in the trenches in Flanders. His younger brothers, Billy and Teddy, were too young to go to war.

My granddad stoked boilers at the photographic film factory, Ilford Films Limited, which produced film for air reconnaissance, where his eldest son, my uncle Tom, also worked, as a packer. I remember its tall boundary wall, at one end of which was the pub. On the other side of the road, and behind another high gaunt wall, was the Plessey factory where they produced RADAR and other equipment and military instruments. During the war both factories were strategic targets, continually attacked by the Luftwaffe.

I was seven years old when the war started and can remember my father and Uncle Sid digging the hole for the underground corrugated steel Anderson air raid shelter at the end of Grandma's yard. I tried to help them dig a pit in our back garden too, six feet by ten and about five feet deep. People who did not have a garden were given a reinforced steel table called a Morrison shelter to crawl under during an air raid.

When the Second World War was declared, Uncle Teddy was drafted into the RAF; Uncle Billy was deemed to be doing essential war work in food distribution; and my other uncles, Tom and Sid, and my father joined the Home Guard. Sid was in the same platoon as Father, who was promoted sergeant and rode around his patrols on a bike with a 303 rifle and bayonet slung over his shoulder. Sid was in charge of the fireworks used in training to simulate battlefield conditions. Their antics and stories were no different or less hilarious than those scenes in the *Dad's Army* TV series.

Not long before the war, in about 1936, when I was four years old, Granddad died suddenly of peritonitis. I can still remember vividly the family's shock, deep trauma and prolonged sadness after his death.

My Parents

My mother Cissy was born in 1902. Her father, Walter Baxter, died when she was a young child. Her mother was a midwife in the East End working all hours of the day and night, which usually left little Cissy sitting outside on the doorstep waiting for her mother to return. Cissy's life became more lonely and difficult when her mother remarried a widower who had a son and two daughters of about the same age. Her step-siblings treated her badly (and having met them briefly a few times over the years I could well understood why she had a hard time with them). It was only much later that Mother told me about the way they had treated her. She carried these girlhood wounds for the rest of her life, scars which must have helped to strengthen her habitual fortitude and independence.

She met my father Joe when she was in her early teens, and from then on spent more time with the Saunders family than with her own. According to my mother, Joe was the brightest of the family. Although his school days had ended at the age of eleven he could rattle through moderately difficult crossword puzzles: his extraordinary vocabulary must have been gleaned from his reading of paperback cowboy westerns, gangster books, and newspapers. While he was still at school, an inspector from the Royal Mail visited my grandmother, hoping young Joe would join the post office management training scheme. It was an opportunity only offered to talented boys but Joe was not interested. I have no idea what he did between leaving school until he was sixteen, but like many other young boys he lied about his birth date in order to join the army in 1916, to be alongside his elder brothers in France. He was promoted to corporal and trained to be a sniper.

While Joe was in the trenches, Cissy worked in the local munitions factory. Somehow she managed to save five shillings (twelve pence) a week to pay for an upright piano and taught herself to play even though she could not read a note of music. Later in life she was always welcome at Christmas and other family parties because she could play by ear all the popular songs on the radio.

At some point, Mother's stepfather died when she decided it was her duty to take care of her widowed mother. This led to a frustratingly long courtship with my father because she believed it was wrong to be married while having to live in the same flat as her mother. They married eventually, in about 1926, once her mother had died. June was born in 1928 and I arrived four years later.

Two years after the war had ended, Father began work as a porter in Stratford's East London wholesale market, a job he kept until the Great Depression in 1928 when he was made redundant. He got a bricklaying job on the Dagenham estate, building houses for the new Ford car factory on the Thames until he found another job in the wholesale fruit and vegetable Borough Market in Southwark where he was employed as a porter by Marshall and Masters (later promoted to salesman). He worked there for the next twenty-five years.

Windsor Road, 1932–1942

Apart from the first few months of my life, the next ten years were spent at a rented late-Victorian, end-of-terrace house in Windsor Road, Ilford. Inside it was dark and gloomy and, like Granddad's house, was painted either a yellowy cream or green. The small back bedroom had been converted into a bathroom; the outside lavatory was hardly ever used.

It was not a happy home. Well before the real war started with Germany, there was another 'war' going on between Mother and Father. Once, the fight was so frightening that I ran into the street calling for a policeman. In between the arguments an uneasy truce reigned, and it was in these times that they would meet up after Father had finished work in the market and go to a West End cinema or a show at the Palladium – his favourite theatre – while Salvation Army Aunt Annie looked after June and me.

Sunday mornings were the best times as this was when either Uncle Sid or Uncle Teddy came to see us. They always seemed to be smiling and enjoying life, despite the war. Through these early years, whenever I needed to escape the frequent arguments and uproar at home (probably due to Father's mid-life crisis and Mother's post-menopause stress) I would walk to either Uncle Sid's or Uncle Teddy's home to be with their family fun and laughter. Of course, the wartime, and especially the two years of the Blitz when every night we slept in the air raid shelter, was frightening but life in general was downright miserable.

Occasionally I played with the other kids in the street. Once, one of them invited me into his house when it was raining: I remember thinking that their hall and living room floors, covered in shiny bare red-and-green patterned lino, were horrible. I knew then that I did not want to have to live on cold lino or be one of the kids with poverty scarred across my face.

Most times I played soldiers in the garden, charging over the air raid shelter with a wooden gun, bayoneting it against the elm paling fence, under the long avenue of elm trees that separated Windsor Road from the houses at the back. I made friends with Tommy Arthur, who lived on the other side of the fence and was about four years older than me. Squatting under the line of towering trees, he told me enthralling exotic tales about his brother who had emigrated to Australia and killed giant snakes and other dangerous animals. Eventually, Tommy wanted me to watch him masturbate and I can still vaguely recall the pungent smell. All this was going on before I was ten years old! I cannot recall whether I gave him a helping hand but I know I was getting wet dreams at this time.

Our next door neighbours, Mr and Mrs Clements, would chat to my father at weekends about the tomatoes and vegetables they had planted in the garden to help *dig for victory*. Clem was a tall man with glasses who sucked on a pipe, even when talking. Mrs Clements, always dressed in a floral wraparound apron, was a wizened, slight woman with a brown nicotine smear across her top lip, stained from chain smoking cigarettes. Next-door-but-one lived Mrs Allen who had a tribe of grown-up children and occasionally gave June and me a plate of the most delicious chips fried in oil: better than Mother's home-cooked chips fried in lard or those from the fish and chip shop.

Evacuation to Wales, March–October 1939

About a year before the war started, everyone was preparing for the worst, mainly because many Londoners could still remember being bombed by Zeppelins twenty years earlier. When Hitler invaded Czechoslovakia in March 1939, war became inevitable.

A government official instructed my grandma to provide accommodation for Erik Alcock, a young Welshman from Ebbw Vale, who was to be drafted for essential war work at Ilford Films Limited. Eric, she was told, would be billeted with her for the duration of the war. This sparked a Saunders family decision to evacuate all the young grandchildren to Ebbw Vale, which made us among the first of the general exodus of young Londoners to safer parts of the country. So, in March 1939, even before the war had started, we were packed off to Eric's remote rural village where June and I found ourselves living with his devoutly religious parents.

Eric's father owned a small opencast mine on the side of a barren mountain, a fair distance from the village. Close to the mine he had built a terrace of six cramped cottages, with six outside lavatories tacked on the far end of the block. The lavatories had no running water so, to use the toilet allocated to the Alcocks, we had to struggle past the five other cottages with a pail of water.

The cottage was as bleak and foreboding as the way the Alcocks dressed. Every night at 6.30 sharp, before we made our way to bed past the oversized and rarely played organ squeezed at the foot of a winding stone stair, we were obliged to kiss Mr Alcock goodnight. As soon as we approached him at the table he took a gulp from his pint mug of cold tea, which left our faces wet from drips on his bushy moustache. Friday nights were laxative nights whether we needed it or not.

At seven every morning we were woken by the delicious smell of Welsh rarebit wafting from next door and a clattering noise as the brothers set off with their pony and cart to go totting in Abergavenny. One evening they came back in a state of agitation – they had actually seen a black man in the town! Strangers weren't easily accepted, and the Welsh kids at school treated us badly. We were called Limeys and if June wasn't around to defend me and my younger cousins, we were frequently bullied.

Six months of hostilities in Wales could not be worse than wartime in London. We were homesick, lonely, unhappy and tired of the constant harassment at school, as well as the daily trudge up and down the steep hillside to the village. But our luck was in: in October 1939, ironically just as the war actually started, June and I returned home to the 'smoke' in Ilford, joined soon afterwards by our cousins.

Wartime London, 1939–1945

When the so-called 'phoney war' ended and the real war started, the government removed everybody's cast iron railings and gates to be melted down to make munitions. A few months later when the Blitz began, the schools in London were closed and lessons had to carry on in neighbours' houses.

Nights were spent underground in the garden shelter. The deafening noises from the mobile anti-aircraft guns in the streets and the blast of exploding bombs made it difficult to sleep. Our Dalmatian dog had to be left in the house while we were in the shelter and the poor animal kept scratching out the stuffing from the back of the armchairs, trying to bury his head to shut out the noise. After a few weeks, he had to be put down.

On several occasions, air raid wardens ran around the streets blowing their whistles to get people out of the shelters and into the nearby evacuation centres while the bomb disposal men defused an unexploded bomb or parachuted land mine, or until they had managed to extinguish incendiary fire bombs. Father, wearing his Home Guard issue steel helmet often kept watch outside the shelter, waving the bombers away – we knew that if they were directly overhead, the bombs would not fall on us. Whenever the all-clear siren sounded, we crept out of the shelters not knowing if the house was still standing. Sometimes, in the early dawn, we could still see fires glowing from the bombardment of London's docks and East End.

When I was about nine years old, there was a moment that became deeply buried in my mind: the worst of the Blitz was over when my cousin Lenny (Sid's eldest son) and his wife Vera came to visit us when he was home on leave. We all went out walking in the early evening. While my parents walked slowly with my sister June, who was not well at the time, I went ahead, hand-in-hand between Lenny and Vera. When we stopped outside our house, waiting for the others to catch up, I watched Lenny draw Vera to him and give her a lingering kiss. That moment was vividly imprinted on my psyche, because with it came the sudden sense that no one would ever love me. What I saw and felt was to define the next fifty years of my life. The first time I became consciously aware of this memory, and realised how deeply the incident had permeated and influenced my life, was after I had met Janet and experienced what it meant to love and to be loved.

By 1942, the mass air attacks reduced to hit-and-run nuisance raids. We no longer had to spend every night in the underground garden shelter. One morning at about seven o'clock, when Father was already at work in the market and Mother, June and I were still asleep, I was suddenly jolted awake with the loud drone of a low-flying plane, the staccato rattle of machine gun fire, followed by a violent shock wave explosion. There had been no air raid warning.

The house shuddered violently as the air blast sucked out windows and shattered plaster ceilings, rafters and roof tiles. In our beds, we were covered in plaster and shards of glass. Mother came running into our bedrooms. There was a stunned silence as the dust and debris settled around us. It turned out that the only cuts and bruises any of us had were the lacerations on Mother's feet sustained from running over the broken glass.

The bomb had dropped two houses away, killing all three inside. In the street, survivors screamed for help; the wardens rushed to the scene, dragging people out of the rubble. Our roof had been ripped off and the walls so badly damaged that the house was virtually uninhabitable. When Father arrived we salvaged whatever we could and moved in with Grandma for a few months. Despite our pleading, Mother refused to come with us – whether from the stress and trauma of the bomb or her strong dislike of Grandma I do not know. She stayed camped out in the semi-ruins until the day we moved to Chadwell Heath, seven miles away, to a house my father bought from one of his market friends.

At the time, Chadwell Heath was a little town with trees, green fields, cows, a park, and newly built houses. It was a complete contrast to Ilford and London's East End, and for the rest of the war, only occasionally we had to sleep in the shelter when the air raid warning sounded.

On the morning of D-Day, we stood in awe in the back garden watching the black cloud of allied bombers flying in their thousands over the house. In the deafening roar of the planes, everyone could sense we were beginning to win the war.

Only a week later, however, after an air raid siren sounded, we sat in the shelter listening to a thudding, pulsing sound. Not the familiar throbbing drone of a German bomber. Father put on his steel helmet, scrambled out, and saw a jet of bright orange flame streaking from the tail of the plane: the first time any of us had seen the V-1 flying bomb, something akin to a frightening science fiction weapon. A few minutes later there was silence, then a loud, crunching explosion.

We quickly learned that so long as you could hear it coming towards you, you knew you were safe. The terrifying time was not knowing how close you were to the plane when the engine cut out and the bomb dropped to the ground. Over 2000 flying bombs landed in London, killing many thousands.

But they weren't to be the worst. At least you could hear them coming. Later, in September 1944, the first V-2 rockets rained down on London, more than 1000 of them, and these could neither be seen nor heard. Air raid shelters were useless. We know now, after the post-war release of classified film and documents, that the D-Day allied invasion of France came not a moment too soon: in addition to the V-1 and V-2 terror weapons, a V-3 super gun on the French coast was already assembled and ready to bombard England; Von Braun was close to building a bigger V-2 intercontinental ballistic missile; jet-propelled fighter aircraft were already in production; and nuclear weapon know-how was well advanced. If Hitler had not continually ignored the advice of his generals, the outcome of the war could have been very different, and the world would not be as it is today.

Close to my thirteenth birthday, in May 1945, I was woken in the morning to laughter and singing in the street: the war in Europe was over – we had survived!

Father at Work

When I was about six years old, I remember going to a sports track – it might have been Crystal Palace – for the London Markets' sports day. I watched Father compete in the basket race, where a dozen or so porters had to run carrying seven or eight round wicker baskets balanced on their head.

In those days in the market, there were no fork-lift trucks: everything had to be carried either in a basket on the porter's head or on a barrow. My father's habit of carrying a heavy bag of fruit and vegetables on his head was never lost, and every Saturday and Wednesday he walked from Chadwell Heath train station to home with his cotchall (cockney for 'catch all'). The tradition in the markets was for the retail greengrocer customers not to give the porters a tip, instead, they accepted that twice a week their boxes of apples or sacks of spring greens, or whatever was in season, would be slightly underweight. The porters and salesmen would take just enough fresh food for their own family's consumption for the next three days until 'cotchall day' came around again.

Sometimes, making his way across London Bridge to Liverpool Street Station, Father would call in on his mates in the old Billingsgate fish market to trade a cucumber, a few tomatoes or some fruit in exchange for a crab or skate. At other times one of his local customers might drop off a sack of potatoes or a bushel of shallots for pickling at home.

From Father I learned how to clean and dress a crab and when mussels are in season how to keep them in a large bucket of fresh water and oatmeal for a couple of days to plump them up and clean out the gunge. Fresh walnuts in October were another treat. In the season, he would sit for hours peeling a whole bushel of shallots without ever shedding a tear. They were stuffed into large pickling jars with vinegar, peppers and spices and kept for Christmas and the following year.

I remember so well the few times I went on the train to meet him at the market, ever hopeful that I would see the Tower Bridge lift up as I walked across London Bridge – but it never did! The Marshall and Masters stand was a like a deep garage and basement, stacked with large sacks of cabbages and potatoes waiting to be sold to the retail greengrocers or the old women in black dresses who shelled peas and trimmed sprouts for the West End restaurants.

The 'office', not much bigger than one of the old telephone kiosks, had a wooden lock-up desk and a stable door. One day, one of Father's mates came on to the stand swearing vehemently, using the F- and C-word expletives that at that time were rarely heard. It had to do with something that had just happened in the street. Suddenly, when he saw me, a young teenager perched on the high stool, he apologised profusely to my father: "Joe, I'm so sorry mate. I had no idea the lad was here." No doubt the market language was as 'blue' as it is now, but I never heard my father swear except for the occasional exasperated 'bloody' or 'bugger'.

The markets opened at four in the morning and by eleven o'clock the stands were closed for business and the retail greengrocer customers would be on their way back to their shops. Several afternoons a week Father went to the Loxford Club in Ilford to play cards and snooker. There he won several silver cups (and bets on the side). He also won medals playing in the football league for Ilford Town in the winter, and cricket in the summer.

Mother's forthright drive and pent-up ambition had to be transmitted to June and me because it was lost on my easy-going father who only wanted the sporting life. With his working day finished by 11.30am, or soon after midday, he could see all the sporting events, especially football (which before the advent of floodlighting had to be played in the afternoon) and cricket, or play snooker and cards at the club. Most market men are sport crazy and my non-academic education was largely concentrated on how to pot a red and screw the cue ball back down to the end of the table to pot the black. I never took to the game – it was too cerebral and there was no one to hit the ball back! I could hold my own at most card games, however, and knew the current soccer and boxing stars who worked part-time in the market.

Outside the home Father was a happy-go-lucky, smiling, whistling man, always ready to crack a joke. When we were young he taught June and me to swim at the local baths in Ilford, and when I was a student, I skived off college once or twice to go with him to a Wednesday afternoon international football match (this was before games were played in the evening). On occasional Saturdays we stood in the Chicken Run at West Ham with my uncle Sid, and once we went to the Oval to watch the Len Hutton test match with Australia.

Father's active sport was snooker and I enjoyed watching him play in tournaments at his club. His well-trained sniper's sight had been impaired in 1940 after he was ill with pneumonia, which affected his ability to focus for longer than a second or two. As a result, when it was his turn to play he would stand at the table, eyeing the lay of the balls before making his shot in one quick movement, and without appearing to take aim. Every ball was hit with such speed that it sounded like a gun going off. I think he was disappointed that I was so hopeless at snooker, but I've always liked it as a spectator sport, as did Mother.

Father had a cherubic face, a great sense of humour and loved telling jokes. Every day except Sundays, he had to be up and dressed by 3.30am in the morning to catch the first special cheap fare workmen's train. By 8pm at night he was shaved, tucked up in bed and asleep. Once he was promoted to salesman he wore a three-piece suit, which he laid out in the bedroom with his socks, a clean white stiff collar and knotted tie. In bed he kept on his underwear – long johns combinations in winter – and white shirt: perhaps a throwback to his childhood days when they served as pyjamas. In the morning, when the alarm sounded, he would leap out of bed, rinse his face in cold water, put on the collar and tie and pull on his suit and boots, ready to walk to the station or get a lift from one of his market mates. He never owned a car or had a driving licence. (His first TV set was one his mate had discarded for a new model, and neither he nor Mother ever possessed a refrigerator, washing machine or vacuum cleaner.)

Father always enjoyed trying to croon Bing Crosby-type songs and, from time to time, in a frivolous mood, usually just before going bed, on hearing music from June's gramophone, he would come down after taking the weekly bath wearing his clean long johns and shirt and prance through the living room door, making exaggerated ballet movements. These rare, hilarious performances were strictly reserved for the family. I wonder if, perhaps, he felt the need to joke about something he had great feeling for.

We all had to endure long periods when either Mother was not speaking to us or she was in uproar. I know my father craved a quiet life. The calmest times were when we were playing cards at home on the weekends. Perhaps his tendency to appease, to not rock the boat, and wanting to be well liked came from being the middle child of seven. I know, because he told me, that he thought I was being too ambitious wanting to be an architect. I felt I could never wholly please him, even when I was picked to play football for Essex schoolboys. He died before I set up my own practice but I remember looking up at the sky when I landed a big contract, saying, "What about that then?"

In my mind, he said, "Hmm... It's alright."

Mother at Home

Despite Mother's periods of uproar, as a sport crazy man my father could not have wished for a better 'mate'. These days it is not unusual to see women at a football or cricket match or watching live snooker and darts but before the 1960s it was rare to find a woman standing on the terraces at West Ham United, the East London team the Saunders family supported. My mother would stand with my father and his brothers on the rough boards of the so-called 'chicken run', packed tight with avid, loud, foul-mouthed fans. She understood all the finer points of the game, followed the fortunes of the various teams, knew the names of the sport's stars, had her own set views on which clubs or players were good sports and those who played dirty, and was appalled whenever a footballer changed clubs because it showed no sense of loyalty.

Our house in Chadwell Heath was just four houses away from the sports ground where the West Ham team trained and where, every Saturday and Sunday, amateur football and cricket matches were played. When Father died, my mother stopped going to see West Ham, but she spent hours in the back bedroom watching the games played on the sports ground. There was just one occasion, when she was seventy-six, when one of her neighbours took her to see a live game under floodlights for the first time in her life.

Like my father, Mother was a very good card player. Her favourite game was Solo – otherwise known as Poor Man's Bridge. On Saturday or Sunday evenings, as soon as my hands were big enough to hold thirteen cards I would make up a four with my sister June to play Solo. I also learned to play Cribbage with my dad. Sometimes we had a music soirée: mother on the piano with June singing (she sang like the Hollywood star Diana Durbin), while I scratched out a tune on the violin. (I had started to learn when I was seven but when the war started the lessons were cancelled.) Both my parents loved the cinema and the variety theatre, with its comics, conjurers, magicians, singers, dancers and novelty acts.

My mother never used any form of cosmetics except Yardley's lavender talcum powder on her feet and under her arms. Clothes and fashion were of no interest to her and the only jewellery she wore were a gold watch and her wedding and engagement rings. She frowned upon women like Uncle Teddy's wife, Flossy, who was always smart and well made-up. She had never been schooled in those arts by her own mother, and so my sister June learned nothing from her either. However, Mother was sexually well-charged. There were periods, despite my parents' rows, when I was woken up by the sound of grunting and grinding, the headboard banging against the bedroom wall next to where I slept. Unfortunately for the rest of us, my mother's sensuality was kept to their bedroom, because her cooking could only be described as frugal. Garlic, olive oil, vinaigrettes, spices and black pepper were not in the compass of British cooking in those days: sauces were either brown HP or Heinz tomato and the only dressings were Sarson's malt vinegar and salad cream.

She never had to go shopping for food because Father brought home fruit and vegetables and occasionally, fish from the markets. June and I did all the other shopping for household goods, meat, or fish and chips. Father never cooked, but enjoyed peeling potatoes, shelling peas, pickling onions and cleaning crabs and mussels.

Mother's poor efforts in the kitchen must, out of necessity, have stimulated my interest in food and cooking. I remember those times, impatient for Saturday lunch to be cooked so that I could go out to play football. When I tentatively opened the kitchen door to ask how long it would be she would shout "Get out!" through the clouds of steam. She would be so flustered with the whole business of cooking that she never wanted anyone to see what was going on. Sometimes she wasn't available to cook for us at all: if someone was ill, Mother would nurse them night and day, sometimes leaving us for several days to look after ourselves.

It was hard being around my mother. The slightest turn of phrase or action could be interpreted as being unacceptable, and often unforgivable. Consequently, we could never be certain who was in or out of favour. Opinion was always divided on her merits: either Cissy was a saint or a tyrant.

One day, when I was about fourteen, I went to see our doctor about it. He told me that it was futile to argue or try to rationalise with her. It was better to keep out of her range until the storm passed. This helped me to understand why my father would stoically sit in despair with his head in his hands. Everyone in the Saunders family felt sorry for him; behind his back he was generally known as 'poor old Joe'.

At the time I could only see that June and I were seriously distressed and unavoidably caught up in the often harrowing traumas of their arguments; in hindsight, I have a more empathetic understanding: my parents had striven to lift themselves from their East End background, and had lived through decades of two world wars and a deep global recession, all of which spanned the period from their late teens to middle age. No wonder conflict was ingrained in their psyche.

Perhaps sport's basic appeal for Mother was the winning or losing that came with it: the good guys triumphing over the bad guys. Conflict seemed to be integral to her character. If she had been born sixty years later, leaving school at sixteen instead of eleven, her innate drive and ambition would have been a formidable force. She had an overpowering need to control and thought she knew exactly what was best for the whole human race, how people should behave and live their life. In other words, she had the perfect idealism suited to most if not all of our politicians! But as she didn't have the chance to use these attributes on a wider stage, all of us within her orbit – family, friends and neighbours – had to suffer her iron-willed control and standards of perfect behaviour. This was a mixed blessing for me: she drove me to do well at school and I became the surrogate beneficiary of her ambitions.

Our young school days were interrupted when we were evacuated to Wales and later during the Blitz. Once we moved to Chadwell Heath, the air raids became infrequent and I travelled back to my junior school in Cleveland Road, Ilford, on trolley buses, where I took the eleven-plus exam, called the 'Scholarship'. My excuse for the lack of junior school academic success were the five years of disrupted education and the stress of living in wartime London.

My failure to pass the eleven-plus was bitterly disappointing and a serious setback. A post mortem held in the headmaster's office concluded that either there had been an administrative error or I had suffered a serious lapse of confidence on the day. Whatever the reason, it was decided that I should stay on at the junior school to sit the twelve-plus the following year.

I failed this exam too and was destined to become a pupil at the local secondary modern state school. While Father took a philosophical view and shrugged his shoulders, Mother and I felt it as a terrible blow. In those days, all pupils who didn't pass the scholarship were banished to a secondary modern which ended in the third year. Unless you passed the scholarship to a grammar or county high school, your formal education ceased at age fourteen, after which you would have an interview with the Schools' Employment Officer to establish whether you would be more suited to the job of trainee car mechanic, bus conductor or an apprentice bricklayer. Evening classes were available for the more ambitious school leavers.

My Sister June

June and I spent most of our childhood years in fairly close contact, and yet I can only recall vague images of her. I know from old photographs that she had straight, bobbed jet black hair with a fringe. She was eleven when the war started and, like me, suffered the disruption it caused, as well as the tensions of life with Mother. Soon after we moved to Chadwell Heath she became seriously ill with Sydenham's chorea, a form of rheumatic fever known as St Vitus's dance. She recovered but it left her with a heart condition that may well have led to her early death. Towards the end of the war she overcame her childhood setbacks and enrolled at the Pitman Secretarial College in Cranbrook Road, Ilford, to become a shorthand typist. She had a narrow escape when a V-2 rocket landed very close to where she was walking near the college.

It was my good fortune to have a big sister who had no boyfriends because in my early teens she introduced me to tennis, ballroom dancing and music. Her enthusiasm for tennis and dancing soon waned but music remained a lifelong interest. She had a good voice and often sang songs from the latest Hollywood musicals, accompanied by Mother on the piano.

Her most precious gift was introducing me to opera. In 1945, when I was thirteen and the war had just ended, she took me to the Royal Albert Hall to hear the then greatest tenor in the world, Beniamino Gigli. It was his first appearance in London since the war and when we arrived there was a cluster of protesters outside demonstrating their anger because he had given concerts for Mussolini and Nazi soldiers in Italy. They were soon forgotten, however, when Gigli came on stage. Dressed in white tie and tails, the paunchy singer placed one hand on the grand piano, nodded to the pianist, and sang the most beautiful songs I had ever heard. It was the most enthralling evening of my life. After he had sung his twelve arias the audience would not let him go: he eventually left the stage after eight encores.

During the interval there had been a moment of embarrassment when I asked June about the aria from the opera 'Pagalaki'. My cockney accent and wrong pronunciation of *Pagliacci* made the people sitting next to us snigger. I felt a bit deflated by that but June corrected me quietly and explained a bit of the story which helped me to forget my feeling of humiliation at being laughed at. Soon the tenor was back on stage and I was swiftly swept away by the tingling sensations, shivers down my spine and the sheer exhilaration of hearing his voice.

After this, I began to listen more attentively to my sister's seventy-eight vinyl opera records. I belted out bits of arias in the bathroom, making up words that, to me, sounded Italian, and whistled long tracts of *La Boheme*. At around this time I went through a bizarre period of dressing up in my wellington boots, yellow oilskin cycle cape and black sou'wester hat, miming to one of June's records in the living room. It became a sort of party piece for family and friends. Maybe, like my father's feeling of awkwardness at his enjoyment of ballet, I made a joke of my love of opera in order to reconcile my background with what was seen as a high-brow taste. It made us laugh.

My love of music, and especially opera, led to me thinking seriously in my student days about giving up architecture to sing. I am told that my voice was good enough to have had a singing career but the appeal waned when I thought I might end up as a third spear in *Aida* instead being the tenor lead.

Girls

I am forever grateful to June for introducing me to tennis, dancing and opera but there was one occasion when she did not help my development. Soon after the end of the war we all went to The Nest, a holiday camp near Paignton, Devon. I was a big lad for thirteen, with hairy legs, and my age was usually queried by the teachers running the opposing school or county football teams. Hormones stimulated by the posters on the local Gaumont cinema of Jane Russell in *The Outlaw*, reclining seductively in straw increased my secret wishful-thinking but did nothing to overcome my girl-shyness.

One of the holiday makers was a young twenty-year-old woman who, it seemed, had her eye on seducing me in her chalet. June could see what was going on and spoke to my father who told the woman to leave me alone. I cannot help thinking that if I had been seduced it would have made a difference to my life and future relationships. The episode reminds me of the film *On the Waterfront* when Rod Steiger, who plays Marlon Brando's brother, tells Brando that the mob controlling the boxing cartel had ordered him to 'throw' his next fight. It's a heartbreaking scene when Brando tells Steiger, "I coulda been a contender…"

My girl-shyness was relieved when I found out that the girls' school was entirely separate from the boys', on a different floor of Mayfield Secondary Modern. The school was a two-storey 1930s building built around a quadrangle, with an open, cloister-like perimeter corridor on the ground floor to the main classrooms. There were still anti-bomb blast sand bags and block work protecting the corridor which, when removed later, made it brighter but cold and dangerous in icy or wet weather. The girls' school was on the first floor, we were on the ground. Even the playgrounds and playing fields were separate.

Close to our house in Chadwell Heath was a street called Chadville Gardens. New houses had been built on the north side of the street but the war had stopped construction, leaving an open field along the south side where I used to kick around a football with my friends. We were playing there one afternoon after school when three girls strolled by on the far side of the street. They slowed and stared at us. Something prompted me – probably out of the desire to show off in front of my mates – to stop playing, smile and wave to the girls. When the tallest waved back I quickly rejoined the game to cover up my bashfulness.

I felt even more shy and self-conscious when I discovered that the girls went to the same school as me. Eventually, at the school gates, I came face to face with the tall girl called Betty Mermod. We were both fourteen and began meeting up to go to school together. She lived with her parents, Lilly and Frank, in a terraced house in Manstead Gardens, off Chadwell Heath High Street, about half a mile from ours. Betty was my one and only girlfriend, and seven years later we were married.

2

Mayfield School

1945–1947

If you bring forth what is within you,
What you bring forth will save you.
If you do not bring forth what is within you,
What you do not bring forth will destroy you.
The Gospel of St. Thomas

Malcolm Gladwell's book *Outliers* makes it readily apparent that the successes and failures in any life story are far more surprising than we could imagine and they are largely dependent on when we are born, where we are from, what we do and who we are. Furthermore, *parents*, *patterns* and *patronage* play a vital role in all our endeavours; no one ever makes it alone.

Charles Hicks, the headmaster of Mayfield Boys' School became my first 'patron'. With greying hair and a trimmed thin moustache, he was a fit, smart man, always well turned-out in a three-piece suit. Whenever he walked along the corridors it was at a fair pace, and we all knew he was the gov'nor: a man of steel, yet always ready with a benign smile. With his two long-standing deputies, Mr Ivey, a Pickwick look-alike who taught maths, and Mr Penfold, the chemistry and sports master, they were the backbone of the school.

Hicks was a progressive pioneer. He understood how to nurture and draw out the best in us, and spot those talents that did not fit the rigid selection system – a system that rejected many bright kids in the country's secondary modern schools, many of them late developers, who hadn't been offered places in the grammar schools. Under his patronage I flourished and became the head of the school, the captain of the school football team, and played left back for Essex thirteen year olds.

Towards the end of the third year, Hicks entered me for an exam for 'late developers'. Ever since moving to Chadwell Heath I had wanted to go to the local technical school and this was my chance. It was on a par with a Grammar or County High school but for those less academically orientated. The exam comprised three papers: maths, general knowledge, and English (which included an essay entitled something like 'What I want to be').

A week after sitting the exam, Mother and I went to the technical school in Barking for an oral interview with the headmaster and his deputy. As soon as we walked into the room I took an instant dislike to the two miserable-looking old men. The headmaster (who unknowingly was about to become my second patron) neither spoke to me nor even glanced in my direction. Instead, he turned to my mother and said sarcastically, "So, he wants to be an architect."

"Do I?" I thought. "What's an architect?"

It is still a puzzle how or why he had deduced from my essay that I wanted to be an architect, especially as I had never met an architect and hardly knew what an architect did. The only professional people connected with my family were our doctor, whom we never saw, and a few footballers and boxers who worked part-time in the market with my father. I know I did not use the word 'architect' – it would not have been in my vocabulary. I can only vaguely remember writing something about houses and where best to locate light switches.

Curtly, he said, "If he wants to be an architect this school's not the best place for him. Architecture's an arduous course. At least five years. I doubt that you could afford to send him to college, and your son is neither clever nor talented enough to become an architect. I see little point in continuing this interview unless he has a change of mind."

Mother looked at me and said, "What do you want to do?"

Bear in mind that this was the one school I had set my heart on, and yet without hesitation I said, "I'll be an architect."

We walked out.

When Father heard the news he was shocked, and clearly thought I was far too ambitious. No doubt, too, he was worried about how much it might cost for me to be a student for five years.

The Guinea Pigs

Hicks was incensed when I reported to him what had happened at the oral interview. Later I heard that it was at that moment that he made up his mind to create a breakthrough in secondary state education: soon after, Mayfield became the first secondary modern school to start a fourth year for those who wanted to stay on. Hicks believed an extra year's education could emulate the standards in grammar and county high schools, despite the other schools' better teachers, smaller classes and selected, brighter pupils. Political ideology intervened when the Local Education Authority tried to block Hicks's initiative. They said that the pressure of study would overstress and possibly damage our already feeble brains, and moreover that as the selection system of the eleven-plus scholarship was infallible, it was tantamount to an attack on the state's education policy. It was incredible that the additional hours and hard work volunteered by the staff should receive such a prejudiced rejection.

Fortunately, Hicks prevailed and we avoided being kicked out of the school at fourteen (which would probably be an equivalent age of a twelve-year-old in 2014). Five other boys enrolled with me for the extra year and we set about helping the teachers to clear out the carpentry classroom's wood store. It became our unheated windowless classroom for the next year, and we felt privileged to be there to study our variously selected subjects for a Royal Society of Arts (RSA) examination which I passed at the end of the fourth year. Despite the regal sounding name, it was probably about the equivalent of a modern O level or GCSE.

Hicks then enrolled me in the Commercial Department at the local South-East Essex Technical College in Dagenham to study for the equivalent A level GCE pre-qualifying exams, needed to start a full-time course in architecture. I passed the exams in 1947 and enrolled for the five year course in the Department of Art and Architecture. Several years later I met up with Hicks's son David, a property developer who became a client.

I believe I carried the desire to design and build but it could have remained dormant had it not been for the fortuitous interventions of my mother and my first two patrons: Charles Hicks and the technical school headmaster who rejected me. Patterns of events, parents and patrons help us to have the confidence and courage to realise what, subconsciously, is often already lurking at the back of our mind. I laser-beamed all of my energies into becoming an architect, never questioning that there might be an alternative career (except for a very short period where I thought of training to sing opera).

The Board of Governors

When I finally qualified as a chartered architect I telephoned Hicks with the news. Soon after, I was surprised to receive a letter from the Borough's Chief Education Officer inviting me to become a co-opted member of the Board of Governors of Mayfield School. Hicks said that as I was the first boy from the school to get a professional qualification, it would be fitting for me to serve on the board. I was honoured to be carrying Hicks's banner as living proof of his beliefs and achievements.

Although the appointment might have appeared to have importance and status it carried little power and influence: one was controlled by the politics of the other members of the board because all of them, except me, were appointed by their local ruling political party, more or less as a perk to long-serving senior councillors and aldermen. I soon discovered that I was the only governor on the board who had read the rule book, which stipulated that the board should ensure that simple repairs to the school fabric were made, as well as other improvements, such as glazing in the ground floor corridor. All these recommendations were dismissed by the chairman as being unaffordable and beyond the allocated budget. (The reason was that the bulk of the available budget was awarded to the local grammar schools.)

I did enjoy revisiting the school once every term, reconnecting with Hicks and the other staff members who had been my teachers, and learning about the increasing list of successes at prize-giving and speech days. I continued for a few years until a new local government rule demanded that a local councillor or anyone holding a position such as being a member of a Board of Governors had to reside in that borough.

The year I presented the prizes, Hicks told me that the other boys in the first fourth year guinea pig class had also gone on to good things: one became an architectural draughtsman; another went into the medical profession; one became a fairly high-ranking BBC programme producer; and another an editor of the financial columns for one of the daily newspapers. This was an impressive list of achievements for 'academically failed' secondary modern schoolboys who had begun the revolution in the wood store. Since then, Mayfield has turned out hundreds of kids who have taken degrees and professional qualifications, and who have become commercially successful.

If the standard of education is increasingly declining, it can only be because we, the elders of the tribe – parents, local and national politicians, and teachers – continue to fail our young people by not giving guidance, by not maintaining discipline, respect and politeness and discouraging healthy competition. These simple ubiquitous standards, which have prevailed in societies throughout the world, have been replaced by a cult striving for instant celebrity success. It is a tragic deterioration, driven by political expediency that demands a dumbing-down to meet social engineering targets. The ideological socialism and left-wing radicalisation of the majority of the teaching staff in state schools and universities have done our children, and society at large, a grave disservice. We need courage and the political will to reverse the critical decline. Plato's view was that everyone is innately gifted with wisdom and knowledge, and all the teachers can do is to help us to remember. 'Education' stems from the root *educari* which means to 'draw out'; it doesn't mean cramming in information.

When my sons Mark and Christopher were about to take their eleven-plus scholarship exams forty-five years ago, grammar and county high schools still existed, not yet phased out by the so-called 'comprehensive' secondary schools system. At the time I had the dilemma of what to do if they failed their eleven-plus and had to go to a secondary modern, where, already, standards were still not pleasing. I was earning sufficient money to afford to send them to a private or minor public school, but I didn't know which to choose and whether they would want to go. Fortunately, they both passed and attended the Hornchurch Grammar School.

Whether or not I was destined for a career in architecture, I do believe that by the age of twenty-eight or so it is likely I would have been setting up something on my own account, even if I sold matchboxes. Leadership, like being born with blue eyes, is not a virtue: it is simply a part of one's nature and make-up – which, in my case, involves an intuitive sense of how and when to delegate and a desire to be well regarded by others. The ambitious drive inherited from my mother pushed me to operate to a higher gear or capacity than, perhaps, I would have settled for under different circumstances. On the other hand, sometimes I feel that aiming for a high level of achievement necessitated such a concentration of effort that it left no capacity for enjoying the world passing by, or stopping here and there to pick the daisies that were there, unnoticed, on both sides of my chosen path.

Whether it had been matchboxes instead of architecture, a chosen career is a vehicle to satisfy particular personality traits. Think of a playwright who has something to say and chooses a plot as a vehicle for expressing a particular philosophy, inventing a situation around which he can weave his ideas. Perhaps it is a therapeutic process to resolve a burning subconscious ache, and in this way the playwright, poet, or painter often keeps producing different words or images to express the same basic theme. Human nature has a remarkable capacity for inventing situations, careers and occupations to fulfil a particular personality need. Actors, for instance, learn to perform because there is a need in them to identify themselves in a set, predetermined, predictable pattern, to create stability in their lives.

Looking at the events in my early life and thinking about the importance Malcolm Gladwell gives to Parents, Place and Patronage, I cannot help but marvel at my luck: if our house hadn't been bombed my parents would not have bought a house in Chadwell Heath where the local secondary school was run by Hicks. Through him I met my second patron, and my local college and school of art and architecture happened to be one of the finest in London. How lucky can you get?

Stone

A year after we left Mayfield School, Betty found a Friday and Saturday job on a department store's haberdashery counter in Ilford. Her mother Lilly was an expert dressmaker, a pleasure to dance with and a fun-loving, attractive woman. Her father, Frank Mermod – the name had French or Huguenot origins – was born on a farm in Minehead, Somerset, where he was orphaned at an early age. He had no interest in dancing, the cinema or having any social contact.

From time to time I went with Betty and her parents for weekends to Stone, a place on the estuary of the river Blackwater in Essex, where her father had bought a few plots of low-grade land protected by the sea wall. There were two pubs, an all-purpose corner shop and a rickety timber structure used as a sailing clubhouse.

You can still walk from the nearby village of Bradwell to Dengie Marshes overlooking the North Sea where there is the oldest chapel in the UK, St Peter in the Wall, that dates back to Roman times. The marshes are a well-known bird sanctuary and across the estuary is Mersea Island, famous for its oysters. The virtually uninhabited flat farmlands, protected from flooding by high sea walls along

44

both banks of the river, create a serenely beautiful rural river-scape, especially when the wide stretches of mud flats are exposed below the stone beaches at low tide. The view across the water to the far bank, shrouded in the early morning sea mist on a hot summer's day, with the Dutch eel boat chugging up river to Maldon, could transport you to any other remote, exotic part of the world. (Unfortunately, the peace and tranquillity of this part of Essex has been marred since the sinister nuclear power station was built.)

The Blackwater has a twice-daily tidal range of about seven or eight metres and at full tide runs at seven knots. It races even faster around Osea Island where it is constricted by the narrow passage between the island and the south shore. There was one large farmhouse on the island which Charringtons the brewers bought in 1903 for the rehabilitation of alcoholics and drug addicts. When a causeway was built connecting the north shore to the islands at low tide it became a clandestine highway for transporting booze to the inmates. In 1917, the navy commandeered the island and more recently the building has become a private hotel.

On the south shore are the archaeological remains of Stansgate Abbey, on the land owned by the late ex-Viscount Stansgate, otherwise known as the left-wing politician, Tony Benn. His son Hilary, who was the Environmental Secretary of the last Labour government, ran into controversy when the Benns closed off the river wall to their land. In 2008 he was accused of singling out his stretch of the river for special flood prevention treatment at the expense of other more deserving cases.

Before the war, the plots were camping sites, but in the 1950s, Stone became a popular weekend retreat for the people of north Essex and East London who were fortunate enough to own a car or motorbike. Plot owners had already started to install permanent caravans, wooden huts, and tin shack 'cottages'; and even a pair of brick houses were built by a local farmer. Frank had chosen one of his large, corner plots to convert a second-hand prefabricated, ex-RAF timber dormitory 'shed' into a three-bedroom hut with an outside chemical toilet. In the 1960s, the hut was replaced with a new brick-built bungalow.

Apart from going to the pub at night, Betty and I took long walks along the sea wall to find a secluded spot for some frustrated heavy petting. We were sixteen years old when I told Betty we would get married and have two sons. I told her the eldest would be called Mark but I could not 'see' the name of the second boy.

Learning to Sail

About this time, her father decided to buy a boat from one of the local weekenders: George, a second-hand car dealer. Frank was neither a man of generous spirit nor a keen sailor; it was a mystery why he decided to buy a dinghy. His passion was for anything with petrol engines (his car, lawnmower and even his push bike, used on his insurance-collecting rounds which had an engine contraption) and it may be that it was the attraction of an outboard motor that induced him to acquire a boat. He only ever ventured on to the water twice, however, and those were the only times the outboard engine was used. Sailing became our passion.

The boat, according to George, was an inverted clinker, ex-navy dinghy about four metres long. It had oars and rowlocks, a gaff rig (similar to the Nile *falucca* boats and a most inefficient sailing rig), and a heavy galvanised centre plate. Betty christened it Nimbus, a storm cloud formation not being the most auspicious association to have for a boat. I sank an old bucket in the mud at low tide, fixed a mooring chain to the handles and an empty petrol can for a buoy. We were complete novices, but gradually learned how to sail the boat and turn with the tide, rather than having to use the oars to get back to the mooring. Unsurprisingly, after a couple of years, the handles were wrenched off the bucket in a heavy storm and the mooring chain and boat were lost. Years later the wreck was found on a deserted beach near Osea Island.

Postscript

To Lilly's dismay, Frank sold off the spare plots at Stone too cheaply. Even greater despair occurred when he answered an advert in the local newspaper looking for a person to go into partnership with the owner of a sweetshop. It all ended in tears when he discovered he was being cheated. His last enterprise was opening a pram and babywear shop, which was a full-time job for Lilly. Betty could see her mother's workload was having a serious effect on her health. It was a continuous worry to her and I believe Betty's father's commercial activities had such a profound effect on her, so much so that she developed a deep distrust of anything to do with business affairs.

3

Student Days

1947–1953/4

In September 1947, I enrolled in the Commerce Department at the local South-East Technical College to study for the equivalent of the current A levels to pre-qualify for the Royal Institute of British architects (RIBA) course in architecture. By June 1948, I had passed the required exams and during that summer, I found a job on a local farm picking potatoes and worked on a building site. In September I became a student architect in the same college's art department.

At the time, I had no idea that the department was blessed with such distinguished lecturers and that it enjoyed the reputation of being one of the best schools of art and architecture in London. (It later became the University of East London and has since been demolished and developed for housing.) As a seventeen-year-old first year student I found myself among third and fourth year students who were veteran ex-army and navy officers taking sandwich courses; and some of the teaching staff had been on active war service as well.

Regrettably, I cannot claim to have had a distinguished student architect career; neither can I remember too much of the five years of sheer slog it took to produce design and presentation drawings, either in the studio until it closed at ten at night or squeezed between the edge of my bed and the drawing board perched on top of Mother's Singer sewing machine in the little front bedroom.

Every day in term time, except in very bad weather, I made a five-mile bike ride to the college carrying rolled up drawings and materials. I played basketball for the college until so many fingers were stubbed on the ball that I could not draw; and at lunchtimes I ate chip butties and played squash with a gloved hand or played cards or darts to earn beer money from the well-paid Ford engineering students.

Throughout my student days I worked for the Royal Mail at

Christmas – as did most students at that time – and on building sites every Easter and summer holidays to provide enough cash to live on. The first time I worked at the local post office sorting depot, I was a telegram boy because I was too young to deliver mail. They gave me a pouch and a hat with a chinstrap, and for three weeks I rode my bike around Barking delivering telegrams. The size of the tip depended on the message. For the next five years I was old enough to work in the sorting office in the morning and then to carry the canvas bags of post on two rounds of house-to-house deliveries every day from early December up to Christmas Day.

Building sites are arenas where the raw edges of life can be experienced. Most Easter and summer holiday times I worked on the Harold Hill estate, near Romford. This was a huge ten-year London County Council residential project where I had various labouring jobs: one year I was a hod carrier for the roof tilers; the next, a carpenters' mate and digger of the water main trenches. One summer I got a very cushy job as a chainman for one of the surveyors, whose job it was to set out the pegs to mark the line and levels of the roads and drainage. When three of the surveyors went on their annual holidays, and because I said I knew how to operate a theodolite and level, I was promoted to the status of surveyor and given my own chainman to carry the equipment, hold the staff level, and hammer in the pegs. Here I first met Len White, who was in charge of the team of surveyors and who, several years later, became a good friend and sailing partner.

One Easter, working on a building site near Whalebone Lane, Chadwell Heath, I was happily digging drainage trenches when the site agent asked me to deputise for Taffy, the wages clerk and timekeeper who had to be away for a month to look after his mother in South Wales. At first I said I would rather stay working in the field, as I enjoyed the physical exercise and did not want to lose my weekly bonus. I relented when he winked, telling me that the wages clerk was also the bonus clerk!

The RIBA curriculum for the first three years was devoted to passing the Intermediate examination before being allowed to go on for the next two years to the finals. We had to prepare a portfolio of design drawings, a measured survey and drawings of part of a classical building, life and plant life drawings, the theory of structural design, the history of architecture, and so on.

One subject I excelled at was freehand life and plant drawing, having spent three hours a week in the art department's life class studios under the tutelage of Bernard Carolyn, who was a brilliant pencil artist. Later, most likely in the 1970s, freehand drawing was omitted from the RIBA curriculum and computers took over, with the tragic result that now the majority of qualified architects have no ability to use a pencil or drawing pen. Fortunately, the trend may be returning: since 2009 our daughter-in-law Ilga, who is a professional artist, visits many of the larger practices in London where she teaches life classes.

Every Wednesday was reserved for the weekly sketch design; we were handed a brief at 9am, and for the next six hours we had to produce complete design drawings with perspective illustrations, which was part of our preparation for the RIBA exams. One particular Wednesday, my father had two tickets for an international football match between England and France at Wembley (before the days of floodlighting, Wednesday afternoons were reserved for such sporting events). Rather than miss either the football match or the Wednesday sketch design, I had to produce my six-hour exercise in three hours so that I could rush away to meet my father at Aldgate East Station by 1.30pm. I dashed off the design, made some excuse, and left my work with one of the other students to hand in that afternoon at the end of the session.

Surprisingly, this sketch design, done in three hours instead of six, was awarded a Mention Star. It was the highest mark I ever received for anything and remained a personal record!

My best subject was the history of art and architecture, 3000 years of which the general paper covered with a choice of one special period, such as the Gothic era. I chose twentieth-century modern architecture. The history lecturer was Charles Handley-Reid. (When I first saw John Wood, in the principal role in *Travesties* at the Aldwych, I thought it was Charles using a pseudonym.) The lecture room was always packed with art and architecture students wanting to hear his enlightened illustrated lectures: his performances were delivered with such style and elegance that they had become popular entertainment.

At this time, in the early 1950s, the extent of my travel experiences reached no further than my evacuation to Wales, visits to parts of London, Stone in Essex and a trip to Glossop in Derbyshire. The slideshows of magnificent works of art and architecture opened my eyes to a wondrous world, and fostered a burning desire in me to see these works in the flesh.

Apart from Handley-Reid's lectures, I was deeply interested in the general and special history subjects and at the RIBA Intermediate oral exam the examiner offered me congratulations on my two written papers. All the other subjects could be classified as a 'scrape through' but I probably tipped the balance in my favour because I presented well at the interviews, with the exception at the design oral which could have been a disaster. For this exam, we were given a choice of three different building types to design within the allocated three and a half days. We had to produce a finished sketch design with rendered perspectives and notes to illustrate the whole concept. A week later, we had to return to the RIBA headquarters for the oral interviews.

On the day, there was an array of ominous-looking examiners for each subject. I was directed to a short man with a waist-coated paunch protruding over the green baize table. After discussing my exam piece he asked to see the drawings which represented the past three years of my studio work. I had made a portfolio of two sheets of hardboard, lined with a protective hessian canvas to carry the bulky weight of three years' worth of large presentation drawings. As I heaved the weighty portfolio on to the table, I trod on the man's toe. Ignoring his pain, I proceeded to display the drawings. To my further dismay, they were turned back to front and because the examiner's stomach was so tight to the edge of the table, the only way I could deal with the large sheet of hessian was to tuck it over his waistcoat like an oversized brown napkin while I turned the pages of drawings. When I carefully peeled off the 'napkin' it left traces of hairy hessian on his blue serge suit.

Passing the RIBA Intermediate exam in 1951 was also marked by my winning a house design and construction competition, open to all third year students in every school of architecture in the country. It was sponsored by Marley Tiles, a company which still manufactures various types of building materials and components. The prize money was £25. I was spurred on not only by the cash winnings, but also by a fellow student everyone considered to be the favourite to win and whom I disliked intensely because his dad was a bank manager in Romford who could afford to give him plenty of money so he could run a motorbike. (If necessity is the mother of invention, so envy is the father of ambition).

There was another factor contributing to my success, one which I wish I could claim to be a conscious piece of gamesmanship but was simply due to my ignorance. I had never heard of Marley, the sponsors of the competition, who manufactured floor tiles, roofing materials, wall tiles, blocks and other building goods, so it was no surprise that my design and technical drawings specified using the name of every other manufacturer's materials except Marley's. It was not until all my fellow students' competition drawings were on display that I became aware that the other competitors had, without exception, labelled every material as 'Marley', whether Marley produced the building component or not.

Post-War England

Even six years after the war had ended there was evidence everywhere of derelict bomb-damaged sites scarring the towns in the south-east, and London in particular. Strictly rationed building materials eliminated any form of architectural embellishment and most building works were restricted to war damage repairs. 'Modern' design, such as a flat roof for housing, was considered to be too avant-garde, un-British and out of keeping with the pre-war traditional Lutyens pitched roof styles. Of course, we students were encouraged to design freely outside these traditional parameters.

1951 was also the year of the Festival of Britain Exhibition, which changed design attitudes and exorcised the trauma of wartime, despite the continuing ration book controls for clothing, meat, food stuffs and furnishings. Mantovani and the Glenn Miller-style dance bands were top of the charts; miniskirts, the pill and the Swinging Sixties were a decade away. The BBC was the sole TV channel; all broadcasts were in black and white and remote controls had not been invented. Home entertainment was dependent on popular BBC radio stations and wind-up gramophones.

Every town had three cinemas where the queues were often four deep, encircling the building. Each performance included one 'B' film before the 'A' film main feature. Before the main film in the major West End cinemas there were hour-long live stage shows, whose entertainers were mostly young comedians and singers such as Tommy Cooper, Vera Lynn and many others from ENSA (Entertainments National Service Association) who had been recruited to tour the British forces during the war. Many others became well-known TV personalities. On screen, couples were not allowed to be filmed in bed unless it could be seen that they were fully clothed and kept one foot firmly on the bedroom floor. The Windmill Theatre girls could pose bare-breasted but were not allowed to move on stage.

Divorcees and gays were social outcasts; illegitimacy remained a lifelong stigma; young couples formally announced their engagement and celebrated with a diamond solitaire ring, and society unrealistically expected a woman to save her virginity until after the wedding bells had rang. Today, in the twenty-first century, when a teenager speaks of their girlfriend or boyfriend, it is often assumed they are sexual partners, but in the 1950s, as in my own case, having a girlfriend usually meant that plenty of petting, fondling and heavy breathing went on in the back seats of the cinema. Sometimes, in addition, I got a romp on a sofa or on the beach at Stone when the opportunity arose, but without, as the *News of the World* would have put it, full 'intimacy taking place'.

Boots the Chemists refused to sell contraceptives because it was a Catholic family business. Condoms were available at other chemists but these were kept hidden away in a drawer under the counter. Customers would ask for a packet of Durex in a low whisper, or even with a nod or a wink, and the counter staff would slip the goods from the drawer into a plain paper bag to save the other customers from embarrassment. Only the mens' barber shops displayed cardboard adverts for Durex.

Talking of Durex, I was a student in the same year as a boy called Derek Amos. We were good friends, and some twenty years later he became a partner in my practice. Derek shared a rented house with four or five other younger students, including one called Tony, all of whom treated Derek as their surrogate brother for guidance and wisdom on the main subject of interest that controlled and dominated their lives – SEX. Tony was the only one of the flatmates who had a regular girlfriend and the obsession to experience sex had gripped Tony for several weeks.

While Derek listened patiently to Tony's various strategies to get his girlfriend into bed, he urged him repeatedly to buy a packet of Durex condoms in the unlikely event he would achieve his goal. Tony had hoped to be asked discreetly if he needed "anything for the weekend, sir?" but instead found himself walking out of one chemist shop after another without ever buying the condoms. According to him, there was always a middle-aged woman serving behind the counter who reminded him of his stern mother. Anyway, after buying countless unwanted razor blades and toothpaste, eventually he found a man to serve him.

One evening not long after, my friend Derek arrived back at the house at about six o'clock to find Tony anxiously pacing the sitting room floor. His girlfriend, who lived close by, was apparently going to be on her own that evening as her parents were intending to go to the local cinema to catch the last performance. She had told Tony to meet her at her house at eight o'clock and they would decide then where to go later. Derek calmed Tony's nerves, suggesting that the opportunity might be more promising if Tony had a bath and put on a clean pair of socks. Tony baulked at the idea of a bath, especially as it was only Tuesday. Derek also suggested that he might consider changing his underwear and washing off his Brylcream, as it might stain her pillows – just in case he got that far. Finally, Derek reminded him to keep the Durex handy.

At 7.15pm Tony presented himself for inspection. Derek looked him over and told him to take his hands out of his pockets. Tony ignored the instruction. He told Derek he was feeling nervous and asked him to walk with him to his girlfriend's house to make it look more casual. After a few steps along the road, Tony began to lag behind, his hands still thrust into his trouser pockets, legs looking like they were buckling under him. Suddenly he grabbed his flies.

"What's the matter with you?"

"I can't go on," said Tony. "It's off."

"What do you mean, it's off?"

"The Durex."

"What about the Durex?"

"The bloody thing's come off!"

When we had the cash, I used to take Betty to the Saturday night Students' Union dance to a live, twelve-piece band playing in the college main hall, which was as grand as a Mecca Ballroom dance floor. The college rugby club controlled the doors. During the interval, many of us surged across the road to the Robin Hood pub for a quick savaloy and a pint of brown ale before dashing back, either to catch the second half of the dance or to try and find some secluded place – usually in the bell tower – for more frustrated petting. For me, it always stopped at fumbling because, like Tony, I was naïve, and never armed with a condom.

Many of my fellow students who had served in the war had adult girlfriends and one or two were married. I was intensely jealous of their sexual activities, especially so one weekend when Betty and

I went away with my student mate John and his girlfriend to stay with her family in Glossop. We hired a pre-war taxi (in those days the driving seat door had no glass to protect the driver who was completely separated from the passengers at the back). It was a slow journey and we stopped off in cheap bed and breakfast places on the way. John and his girlfriend shared a bed but again, to my frustration, Betty insisted we slept apart.

Of course, the college was awash with attractive young women and later, in hindsight, I regretted that in my ever persistent girl-shyness, my loyalty to Betty, and the total focus on exams, I remained celibate until we married.

Exams

In 1952, I was a twenty-year-old third-year student when I passed the RIBA Intermediate exam and won a bursary of £360 a year, enabling me to go on for the final two years. This marked the beginning of the next ten-year cycle.

The only other significant part of my student life was initially a rather negative one until some years later when I recognised it as a non-failure. Frank Risdon, the head of the Architects Department, while carrying out his full-time duties as head and senior lecturer, also ran a successful small practice in London. He coerced many of the senior fourth and fifth year students to produce drawings and details for his private work for the odd five or ten pounds. I considered it to be slave labour and, in any case, was never invited to participate. Gradually his practice flourished and, with just one exception (me), after graduation many students accepted the offer to work in his firm, some leaving soon afterwards, a few staying for longer periods.

Later, when my own practice was flourishing, I treated the episode as something positive, even a bit flattering: while I respected and regarded him highly as the head and senior lecturer, I could never have succumbed to his demand that everyone had to be a cardboard replica of himself. One was either a dedicated disciple or discarded.

The RIBA final exams included a written thesis. I decided to write something about boat design or marina planning. One day on the District Line I sat next to a man wearing a Port of London Authority uniform and we started chatting about the Thames as a subject for a thesis. He suggested I looked at the boats moored in Chiswick and Chelsea. Eventually, the historic associations with houseboats on the Thames in Chelsea became the subject of my thesis: *The Redevelopment of Chelsea Bay*. At the time, in 1954, to preserve the historic character along the length of Cheyne Walk from Chelsea Bridge to the Worlds End, all bus routes, red post boxes and telephone kiosks were banned. During the long walks from Sloane Square to research the locality and meet the people living on the moored boats, I remember looking up at the elegant Georgian houses along Cheyne Walk and thinking, *I will live there one day*. Several years later the thought became a self-fulfilled prophecy.

Traumas at Home

With the exception of the immense pleasure the research and writing of my thesis gave me, I look back on those two final years as a period of extreme hard work, deep unhappiness, and emotional chaos. I was stressed out, preparing to sit the final exams while preparations were under way for our wedding. I was also having serious doubts about marrying Betty. There were inklings that our ideas about where we would hope to live in the future, my business ambitions and social horizons were not in accord. My problem is that once I set a course it is difficult for me to change tack.

Another problem was Father losing his job. Marshall and Masters' main office and stand was in Spitalfields market with a subsidiary stand in the Borough Market, Southwark, where Father had been promoted from porter to salesman and where Jack was recruited as his porter. Father had started to treat the sales as his own satellite business which, eventually, led to him getting the sack. Mother was mortified and prepared to get on her white charger to ride into Spitalfields to defend her wronged husband but he was saved the ignominy when it became apparent that he had indeed been siphoning off a top layer of the profits.

It was kept secret. Every day Father left the house as usual to search for jobbing work in the markets. Eventually I was told about it once he had been taken on by a friend in Spitalfields, but he never recovered from the stress. One day, out of Mother's earshot, he asked me to lend him a quid, which I could hardly afford, for stake money for playing cards at the club. He folded the pound note and pinned it to the inside pocket of his suit. Within a week the money was repaid. It was a sad and distressing period in all our lives and one that must have contributed to his untimely death four years later.

About nine months before the final exams, another major household crisis arose when June told our parents that she planned to marry Rustum Cooper in Kensington Registry Office, just a few months before the date Betty and I had decided on for our wedding. Before June met Russi, as far as I know she had only had one girlhood crush, on our second cousin Ronnie who was killed in the war when his plane crashed, and after the war she briefly went out a couple of times with a Canadian Air Force pilot. At eighteen, after graduating from Pitman Secretarial College, she went on to work for a couple of firms in the City of London before taking a job with Scindia Steamships Limited as the secretary to Russi, their marine insurance legal advisor. He was a most handsome man, who looked like the film star Omar Sharif without the moustache. June was in her early twenties when she fell in love with him.

Towards the end of the war, Russi had played cricket for an Indian combined eleven, and in his student days at the London School of Economics he played Middlesex County Cricket for three years as their number three in the batting line-up, alongside famous names like Dennis Compton. After graduation, he was employed by Scindia and both he and his brother Burjor played cricket for the amateur Indian Gymkhana team. June travelled with him to all his matches and became Gymkhana's chief scorecard keeper.

Although I rarely saw Russi before the wedding, I thought he was a good and gentle man, well-suited for my sister. My parents were deeply concerned and disappointed and I too felt sad that they had made the decision to live permanently in India after their marriage. They liked Russi but were worried about the couple's racial, creed and colour differences. Many anguished arguments ensued. In India there was a similar reaction from Russi's family: they would have preferred him to marry a nice Parsi girl, and they probably thought of June as a trophy English rose.

In addition to the stress and sadness of June leaving the country to live in Bombay there was also Mother's disappointment that her vision of a white wedding with Father leading June down the aisle was to be dashed because Russi was a non-Christian. Never mind that neither he nor June wanted a church wedding, or any other form of religious ceremony. It didn't change the fact that Mother wanted June to be like every other English bride, dressed in white with a veil and bridesmaids. In other words, 'properly churched'. Apart from Salvation Army Aunt

Annie, no one in the Saunders family was devoutly religious, and churchgoing was restricted to weddings and funerals, but nonetheless, Mother wanted people to know that her daughter would not be barred from a Christian marriage ceremony just because Russi was Indian.

For a quiet life, June succumbed to Mother's persuasion and agreed that if she could convince the Bishop of Barking to marry a Parsi in church then they would go ahead with a church wedding. June was certain the bishop would not approve, but she underestimated Mother's extraordinary willpower and, for whatever reason, the bishop agreed. June and Russi still refused, however, and went on to marry in Kensington Registry Office as planned, quickly retreating to India afterwards.

The traumas gathered strength: not only had Mother lost her battle over the church wedding and her daughter was leaving England for good, but she realised she had no control over my marriage arrangements either, as they were being organised by Betty's parents. There were tense discussions and fierce rows over how many guests could be invited and who should sit next to whom. I burned with envy that June would live in India and escape the cauldron and chaos of our parents' household.

Six months before our wedding, I left Chadwell Heath to get away from the destructive home life and went to live in Barking with a student mate, Roy Jones, and his widowed mother. I made no contact with my parents until the eve of the wedding, when I arrived unannounced, and hoping to effect a reconciliation. Within minutes, the onslaught of abuse flared up. I hurriedly left, still having no idea whether they would turn up at the church or not.

The look of surprise on my face when I saw my parents in the congregation must have registered with some of the guests. After the bitter acrimony I had experienced the night before, it was an astonishing transformation to see their smiling faces, chatting away as if they were in a state of bliss with me, Betty, her parents, and the world at large.

4

Marriage

1954

Betty and I were married soon after I had left college. She was a secretary in the City and I was a 22-year-old low-paid assistant architect commuting to offices in the West End. We were both exhausted and drained. No wonder the wedding itself, our first night together, and the honeymoon on the island of Sark were not joyous affairs.

Our home was a rented first floor one-bed flat in Wanstead, East London, in a cul-de-sac called Woodbine Place. Wartime rationing of meat, furniture, clothing and other goods was still in force and our joint earnings just about covered our living and travel costs. Not too long after we moved in, Betty's father Frank surprisingly offered to talk to a contact at the Liverpool Victoria Insurance company about their special rent-controlled flats that occasionally became available. What luck! Within a few weeks we moved to a first floor three-bed flat over the offices of the *Romford Times* newspaper in a parade of shops along Corbets Tey Road, the main high street of Upminster. From time to time my father came to see us and on a few weekends helped me wallpaper and paint a couple of rooms. Very occasionally I called in to see Mother. She only ever came once to the flat, to see baby Mark, and that was the only time since our wedding that she had seen Betty.

Birth of Mark

The events surrounding the birth of Mark are vague. It was 1956: I was at work in the City when a telephone call from the hospital told me that I was the father of a baby boy. Why Betty was taken twenty miles to Plaistow hospital in the depths of the East End of London was puzzling, and why expectant fathers were not allowed to be at their baby's birth has been a long-held regret.

I rushed from Park Street near Marble Arch to catch the Underground train to Upton Park station. At the hospital everything surrounding the birth was sanitised, distant and almost secretive, as if I had no part in the whole affair. When a nurse told me my visiting time was up, I went on to see my father in Spitalfields market. He was delighted, and after a celebratory drink, and feeling somewhat heady, he came with me back to the hospital to see Betty and the baby that afternoon. Betty's parents took them home to our flat in their car. From the day Mark was born and all through his early years it was a joy to see him so animated and aware of everything going on around him.

When he was five months old, a cold 'truce', rather than a reconciliation, was made between Betty and Mother. It had occurred unexpectedly when, at Father's instigation, we were invited to Chadwell Heath to spend the weekend with them. Nervously, we arrived after lunch, in time to watch the 1957 Cup Final. Father sat with baby Mark on his lap in front of the tiny TV screen until the final whistle and celebrations. I will always treasure the memory of Father cuddling Mark throughout the match in total peace and contentment.

Father's Death

Father went to bed as usual about eight o'clock that evening. We went to bed an hour or so later to get away from the tension of being alone with Mother. In the middle of the night we were startled by a commotion in the other room: with his last breath, Father had called out in agony before dying, instantly, of a heart attack. He was just fifty-seven years old. For the next forty-five years of widowhood, Mother saw as much sport as she could but vowed never to watch an FA Cup Final ever again.

After the burial at Whalebone Lane Cemetery the house was packed with Saunders family, close neighbours, and thirty or so mates from the markets and his snooker club. Father had been a popular man, always ready for a joke, and everyone spoke of him with such fondness. I had not met most of his market friends but as each one came to talk to me it became uncannily apparent that three days before he died he had gone to the markets in Covent Garden, Spitalfields and his own market in the Borough to see his mates. Now that he was dead they understood that in a strange, prophetic way, wrapped up in general chat, he had been saying goodbye to each one of them.

A few months before he died I had the impression that since both June and I had left home, he had become resigned to life with

Mother which had settled into a quieter pattern. Maybe he had just had enough. Perhaps he felt he was seriously ill or had simply decided it was a good time to go.

I know that sometime during my mid-forties, I have had three or four fleeting moments when I have caught myself in such a state of bliss and total equilibrium with my life and the world about me that I felt that it would be the perfect time to pass painlessly away, completely contented with what I had done or not done, with nothing more to do, and nothing needed, wanted nor desired. It could well be that Father's 'farewell' to his mates that perhaps, he may have been in a similar frame of mind for several days before he died.

Father's unsociable working hours, my late-evening student working times, the frequent weekends away with Betty's parents, and then having a family of my own, meant that I'd had little contact with him. In the past, when I had been with him, we would swap jokes, go to sporting events and share in our joint woes about Mother. Regrettably, I cannot remember ever having had a meaningful conversation with him. I could not understand why he never found the courage to look for peace and tranquillity elsewhere. I loved him and loved being with him; we had some pleasurable, fun times together. But his life reminded me of *Pagliacci* – outwardly playing the clown; inwardly nursing heartbreak. In June's eyes he could do no wrong and was the victim of Mother's oppressive paranoia.

Despite the earlier traumas and strife over June's planned marriage, Mother and Father had wanted to give her a big wedding reception at a hired hall with caterers, free drinks, a dance band and the usual trimmings. They had no savings and had arranged to re-mortgage the house to raise £800, turning a blind eye to the mortgage lender's refusal to renew Father's life insurance when he failed the medical test. Giving their only daughter a grand wedding and send-off to India far outweighed any thought of the likely risk of Father's early demise.

His sudden death and the deep emotional numbness that followed were shortly compounded with very immediate anxieties. Mother had been left in serious debt. On her own, it would be impossible to pay off the mortgage and have enough money to live on. I had a wife and young baby to support on a meagre salary, which left us with very little cash to spare. June's family in India were financially well-off but at the time there were stringent restrictions on foreign exchange. After much lobbying and knowing the right people, Russi and his brother

Burjor managed to get permission for June to send Mother two pounds sterling a month.

By Mother's own admission, the idea of sharing her house with anyone else, or letting out a couple of rooms to a teacher or nurse, was repugnant. (Even the German Luftwaffe had not been able to induce her to leave our bombed-out house to live with her mother-in-law!) She could not accept the reality there was an outstanding uninsured mortgage on the house that had to be repaid, and that her widow's pension was never going to be enough.

Finally, financial pressures did persuade her to move in with her stepsister and let the house to a married couple with a baby, but within a very few months she was back at her own house and the couple moved on. June and I managed to scrape together enough cash to keep up the mortgage repayments until, in the mid-1960s, once the practice was going well I was able to pay off the mortgage.

Two years after Mark was born, the threat of my having to serve two years' National Service loomed over us. I decided that if I was conscripted, I would sign on for three years, take a short-term commission and buy a house on a mortgage which the government would subsidise. In the event, although I avoided conscription, we still bought a newly built semi-detached house for £2800 in Nyth Close on the River Estate, about a mile from the flat in Upminster.

Birth of Christopher

A year or so later, I remember lying in bed thinking, "Why not? Let's have another," and in 1958 Christopher was born. This time we planned a home birth: it was a precious, closely bonding experience. The midwife was late, and I did whatever I could to help. The doorbell rang just as Christopher's shiny, black-haired head popped out; the midwife had arrived at last, just in time to take over.

Betty was a loving and caring mother. While she looked after the home and family, I was at the office during the day and most evenings. I worked on private jobs at weekends too, making the extra cash we needed to buy household things like a refrigerator and a washing machine.

Business Conflict

Three years after Christopher was born, I started my own practice from our small front bedroom. This was something I knew I had to do, and in my mind there was no chance of failure. (In any case, if you don't have anything, you can afford to risk everything you've got!)

Betty accepted the situation and, in between being a mother and housewife, she typed letters and helped with the office work. Understandably, she was anxious: undoubtedly, the financial risks involved us all – but not for one minute did I share these concerns. On the other hand I recognised that her fears were rooted in her father's business failures and we could find ourselves in the same financial meltdown.

As the business began to flourish I could afford the hire purchase payments to buy my first car, a Ford Popular. This allowed us the freedom to spend occasional weekends at Stone and to go to the pub while Betty's parents looked after the babes. Other than that, there were few times when we went out together because Betty was never comfortable about leaving the boys, and declined offers from neighbours and friends to look after them. Even when I started to earn good money, she still resisted having anyone to help with the housework or babysit.

Her reluctance to take pleasure or participate in the growing success of my work was frustrating. Perhaps her abhorrence of 'business' may have led her to believe – as I have heard since – that my success could only have been the result of malfeasance or dodgy crookedness.

During the early days of the practice, I was commissioned to act on several house projects in Kensington and the West End. That way, I became exposed to other lifestyles, ones that contrasted with my insular, suburban life on a new estate in Upminster. There were so many films and plays that I wanted to see, especially those at the Aldwych Theatre (at the time the home of the Royal Shakespeare Company), so that gradually, I started to go to these places on my own. Invitations for dinner or lunch with clients or friends either had to be turned down or I went alone.

I had met the sculptor Jack McCarthy when we were both part-time lecturers at the college of art and architecture at the Walthamstow Technical College (now the University of East London). The few times I went to his studio for dinner, Betty declined to come with me. Jack had been a young, conscripted midshipman in the Royal Navy and was one of the comparatively few sailors who had survived serving on the murderous Murmansk Arctic convoys. After the war he had studied to become a sculptor, and now lived in Chelsea Mews with his wife Molly and their two children.

Their living quarters opened out onto a cavernous, church nave-like studio with a north-facing 'transept' window where the statue of Eros was cast in 1893. The workbenches were covered with sheets of steel, plastic mouldings, long strips of bronze, sacks of plaster and an array of metal and stone working tools. Crammed on the perimeter shelves were Jack's pieces of sculpture – a sort of memory bank of miniatures, models and paper sketches. Looking at them, I always felt as if I was meandering intrusively through the private intimacies of his mind.

I wanted to enjoy these new and exciting experiences with Betty, so that we could expand our way of life, but it was a lost cause. She showed no interest outside the comfort zone of her small local coterie and I found it impossible to accept that we did not share the same hopes and ambitions for the future, including where and how we wanted to live. In hindsight, I realise we both had valid, heartfelt views on life-fulfilment, which simply did not coincide. The issue was not a question of judgement; neither of us was right or wrong. Quite simply, for whatever reason or underlying motives, our horizons and lifestyle aspirations were on a totally different course. Inevitably, conflict ensued.

Family Holidays

We did manage to relax and enjoy time together when we travelled abroad with Mark and Christopher and were able to give them opportunities we had never had. They were as young as six or seven years old when we first ventured to Rosas on the Costa Brava on a cheap package tour. After that, as the practice developed, we could afford to take regular holidays to Spain, Majorca, Ibiza, Venice and the Lido, and car trips to Normandy and Brittany.

The grand adventure came in 1967 when we travelled to India; the boys were nine and ten years old. We spent three weeks with Russi, June and Dinaz, touring from Bombay to Agra, Jaipur, and Fatehpur Sikri. The erotic Hindu temples of Khajuraho were a special fascination for the boys and, undoubtedly, were of particular interest to me!

These travel experiences not only broadened our horizons, they also gave me a deep satisfaction that I was able to share the benefits of my business success with my sons. These precious holidays with them compensated, to some extent, for my own growing discontentment. I knew there was more to life and living than I could find in suburban Upminster.

Mark and Christopher went to Engayne Primary School, a five-minute walk away in Severn Drive. They both passed the eleven-plus scholarship to Hornchurch Grammar School, which at the time was considered to be one of the best state senior schools in the country – fortunately before various governments decided to 'improve' our education system! At the time, we did not appreciate how lucky we were to live in the catchment area of such good schools.

At school, they enjoyed sports: Christopher was a keen footballer and had a good eye for other ballgames; Mark's forte was swimming (he always looked the part in his soccer strip but had little ball-eye coordination). Often, I spent long hours on a weekend waiting for the team coach to arrive back from an away gala, sometimes in the early hours of a Sunday morning.

Mark was the butterfly sprinter and relay specialist. A Doctor Alladyce was the official team coach, whose daughter Lesley was already destined for Olympic success. Mark was only thirteen when he was offered a place to train for the next Olympic Games. We left the choice to him but were relieved when he declined the offer (it would have meant hours every day with his head immersed in chlorinated water).

By the time my practice began to flourish, the Stone Sailing Club had blossomed into a formidable racing centre. Len White, whom I first met when he was the site engineer I had worked for in my student days, and his wife Bonny were keen members of the Club and encouraged us to join. I bought a five metre Enterprise class racing dinghy and often Betty crewed for me or I raced with Len or Bonny.

At about this time, in 1966/7, the boys became interested in sailing. They joined the club and raced their own sailing dinghy in the cadet class. For the next five years, from May to the end of September, all four of us spent most Saturday afternoons and all day Sunday dressed in wetsuits. Even in the most horrid British weather conditions, despite occasionally capsizing I enjoyed the exhilaration of racing round the buoys. Disappointingly, I never crossed a finishing line first and could never find solace in the adage that it is more important to take part than to win!

In 1968, six years after I started the practice, I bought a detached house for £11,500, next to the golf course in Hall Lane, known locally as the 'Beverly Hills of Upminster'. I built an extension at the rear, totally refurbished the house, and landscaped the garden.

Mother in India

While we were in the throes of moving from Nyth Close and getting the new house ready, June and Russi invited Mother to stay in India. Perhaps she wanted to reach a reconciliation that would resolve the acrimony between them, or it may have been that June intended to mark the end of their relationship. Mother had a fear of water and had never travelled beyond the shores of mainland England until the day Father persuaded her to take the ferry to the Isle of Wight. Now, aged sixty-six, she plucked up courage to accept June's invitation, despite the deep concern that once in Bombay she would be unable to get the bus home if things did not go to her liking.

I alerted the airline that she was a first-time traveller abroad. She enjoyed the flight and everything went well for a few days until she fell ill with Delhi belly. It was then that she started to find it impossible to cope with Bombay and the Indian way of life. Uproar and chaos ensued for the duration of her stay. She returned in utter desolation and despair.

Soon after, June turned up at Mother's house unannounced, kissed her goodbye, and never saw her or contacted her again. Thereafter, she would not even open Mother's letters. From time to time I pleaded with her to write to Mother – an occasional note to say the family was well, that Dinaz was happy, what the weather was like, and that they all sent their love. Not only would it have made Mother's life easier but it would have been a great help to me to keep her on an even keel. But June could not bring herself to make any form of contact, convinced as she was that her mother was the cause of the stress, unhappiness and early death of Father.

June's sudden death in 1985 at the age of fifty-seven dashed all hopes Mother had for a reconciliation. Without June's compromise or forgiveness, her sorrow deepened while the emotional charge kept churning.

Although Mother never recovered from the shock of losing Father, for me it was a relief once she regained her sense of independence. She started working for the local council as a home help, looking after the old and infirm in the district. She put in more hours than her employment required, and the work served as a safety valve for her pent-up and abundant energy, which for most of her life she had been able to maintain on just four hours' sleep a night. At the age of sixty, when the work became too strenuous, she changed jobs, and for the next few years enjoyed working in the local bakery, decorating cakes and squirting cream on to pastries. After she retired five years later, she spent her time gardening, going to whist drives, playing bingo at the local cinema and watching sport. Her next door neighbours dropped their newspapers through her letter box and she read every page, keeping well-versed in the politics and conflicts of the day.

Another thing that kept her active and occupied for the next twenty years was watching snooker. She had often watched Father play tournaments at the club in Ilford and later, when it became popular on TV, she watched for hours whenever it was broadcast. Her favourite player was Steve Davis, her blue-eyed, clean-living East End boy, and she clapped and cheered with the audience. She insisted she did not want to change her old black and white TV set, until finally it broke down. I bought her a bigger TV and when the engineer tuned in the colour she went into her 'uproar' mode until he turned the screen to black and white. The engineer clearly thought she was mad, or maybe partially blind: how could she watch snooker without being able to see the different coloured balls? (He was not to know how right he was: she was both partially blind and a bit mad, and for her, everything in life was either black or white!) She continued to watch the TV without colour for the rest of her life.

At least every fortnight, and sometimes weekly, I went to see Mother with a box of fruit, vegetables and other goodies. Provided we only talked about football, snooker, her gardening or politics, I could leave her after an hour or so in an easy mood. Otherwise, more often than not, I had to spend the times with her trying to calm her constantly churning state of agitation, which would surface over her disappointment with my marriage, her dislike of Betty's parents and, particularly, the upset with June and her family in India. To the outside world, though, Mother always projected the image that she and everyone in her immediate family were in a blissful state of peace and happiness.

Christmas was always joyless. Mother would come with us to Betty's parents and usually by the time Boxing Day had dawned, something trivial would annoy her and she would be off, storming out to catch a bus home. Betty had no empathy towards her, and there was little contact between them except on rare occasions. Betty blamed our eventual divorce on Mother's unbending attitudes and state of mind. Mostly the incidents that occurred were relatively minor; it was only later that situations became explosive, with the emotional eruptions and bitter recriminations that frequently arose over June's silence and Betty's parents.

Divorce

At some time in 1971, Russi's younger brother Burjor travelled to London on business. We arranged to meet for supper at one of his client's hotels. He was obviously on a mission on behalf of June to talk to me about Betty and our rocky marriage. He quoted Reinhold Niebuhr (often attributed to Kahil Gibran): 'May you have the courage to change that which you cannot accept, the tranquillity to accept that which you cannot change, and the wisdom to know the difference.' I don't know if the outcome was what he, June and Russi had been hoping for, but it certainly made up my mind. Betty and I were living emotionally isolated lives and the breakdown of our marriage was inevitable.

Mark and Christopher were in their early to mid-teens when we spent our last family holiday together on a three-week safari in Kenya and Tanzania. A few months later, I walked out of the house and moved into a rented a flat in London. I loved my sons and took great interest and pride in the way they were growing up and, had it not been for my wanting to be with them, I would have left Betty much sooner.

I knew that I risked losing the boys' love and respect, but I had a compelling need to get away from a loveless, unfulfilling marriage. My sense of guilt and failure was compounded by the knowledge that it is never a good time to leave ones' children. Whatever their age, they will always feel abandoned.

Later, whenever Mark and Christopher met me in London for a weekend day out, feelings of acute heartbreak, trauma and despair welled up in me. Matter-of-fact, stilted conversations broke up the long, tense silences. The love and ease we had had between us had disappeared into despair, and I felt their sadness and alienation. Then, after having driven them back to Betty's at the end of the day, I would sit with them outside the house in the car, feeling the pain of saying goodnight.

Within a few weeks, Christopher decided it was too much for him to bear and wrote me a touching letter telling me he would prefer not to see me for a while. Mark stayed in contact and felt relaxed enough once he'd started university to stay with me in Bethnal Green, which we both enjoyed. About two years later, I organised a Halloween party and suggested to Mark that he should mention it to Christopher in case he would like to come too. He arrived with a girlfriend as if we had never been apart.

Gradually, spending more time together and going on sailing and skiing holidays helped to heal some of the wounds we had all suffered. Mark treated my house as his London home until I helped him buy a ground floor flat in Battersea. Christopher continued living with Betty until he was in his early twenties when I also helped him to buy a flat in Wandsworth.

In spite of the healing of rifts, I was still an unhappy and troubled man. In 1975 I wrote to a friend:

> No doubt many men would envy my situation – being moderately well-heeled from my own efforts, successful in the eyes of the business world, well-travelled and having two handsome, talented and clever sons who looked more like my friends than offspring. I had the luxury of household staff to deal with dinner parties, enjoyed good health, and was happy to be unattached. And yet, what did I want? No – what else could I possibly want? Above all, I longed to be with a woman with whom I could share my life and to whom I could give myself – everything I have as Tom Saunders – not what I own or what I am but simply me – who I am, the naked me.
>
> Maybe, one day…or am I asking too much?

Could the divorce and dissatisfaction with my lot be dismissed as the proverbial mid-life crisis, or be more to do with a growing awareness of my mortality which posed the questions: "Who am I?"; "Why am I here?"; and "What is my destiny?"

The Intervening Years

After the stormy waters of the divorce had calmed somewhat, I chartered a skippered four-berth boat to sail with Mark and Christopher around the Aegean Sea to Piraeus and through the Corinth Canal. The following year I chartered a ten-berth boat to sail with Mark, Christopher, David King, Jamal Khanafani, Raymond Maggar and three other friends for an all-blokes cruise from Corfu to Cephalonia. The owner of this pre-war, timber-built boat had restored all the original rigging, which took most of us to haul up the main and fore sails.

There were moments of mild personality conflicts – especially when Jamal refused to take his turn to wash up the dishes (on the basis that a Lebanese gentleman does not do that sort of work!). The cruise was great fun and I had the opportunity to practise my newly learned navigation skills.

A letter to a friend who lived in America, dated 8th January 1976:

> ...I must say that one of the most positive and important things in my life is to be with my sons and, of course, having had children, especially when they are mature and become good mates... The past few months have been a good time, spent straightening out Mark to overcome the knock he took from not getting the results he had hoped. Now, he has settled well, everything is going fine and in the last few months all seemed to have improved enormously. Things weren't that bad but he was in a frame of mind which blocked him. It has also helped me to regularise my life rather more and spend time enjoying him and my home. My other son is in good shape mentally and physically and our relationship has become good also. So – how can I complain? I certainly do not have enough time to do everything I want and suppose one is for ever hoping that one will meet the person with whom one can have a deep mental and physical relationship but this may be pure fantasy and romanticism on my part... At the end of the month we go skiing in France and then I am back to Saudi Arabia and Egypt on business.

A signifier of future tendencies became evident when Mark was about seven years old: he argued with one of the teachers who had reprimanded him for picking flowers from a front garden on his way to school. No doubt, had he acquired the necessary exam grades, he would have been destined for a career in the legal profession, but he was bitterly disappointed when he was rejected. Instead, he opted for History at Norwich University, but before the first term ended, he returned to London to tell me that he had quit the course.

Timorously, he said he was really interested in becoming a journalist or filmmaker but had no idea where he could read the combined subjects. I suggested that he create his own 'university' by studying a couple of languages and attending writing courses, and that as I had met David Bailey and knew one or two other well-known photographers, I could arrange for him to train in their studios for a few months at a time. This did not appeal, and instead he enrolled at the London College of Printing where he got the technical training he wanted, although at that time it was a hot-bed of Trotskyite indoctrination.

From the time Mark was a young teenager until soon after he became a student, he had worked at several part-time jobs: Friday and Saturday evenings pulling pints at the local pub; as an agent selling insurance, at which he made good money; as expert cocktail shaker at Joe Allen's restaurant in Covent Garden; and as occasional DJ at the Alibi Club in King's Road, Chelsea. Then, in his mid-twenties, the influence of the London College of Printing changed his attitude to commerce and making money.

As a graduate, he worked for The Arts Project for eleven years before setting up his own independent studio, fully equipped to film, edit and produce TV documentaries, which included a couple of award-winning videos of the Poll Tax riots in London and the plight of the Turkish immigrants in Germany. He script writes all his own material and has devoted his working life to defending those who are the victims of injustice; like a knight warrior, crusading to right the wrongs. If there is strife or trouble, he will be there to film it. Many seemingly lost causes have certainly benefited from Mark's intervention.

Christopher's characteristic talents were illustration and design, which were evident when he was at the grammar school and well-recognised by the head teacher who asked him to draw a cartoon to illustrate a piece of text for the school magazine. His first drawing was clever, beautifully drawn and fitted the text, but he was not satisfied. For the next few days he was in a stressed state of mind, persistently redrawing the cartoon and changing the whole concept until the final deadline when the teacher demanded a finished sketch. Luckily, he retrieved the original drawing, which was far superior to anything he had subsequently produced, and the published cartoon received great praise from the school. Even without the necessary O and A levels, the Central St Martins School of Art (now part of the University of the Arts London) accepted him for their Foundation

Course where he thrived until, for whatever reason, he quit at the end of the first year.

Perhaps Christopher's multi-talented gifts scattered his abilities and focus. From time to time I encouraged him to concentrate his energies on just one thing for, say, six months, such as working as a photographer or illustrator, or doing something positive with his creative, Monty Pythonesque comic imagery. He did get a job working as an illustrator on the film *Highlander* but it was a fairly short-lived appointment.

Christopher rarely seemed to be gainfully employed, yet he too, somehow, managed to thrive – or at least to survive. As well as being a talented artist with an unusually comic sense of the bizarre, he was also a naturally gifted photographer of buildings, and several London property agents commissioned him to take photographs for their sales brochures. Again, he never pursued this aspect of his work. Later, it emerged that he was driven to emulate the sort of work Mark was doing, but attempts at collaborating with him to write TV scripts only led to brotherly conflict. I cannot understand why he felt so overshadowed, but maybe that is sometimes inevitable between brothers.

I did not see Betty again until Christopher married Christa, twenty-five years after our divorce. Betty had remarried a few years after we had broken up and her new husband was a Doctor McCrae, the brother of the wife of her next-door-but-one neighbour in Hall Lane (a man who had been the locum doctor when Christopher was born). When her husband died a few years later, she began teaching English. She still lives in the same house we bought forty-five years ago. Other than one other meeting, at Mark and Ilga's wedding, we have remained out of contact for these past forty years.

Mother at Home

Mother's active daily routine carried on until she was about eighty-nine years old and could no longer climb the stairs. She refused to allow me to set up a bed on the ground floor and, in any case, found it too uncomfortable to lie down. The suggestion of moving into a comfortable hospice or home was impossible for her to contemplate. Instead, I bought her a throne-like, well-upholstered high-backed upright armchair, which she sat in for the next four years, and I paid for two private nurses to attend to her three times a day on a rota system. Fortunately, they were professional enough to ride out Mother's tantrums.

Incontinence and sitting in the same position for four years eventually led her to develop sores that turned gangrenous. Her indefatigable spirit staved off the inevitable deterioration until one evening the nurse phoned to say Mother wanted to see me urgently. By this time, in 1995, I was living with Janet, who sometimes came with me on my regular visits. This time, however, I went alone and found her in a seriously poor state and failing fast; her neighbour June was there, trying to help the nurse. Mother whispered to me that she had read somewhere that euthanasia was now legal and that if I found three doctors they could jointly certify that she wanted to be given a lethal injection. Knowing she was in such pain, it was heartbreaking to tell her that it was still not allowed in England.

The nurse said that Mother had always refused to take the sleeping pills and painkillers prescribed by her doctor. She showed me where they were kept in a kitchen cupboard. I asked the nurse and June the neighbour to go back to her own house across the road and wait for me there. By this time, Mother was exhausted: her life energy was ebbing away from her. She asked me to give her all the pills. As her life energy drained from her, I held her for half an hour or more, kissed her, told her I loved her, and left when she was asleep. Across the road, in the neighbour's house, I told the nurse to leave her in peace as she was unlikely to survive the night. When the nurse returned for her morning visit at 7.30am she found Mother in a coma, and a few minutes later she died. She was ninety-three.

Two or three of Mother's neighbours, the two nurses, and my cousin Kenny came to the cemetery where she was buried in my father's grave. It was a sad, impersonal affair, at the end of which, we left the graveside and went our separate ways. Although I felt the burden of my life had been lifted, I know I have never really mourned her death.

It has been my good fortune that I inherited my mother's long-life genes, her love of music and sport, her tenacious independent spirit, drive, energy as well as, regrettably, her stubborn streak of *knowing I am right*. I still need to control situations and challenge bureaucratic incompetence, and have never fully overcome the sense that I am an outsider, rarely acknowledging that I was ever accepted in a group or social gathering. During Mother's lifetime and since, I have spent a lot of time and money on psychotherapy, trying to understand and exorcise my relationship with her, and resolve my relationships with women.

PART II

Thomas Saunders
Chartered Architect

5

Gainful Employment

1954–1961

Assistant Architect

My first permanent employer was Percy Bilton Limited, a firm of developers and civil engineering contractors, who paid me £10 a week as an assistant architect, designing their speculative factory buildings and repairing bomb-damaged buildings in Bermondsey. This soulless work paid me more than my fellow graduates were earning and gave me the chance to experience the inside operations of a building construction company. However, there were two pressing matters which had to be addressed. The first was that RIBA graduate students had to have two years' employment and experience with a bone fide firm of chartered architects, who had to monitor and report their progress, before being allowed to sit the final Professional Practice exam to become a fully qualified architect. The second matter was the dark cloud of two years of National Service conscription that had hung over me since I was eighteen years old. Students were exempt up to the age of twenty-five, but I would only be twenty-four when I took the final Professional Practice exam.

I left Biltons to join a large firm of architects in Bishopsgate in the City, called Ley Colbeck and Partners. Its reputation was based mainly on their designs for industrial buildings, as well as the Vickers Armstrong Polaris submarine bases in Barrow-in-Furness in the north of England. More importantly, they were extremely efficient at administration control and good business systems – the very experience I needed to pass the Professional Practice exam.

At the same time, my evenings and weekends were spent on private work, designing shop fronts and interiors for a small firm of shop fitters in Hornchurch, and other drawing work for a few local builders in the Upminster area. I also returned to the college art department for an evening course on perspective drawing and graphic illustration to further develop the rendering techniques I had learned in the third year.

At Ley Colbeck, I worked in the main studio in Bishopsgate with about eighty other architects of varying status. I was assigned to work as an assistant on a new headquarters building for Barclays Bank. The project chief had been a set designer at Shepperton Film Studios, and it was no wonder the scheme looked theatrical. A month or two later, Ley, the senior partner, summoned me to his office to tell me that one of his major industrial clients had commissioned the firm to design a new staff sports pavilion and he wanted me to produce the initial sketches.

My design drawings did not meet with Ley's approval. He agreed with the planning and layout, but the modern treatment was not what he'd had in mind: he wanted a 'pavilion' pastiche of early Edwardian bandstand architecture with a clock tower, pergolas and planked white woodwork. It was as if strains of the 'Eton Boating Song' had evoked his visual concept of what a sports pavilion should look like. He didn't disguise his displeasure with my sketches and my colleagues tried to calm the stream of abuse I hurled at Ley after he left the studio.

In fury, I set about redesigning the elevations and perspective illustrations. Within a couple of days, the new design sketches incorporated bits of Wren, Hawksmoor, Lutyens, together with some of the nineteenth-century garden follies so popular among the nouveaux riches of the Surrey Hills, as well as a W.G. Grace silhouette weathervane adorning a clock tower. The exercise was therapeutic, as well as being amusing to the others in the studio, although my immediate boss was concerned that it was too mockingly scornful. Before I could make any changes, Ley came to my drawing board to see how the revised scheme was going. It was an astonishing anti-climax: Ley said he was delighted, and that I should add the finishing touches to the drawings as soon as possible because he wanted to present the scheme to the client personally! Indignation and disappointment urged me to resign on the spot but the need for the credentials for the Professional Practice exam and the daunting thought of the pending conscription restrained me from leaving.

Clearly, Ley Colbeck and Partners were not renowned for their architectural design work and to my relief, shortly after this episode,

I was transferred to the small design team annexe located on the second floor of Abdullah's Ships' Stores, in Helmet Court, a narrow alleyway that no longer exists, where the staircase to our five-man design office oasis reeked of Abdullah's oriental spices. I am sure our little team working on office interior design, reception entrances and display areas, was kept away from the main office studio to avoid corrupting the others with any fancy ideas. One major project was the refurbishment and conversion of a grand private mansion in Barrow, for the use of the Vickers Armstrong directors and their client visitors. Most of the time I was left to get on without too much interference from Ley and the other partners who seemed relieved that this type of work was being taken out of their hands.

In the meantime, I had a steady stream of private projects. Soon after Mark was born, we moved to a newly built semi-detached house on a housing estate. Everything was progressing well until, on the same day that I was notified that I had passed the Professional Practice exam and was now an RIBA chartered architect, I received an official buff postcard, directing me to attend a medical examination in London.

Conscription, 1956

The war in Korea had ended and the threat of a full scale war caused by the British and French Suez Canal invasion fiasco had abated. Since peace had broken out the armed forces were overcrowded. The media reported that National Service would soon be abandoned or, at the very least, the two-year period reduced. The decision was dependent on politics and economics; one side insisting that we should be armed to the teeth, the other demanding 'butter, not guns'. I thought a twenty-four-year-old qualified architect could contribute more to the economy as a civilian than being trained to kill people.

When the first batch of call-up papers arrived, I decided that if I had to serve for two years I would rather sign for a three-year short-term commission with better pay and conditions, and to train to be an airman or sail boats in the Air-Sea Rescue regiment.

I had gleaned many stories from my fellow student ex-servicemen about the 'dodges' their subordinates had tried in order to avoid call-up or service duties. I thought that the most promising excuses I could come up with were migraine headaches and back problems.

Since leaving Mayfield School, migraine headaches had periodically plagued my student days, and there was sound medical evidence to prove it. Back problems were not unusual for architects because we spent our working hours bent over a drawing board.

I'd had one bad-back incident. Shortly after starting work at Biltons, I had stooped down and, as I did so, the muscles had grabbed a vertebra. I was in agony and by lunchtime had to go home. On the train it was too painful to sit down, and at Mile End station I lurched to get out before blacking out on the platform. I partially regained consciousness when the two ambulance men lifted me into a chair-like stretcher and carried me up the long flight of steps. It was then that, quite suddenly, all muscular tension was released and the pain vanished. The only person now in any sort of discomfort was the ambulance man facing me. In order to carry me in the chair, he had tucked one of my feet under the other, but with each step up, one foot dislodged itself under the ambulance man's crotch, causing him to wince in agony.

At the time of joining Ley Colbeck, it had not occurred to me that their work for the Vickers Armstrong Polaris bases could be used to apply for exemption, even though my contribution was in creating a private hotel for the visiting directors and clients. The partner in charge of the project was concerned that I was about to leave for military service, especially as the Vickers Armstrong directors were impatient to have their own hotel instead of having to book into less salubrious establishments. He wrote to the Ministry of Defence, telling them of my professional work connected to Polaris, my important position in the production team, and how my expertise was vital to the overall project, without ever specifying my actual role. The Ministry acknowledged receipt of the letter without referring to the request for exemption.

On the morning of the medical, I filed into the nineteenth-century civic centre hall with about 500 brash eighteen-year-olds. I had not slept for over thirty-six hours and, as well as having drunk a lot of alcohol, just before arrival I swallowed a substance given me by a student friend, a recently qualified pharmacist, who had guaranteed that the albumen content in my urine test would dramatically increase.

Bench seats were arranged in front of seven or eight doctors, sitting in partly partitioned-off cubicles, each one of whom specialised in different parts of the human anatomy. In the centre, a group of three doctors served as adjudicators, appraising the findings of the specialists, before grading everyone's overall fitness. The layout was like a primitive tribal encampment. All the doctors looked tired, and a bit tired of life.

The first doctor I approached was in his late fifties. He gasped for breath through his nose like an overbred snub-nosed Pekinese dog: I stifled a laugh when he announced that he was the ear, nose and throat specialist! He began a cursory hearing test, turning away from me and whispering phrases like, "Fish and chips...Westminster Abbey". My ability to repeat his words was considered sufficient medical proof that I had perfect hearing. Then, after a brief look down my throat, he asked how I felt. I told him that although I had suffered from severe migraine headaches for many years, the main problem was my weak spine and described in detail how I had blacked out on Mile End station. Totally uninterested, he decided that I was now fit and the back trouble was nothing to worry about.

"Sit down, Sonny," he said, picking up a syringe-like instrument that looked like it was designed to be used to artificially inseminate an adult elephant. I jerked away, telling him that if any medical treatment was needed, my own doctor would do it. He snuffled something about it being a free country and my right to choose my own doctor, then telling me that he could not finally grade my fitness until my ears had been treated. Frustrated and peeved, he ushered me out of the cubicle, shouting, "And don't forget to get the ears done."

I moved on, removing an item of clothing to reveal the relevant part of my anatomy for each doctor's speciality examination. My answer to each identical bored question, "Sonny...how are you?" was as unvaried as their response. Clearly they were only concerned in detecting cases of potential heart failure, chronic hernias, VD or haemorrhoids.

Finally, it was time for the three doctors' overall assessment.

"Now tell us about these headaches."

Trying to sound casually evasive, I said that provided I could lie down in a darkened room I could be up and about again within a few hours. Of course, the occasional vomiting was unpleasant *but* the real trouble was the back and the blackouts. The doctor interjected at that point, wanting to know more about the migraine symptoms. After further interrogation he asked for permission to write to my doctor for the case history notes. It was not easy to look frail and morbid dressed only in woolly socks and a pair of Y-fronts. I signed the declaration form.

"Good," he said. "And don't forget to have your ears syringed, otherwise we can't grade you."

Next, I was directed to another room to join others who wanted to serve in the RAF. After the intelligence test paper that was designed to separate idiots from cretins, and a test for colour blindness, I was interviewed by an RAF officer. The officer said I would be accepted in the Air-Sea Rescue unit but that the final decision would be in abeyance until I had been graded.

I was now resigned to becoming a member of Her Majesty's Services. Three weeks later, another official buff postcard arrived, directing me to the same medical centre, where, I assumed, I would be informed that I was graded as being unfit for duty.

An usher directed me to the same ENT doctor (obviously, the migraines and back ploy hadn't worked!). I winced as the pug-nosed doctor prodded the syringe into my ear. He was astonished and furious that nothing had been done. I told him that I had intended to have it sorted immediately before reporting for duty.

"But I can't *grade* you until your ears have been syringed and inspected!"

Exasperated, he sought direction from the three doctors who looked as though they had not moved since my last visit. I was summoned to the table and pleaded that I had every intention of having it done and wanted to cooperate but...they had wasted a whole afternoon of my time which was vital to the Polaris submarine programme!

The approach of my twenty-fifth birthday increased the tension of an uncertain immediate future until another plain buff, officially stamped envelope arrived containing an identity card, which stated that Thomas Saunders had been graded 'three, unfit for service'. Was it the medical condition or Polaris that had done the trick? Friends well-acquainted with Her Majesty's Ministry of Defence thought my outburst at the medical had resulted in my being categorised as an 'undesirable' and 'troublemaker'!

One month later, conscription was reduced to eighteen months and complete abolition swiftly followed. On reflection, and with some regret, I do think service in the armed forces would have been a worthy experience; it certainly would have profoundly changed the course of my life.

The Swiss Israel Trade Bank

With the threat of conscription now vanished, I continued at Ley Colbeck, working on the hotel in Barrow and other design projects. In early 1957, one of the partners, Mr Dicketts LRIB (who unknowingly was about to become my third major 'patron'), instructed me to accompany him to a meeting with a Mr Solomon of the Swiss Israel Trade Bank. This new client had come to Ley Colbeck through unusual circumstances: when the senior partner of one of the other London practices had wanted to retire, the remaining three partners divided between them their current clients and ongoing projects. One of these partners joined Ley Colbeck on a temporary basis and while he looked for a new partnership elsewhere, he assigned one of his projects, the Swiss Israel Trade Bank, to the firm. Shortly afterwards, when he was offered a partnership in another firm he resigned from Ley Colbeck, leaving them with a prestigious interior design bank project that in no way matched their expertise.

In February we met the CEO, Mr Solomon. He had leased the entire ground floor and double-height basement in Barrington House, Gresham Street, for the bank's London offices. The project included a banking hall, conference rooms and offices on the ground floor, with a new lift and staircase down to an archives room, which was to be built over a new strong room, with space for communications equipment in the tall basement. Solomon needed the initial sketch scheme proposals to be presented in three weeks and the final concept drawings and perspectives to be ready for him to take to Geneva for approval by early April. It was imperative that the opening ceremony took place seven months later, on 25th September.

Dicketts seemed overwhelmed by the demands of the brief. His bewildered glance gave me the opportunity to speak up: I said that the timetable was possible but that I would have to have Solomon's approval for the layouts and perspective sketches by the first week in March, and the contract would have to be negotiated quickly. He would also have to put pressure on the firm of property agents, Jones Lang Wootton (now known as Jones Lang LaSalle), who represented the building's owners, to approve the works without delay. The deal was agreed.

Outside Solomon's office, Dicketts asked me how the hell it could be done. Since leaving college, during evenings and weekends, I had worked for Albert, the boss of a shopfitting firm in Hornchurch, designing layouts and sketches for his mini-supermarket and other shop clients. Here I had experienced how all shopfitters prefabricated everything to enable the fitting-out work to be completed on site within a couple of days. I knew it could be done.

I told Dicketts that I would have to work on the project full-time, and a contract would have to be negotiated with Courtney Pope – the biggest shopfitting contractors in the UK – as well as their building contractor specialists. I would use their team of setting-out draughtsmen to detail all the drawing work from my designs. I told him not to expect to see me in the office except to collect my monthly pay cheque, because I would either be at Courtney Pope's offices or on site.[2]

Geneva approved my project drawings and illustrations. I then started negotiations with the contractors and prepared the smaller-scale technical drawings for building bye-laws and the building owner's approvals. At Courtney Pope's factory and offices they seconded four of their draughtsman to work for me. (Typical of the shopfitting industry, they employed some of the finest draughtsmen who set out on paper every piece of a job for prefabrication to full size on seven-metre-long drawing tables.) Every day I sketched out the details of each aspect of the design for the chief draughtsman who, in turn, instructed his team to complete the fabrication drawings. My time was split between the design work at Courtney Pope's workshops, selecting specialist materials and inspecting the work on site.

The building contractor unit started on site in May to gut the existing areas and begin the main structural works. It was a major construction job: cutting the ground floor slab with a thermal lance to create the access down to the basement for the new staircase and lift; the building of the strong room and archives room; then the fitting-out installation of the finished interior design work of the banking hall and offices.

---

2   The letters 'LRIBA' after Dicketts's name denoted that he was a Licentiate of the Royal Institute of British Architects. The RIBA was granted its Royal Charter in 1837 and anyone could practice and call themselves 'architect' until 1931 when the Architects Registration Council of the UK (ARCUK) allowed all those architects who had been in practice for a certain number of years to adopt the designation 'Licentiate RIBA'. Thereafter there were examinations to qualify as an Associate RIBA. When an Associate had been in practice for six or seven years the designation 'Fellow RIBA' could be awarded. Several years ago the RIBA dropped the letters 'L', 'A' and 'F', and now only 'RIBA' is generally used except by old-timers like me.

During the last two months before the September deadline I was on site every day, including weekends. Here I met Mr Weston, a partner in Jones Lang Wootton (JLW), who would turn out to be another 'patron'. Towards completion, as the design features began to show, his visits, always accompanied by groups of people, became more frequent. One day, when he was conducting a party of Japanese around the site, I overheard him pointing out the ceiling treatment and the light fittings and asking the group if they liked the design of the partitions, the general layout, and so on. I knew he was obliged to report to the building's owners on the progress of the works, but who were all these people? I asked Weston what was going on.

Reluctantly, he admitted that his firm was busily engaged as letting agents for large office accommodation and with the new influx of banks into the City, JLW's surveyors and draughtsmen were carrying out similar projects for their various clients. He had been bringing some of his clients and surveyor staff to the site to show them good modern design work and my choice of materials and fittings. I told him in blunt language that his surveyors would never have any original design ideas of their own, and that one day soon, when I started my own practice, JLW could send their clients to me direct. With that parting shot, I told him and his entourage to leave the site.

Dicketts saw the finished job for the first time when he came to the grand opening on 25th September. He'd had no idea that for the past eight months his patronage had offered me, a twenty-six-year-old assistant architect, a once-in-several-lifetime's opportunity. Shortly afterwards, I passed the Professional Practice exam, qualified as an Associate member of the RIBA, and left Ley Colbeck to work for Sydney Kaye and Partners in their Holborn office design department.

I became one of twenty young architects in the design team, each of whom had their own new office project. Mine was a site in Tottenham Court Road. These were the post-war days of feverish building expansion in London, when architects Sydney Kaye and Partners and Richard Seifert and Partners, and their main property developer client, Charles Clore, dominated the design and construction of most post-war speculative office developments, which changed the urban landscape of the City and central areas of London.

Sydney Kaye's major project, and town planning coup, was a hotel scheme in Park Lane, which, at the time, was destined to be the tallest building in the West End. Controversially, the topmost floor would be able to overlook the gardens of Buckingham Palace. Grand Metropolitan Hotels, Hilton Hotels, and other operators were interested to lease the building when completed, and although each hotel group had its own specific requirements for the public areas and size of rooms, the approved fenestration of the façade could not be changed. Every so often, the whole design team would set aside our individual projects and with rubber guns – like slugs of rubber in a small Black and Decker drill – clean off the gold-back prints and overdraw the new layouts to suit the latest hotel operator's brief. Eventually, Clore signed a twenty-one-year lease with Conrad Hilton and after a boozy lunch at the Mirabelle to celebrate the deal, they swayed in to our office to meet us, the design team.

The Breakthrough

Most mornings I travelled to work on the Southend over-ground train from Upminster to Fenchurch Street with John, a quantity surveyor friend who occasionally asked me to prepare sketches for some of his projects. On the last Friday in January, 1961, he invited me to lunch at his office to talk about one of his clients, whom I'll call Mr B: who was the boss of a freelance entrepreneurial company that searched for speculative development petrol filling station sites for 'one of the major oil companies'. Mr B's problem was the frequent delay between engaging an architect to investigate the planning situation and the production of the design and submission for planning approval. The delay often resulted in losing the deal. John had suggested to Mr B that he should finance the setting up of a practice for an architect like me who could give him first priority in all his projects.

John told me that if I was interested, he would arrange a meeting with Mr B on the Monday after the weekend. He said that there was one important proviso: I would have to start on the first day of March. Without a second thought I decided to quit my job at Sydney Kaye's that afternoon as their rules stipulated that notice must be given on the last day of any month, and it would be another four weeks before I had another chance. John advised me against doing so before the Monday meeting, thinking it too much of a risk, but I was undeterred, convinced that whatever the outcome with Mr B, I had the confidence to get another job.

On the Monday, I met Mr B. Except for his creamy-white shirt, everything else was black – his suit, moustache, hair, shoes and tie. It was all too funereal. In a monotone, he told me curtly that I would be in 'partnership' with his brother-in-law, who was an electrical engineer, and I would be paid a salary rather than fees. My small private clientele of contractors and shopfitters, and a factory extension project, were dismissed as irrelevant because I would only have time for his projects. Any additional fees earned would have to go into the kitty. I struggled to maintain a pleasant countenance, saying that although I was interested, I was bound by the RIBA ethical code of conduct and needed to check that having Mr B's brother-in-law as a partner would be in accordance with the rules.

That afternoon at Portland Place, the RIBA confirmed that a non-chartered architect as a partner was not allowed. Later, I called John to tell him that I could not agree to Mr B's terms. I still hoped we might be able to work something out: it was a gamble but the stakes were good. John called back to say that it would have to be on Mr B's terms or not at all.

That Monday evening I faced a life-changing challenge. At the end of the month I would be unemployed, with a wife and two young children to support. I had the mortgage on our semi-detached house to pay, as well as the cash each month earmarked for my mother, which supplemented June's contribution from Bombay. I would have next month's £100 pay cheque, but I had no savings, and did not even own a car.

I decided that this was the moment to take the plunge and start on my own, despite the news announced by Selwyn Lloyd, the Chancellor of the Exchequer, that there was to be yet another economic squeeze. After all, this is what I had told Weston I would do four years earlier at the Swiss Israel Trade Bank site. When I told an old student friend that I was about to start my own practice he said he was not surprised because when we were first year students he remembered me saying that I would only want to work for myself. It felt like some piece of fortuitous synchronicity was at work.

I placed adverts in the architectural journals, one offering to help other busy practices; the other a service to architects needing perspective drawings and presentation work. I set up a telephone extension and drawing board in our small front bedroom, ready to start work at the end of the month. A friend printed up the headed paper and I borrowed a typewriter. I realised that I would need a car, so I quickly found out hire purchase terms. Getting things done was the easy bit; how to pay for them was another matter.

On 1st February, 1961, in quiet excitement, I started business, with enough work for a week or two. This marked the end of my third ten-year cycle, and the early beginnings of *Thomas Saunders Architect*, which evolved into *Thomas Saunders Associates*, and later became *The Thomas Saunders Partnership* (TTSP).

6

The Practice

1961–1974

Thomas Saunders Architect

Within the first three weeks, I was kept so busy with new shop design work, house extensions, a small factory building for Blagden Drums in Barking, and other minor schemes that I had to refuse ghosting work. It wasn't long before I had to call on old student friends to help with detailed drawing work. A month later, I could afford to buy a Ford Popular on hire purchase.

Often, a client would pay an extra fee for a coloured perspective drawing of his project (bearing in mind this was before we had computers to produce three-dimensional perspective illustrations). The good response to the February adverts for the perspective work was hardly surprising because so few architects had acquired the techniques themselves. There were only two or three professional perspectivists, and they commanded substantial sums for their highly artistic work on major prestigious projects. My charges for perspectives were £25 for a black and white and £40 for a coloured rendering, depending on the size and complexity of the job. (The evening classes I attended at the college were starting to pay off.)

A month after I had set up the practice, my newly appointed accountant, Michael Leigh, who had recently started his own practice, told me that one of his clients might need my services. They were a two-man partnership that had taken over a tuck shop in Cranbrook Road, Ilford, selling cards, tobacco and sweets. At the rear was a small snack bar that served the local shoppers and school kids with sandwiches, drinks and beans on toast. They appointed me to design the major alterations to extend the snack bar area, and a week or so later I presented a set of drawings with coloured sketches showing the interior treatment.

The clients approved the scheme and instructed me to proceed with the detailed drawings for bye-law and planning approval. A few days later, when I returned to the shop to check the existing drainage at the rear, one of the partners greeted me with a despondent look: they had decided to not proceed with the project because they had a cash-flow problem, and the business was not strong enough to warrant the expansion. With this was depressing news, I decided that £35 would be a reasonable fee to charge for all the work carried out to date.

A month passed after I had posted the invoice, I called the client to settle the fee. Michael, the accountant, then told me that his clients had asked if he thought the fee was reasonable, and that he had confirmed that they should pay. Armed with this information, I telephoned the shop again. When the client said he would post a cheque that afternoon I told him to save the price of a stamp as I was on my way to collect it in person, and I put the phone down before he'd had time to argue. Half an hour later I arrived at the shop. Immediately the man became evasive. I lost my temper, reminding that him he had instructed me to proceed, that my fee was more than reasonable, and that I needed the cash. It was fortunate there were no customers in the shop at that point, as I 'eased' him towards the till and gave him the choice of either writing the cheque immediately or after I had 'filled in his face'! He grudgingly wrote the cheque. This was the first and last time I resorted to tactics typical of my East End roots to get money owed to me.

Six months later, while playing some Beethoven on the gramo-phone and colouring up a perspective for an architect's community centre scheme, the phone rang. The caller was Eric Deane (yet another 'patron'), a partner in Jones Lang Wootton, who said that one of his colleagues, a Mr Weston, had told him of his 'conversation' with me at the Swiss Israel Bank. Deane invited me to meet him at his offices in the City.

Eric Deane and two other partners greeted me in the boardroom where they outlined the increasing demand for space in the City by the increasing influx of international banks and other business clients. JLW found that the clients not only appointed them to negotiate the leasing of office and banking hall spaces but also wanted them to carry out the refurbishments and the interior layouts of the premises. Eric said that as his staff were surveyors with no architectural or interior design capability, he would like me to act as JLW's design consultant and perhaps in some cases, taking over certain specific projects myself. Thus began a long, prosperous, and enjoyable relationship that led to the rapid development of my practice. What an extraordinary appointment! No wonder every day I felt energised and excited.

The significance of being associated with property agents such as JLW (now Jones Lang LaSalle), CB Richard Ellis, or Cushman Wakefield Healey and Baker is that they are the first port of call when a business organisation needs a site for development or to lease new premises. The client's choice of architect and the project's professional team are greatly influenced by the recommendations of these powerful, now global, property organisations.

My energy and sense of excitement reflected the country's recovery from post-war austerity, and the revolution in social attitudes of the 1960s. Thus began the new era of youth and youthfulness, hedonism and optimism, with The Beatles, The Rolling Stones, the offshore pirate radio music stations, Mini Cooper cars, miniskirts, Carnaby Street, the Kings Road in Chelsea, and the Pill. Latter-day commentators have said that if you can remember the '60s then you weren't there, implying that everyone was in a haze of cannabis! Certainly I was there, but regrettably far too busy with my family and business to fully enjoy those early days of the Swinging Sixties' social revolution.

At the same time, an economic revolution was transforming the banking and financial centre in the City of London that would become the foundation of the success of the practice. Here, *patron* and *place* could not have created a more auspicious time to be a young architect. It was also fortuitous that I had always been drawn to focus on interior planning and environmental design – after all, it is the inside of the buildings, where people live, work, play and make love – which should dictate the architecture of a building. It makes no sense to design the façade first, hoping it will then fit the use of the interior. It was also my good fortune that most architects have little training, skill or interest in designing from the inside out.

The boundaries of the City, known colloquially as the Square Mile, date back to Roman times, and since the Middle Ages, the area has been the banking and financial centre of London. Its own Lord Mayor and local authority Corporation are independent of the rest of London. The City is London's centre of gravity, where the Tower of London, St Paul's Cathedral and the big businesses of Lloyds, the international banks, and insurance institutions are located. (And in those days, the wholesale markets, such as Billingsgate, Smithfield, Spitalfields and the Borough were to be found there too, before they were relocated.)

The City used to be a largely non-residential zone, isolated from the surrounding urban housing areas. Unless you were an office worker, banker, stockbroker or 'something in the City' – if you lived and worked west of say, Holborn, the Aldwych or Covent Garden – you never ventured eastwards. East End places, such as Bethnal Green, were virtually unknown to most Londoners.

It is still the accepted view of those who work in the City that anyone who has offices west of Holborn must be in the shady business of advertising, theatre agents for show-girls, or mafia-controlled restaurateurs. As for the banks and property companies of Mayfair, they were staffed by pimps and hookers and most of their dealings were on the fringe of the underworld. Of course, the West End businessmen had an equally prejudiced view of the 'Square-milers'! It is true to say, however, that the quest for respectability has induced many West End organisations to swallow the exorbitantly high City rents and join what used to be called 'the bowler hat brigade'. Strangely, there appear to be more entrepreneurs, true eccentrics and 'characters' in the City offices than, for instance, one would find in the music businesses in Soho.

Historically, London *was* the City. Its narrow alleyways and pubs serving good 'Dickens'-type food are (or used to be) peppered with extraordinarily interesting and exciting places. At night the City used to be deserted, with very few restaurants and pubs open in the evening except a couple of nightclubs, the Mermaid Theatre (before it was abandoned), the new Tower Hotel, and St Katherine's Dock, which attracted those adventurous people prepared to travel around the area at night. Some West-Enders ventured to the river areas like Wapping when it was discovered that Princess Margaret and Lord Snowden were having clandestine meetings there, but generally it was, and still is, of no interest to the inhabitants of Chelsea and Knightsbridge.

Later, in the 1980s, the residential development of the Barbican flats, office and warehouse conversions, and the Docklands redevelopment projects rapidly increased the number of people living in the City area.

Cranbrook Road Offices

The booming business with JLW and other newly acquired clients created an urgent need to engage part-time secretarial services and other architects to 'ghost' for me. Suddenly, I had to find proper office space. A chance call, when I was searching for a firm selling second-hand plan-chests, chairs and desks, solved my problem. One office furniture company mentioned their intention to vacate their two-roomed office in Cranbrook Road, Ilford. We arranged to meet at the premises. The offices were over a greengrocer's shop with a side entrance to the upper floors, and immediately next to the ex-client's tuck shop, which was still being run by the man who had to be 'persuaded' to pay my fees.

That afternoon, during the conversation with the greengrocer who owned the building, I discovered that he had been one of my father's customers at Marshall and Masters and had spent many hours playing snooker and cards with him at the local Loxford Club in Ilford. We went on to agree the rent for the second floor space which had one large room at the front and a small room to the rear. Soon after, I moved in with some second-hand furniture and two plan-chests, and advertised for a secretary and an architectural assistant. The Nyth Close 'office' was reinstated as a bedroom. Nine months after moving in I was no longer a sole practitioner and I renamed the practice *Thomas Saunders Associates*. This marked the beginning of my third ten-year cycle. Two years later I expanded into the floor below, when United Friendly Insurance moved out to their new premises.

The tuck shop enjoyed our good business, and we never discussed our earlier encounter. The greengrocer did well from us too. When the fresh walnuts were on display for the three or four weeks in the late autumn, they brought back memories of those few times my father came home with a small sack of the large French variety. Together, after lunch on a Saturday, we cracked open the shells and dipped the nuts in a little mound of salt.

One of the first people I employed was a young man called Derek Joiner, who was a one-day-a-week part-time student at the South-West Essex Technical College in Walthamstow. Each term the college was obliged to send a copy of his report to his employer. These reports were poor and I soon discovered that while he should have been attending the Wednesday part-time courses, he was playing football for the college in the afternoon. By the time he joined the practice he had produced little or no design work for the past two terms and was about to be either relegated to a lower year or expelled completely. I had several meetings with Sandy, the head of the Architecture department, where I made excuses for Derek, encouraging Sandy to keep him on the course.

As the business increased, I employed other part-time students, including Albert Hayden, who talked to Sandy and other lecturers about the practice and the projects they were working on, which earned Thomas Saunders Associates a reputation as a firm worth joining for good experience.

At one of my meetings with Sandy, he invited me to take over the two-hours-a-week Professional Practice and Business Management slot from the current lecturer who was leaving. My first reaction was to decline because during my own two-year postgraduate studies I had felt there was still much more for me to learn. But on the premise that the quickest way to learn a subject is to teach it (and get paid to do so), I accepted. It was a job I would have for the next four years. Fortunately, at the time, there was good backup provided by the RIBA, it being the first professional organisation to publish and run seminars on office management to improve the business administration control in architects' offices.

The RIBA Final exam, after five years' full-time study, still requires a graduate architect to work for two years in an RIBA-approved, professional architect's office, while also attending lectures on Professional Practice. The work experience must be under the supervision of a qualified architect and a log book must be completed, showing a daily record of the work carried out. At the end of their two years, architects can sit the final 'Final', and if successful, are allowed to call themselves 'Chartered Architect'. The examination covers building law, the law of contracts, insurances, professional ethics, fees and general business management.

Based on personal experience, I recognised that the twenty or so students had been immersed in fine matters of aesthetics and design for the past five years and now they needed help to cope with the mundane matters of day-to-day business and administrative management. My first task was to stimulate them enough to want to read about the subject and to evoke a killer instinct when dealing with an experienced adversary. It was also imperative for them to study the building codes and planning law, so that they would know how to manipulate the rules when it came to acquiring the necessary approvals to build their wondrous architectural gems in the future.

My first lecture for each new intake included an actual test case which concerned a milkman. One day, a woman customer found her bottle of milk contained a used rubber condom. The questions were: who was legally responsible? Who could be sued for damages? They had to ask themselves whether the milkman was blameless in the matter because the bottle had been properly sealed, or if he did, indeed, carry any legal responsibility because he had effected delivery to the woman's door. If it wasn't him, would it be the dairy farm? The milk bottling company? The installers of the bottling plant? Or even the man who had deposited the semen in the condom? This got the students busy researching the Law of Contracts!

Most of my lectures were based on the actual experiences and events the students encountered in their work. The most instructive and entertaining lectures arose when one of the students, who only attended two or three lectures a term, was trying to run a part-time practice in parallel with his studies. He usually arrived carrying a pile of files pertaining to one of his many major business difficulties. My planned lecture would then be abandoned and the session devoted to a discussion on how to overcome his immediate problems such as an unpaid fees issue; a small contractor who was about to go bankrupt and had removed all the plant and materials from the site overnight; income tax related to works in progress; a client who was about to sue him for negligence, and so on. His rare appearances always brought a particular aspect of the syllabus into bright and amusing focus. I am pleased to boast that each year, every one of my students passed the Professional Practice exam (although the countywide average pass mark was forty per cent).

One of the other part-time lecturers was the sculptor Jack McCarthy, who eventually joined the practice in 1974 to run the graphics department until 1984 when he retired to live permanently in France. Another part-time lecturer was an Indian (Parsee) who was also trying to establish his private practice and pleased to do some occasional 'ghosting' work for me. (Several years later I was swimming in the pool at the Willingdon Club in Bombay when I heard his voice: "Hello Tom, what are you doing here?" I pointed out my sister and brother-in-law Russi sitting under the shade of the trees.

"Not old Russi. My God, I've known him for years. We went to school together!")

The chief architect at Ilford Films Limited was a man called Edgar (his surname escapes me) who served on the architects' Education Board at the college and was also the chairman of the Essex Cambridge and Hertfordshire Chapter. He said he had heard about the practice from Sandy and invited me to become a committee member of the Chapter: he wanted to recruit young blood to the committee. I suggested that maybe what he was after was young 'bloody-mindedness' and told him that I came from a line of Tom Saunders, two of whom were connected to his firm Ilford Films Limited: my granddad was a stoker in the boiler room and had started up the trade union and my uncle Tom still worked there as the manager of their export packing department. I declined his kind offer due to family commitments, the pressure of running a young practice and the need to prepare for the part-time lectures.

Edgar called a few months later asking if I was going to the students' Summer Exhibition. We arranged to meet there at 7.30. I arrived early to look at the presentations and talk with the students. When Edgar arrived he came into the hall helping a frail, smartly dressed, white-haired old man with a stick. Edgar introduced me, saying that the man had wanted to meet me because, for many years, he had worked in the boiler house alongside my granddad. I listened to his reminiscences, a most touching and poignant half-hour, until he tired and asked Edgar to take him back home. The next day I called Edgar to thank him, saying that I would have gladly gone to see the man, wherever he lived. Edgar assured me that when he had suggested this to him, the old man had insisted that he wanted a night out!

Soon after moving to the Cranbrook Road offices, JLW called to discuss the extensive repairs, renovation and new design work for the Netherlands Bank of South Africa's existing building, located in a narrow passageway off Lombard Street in the City. At the meeting, I convinced JLW that the project was too complex for me to work jointly with their surveyors department. There was also the added complication of the bank needing to remain in occupation during the construction works therefore, the best way forward, I assured them, was for me to take over the complete project. This was my first major bank project, which cost some £200,000 in the early 1960s, the equivalent of several million pounds today.

Domestic Clients

Through one of the other London property agents, I was introduced to John Guest, a well-known society lawyer whose West End offices were in Christopher Place, off Oxford Street. Most of his clients were listed in *Debrett's Peerage* or were fashionable celebrities. John's 'weekend country cottage' was a grand bungalow, originally built by Noel Coward, on the beach at St Margaret's Bay, nestling under the towering white cliffs of Dover. On one of the rare occasions John and his wife had decided not to spend the weekend there, an overnight cliff-fall had crushed the main bedroom, although the rest of the bungalow was left intact. Before the demolished bedroom could be rebuilt, the chalk face had to be injected with a silicone treatment and held in place with strong wire netting, anchored deep into the cliff face.

While the rebuilding work was in progress, John introduced me to one of his clients, Noel Cunningham-Reid, who used to be a driver for the Aston Martin racing team and was a one-time winner of the Monza Grand Prix. His father, Captain Cunningham-Reid, was a World War One fighter pilot ace who became a Conservative MP. (He was later forced to take 'the Chilton Hundreds', a device used by the House of Commons to allow a sitting member to formally resign, in this case because of the social stigma attached to Cunningham-Reid's divorce.)

Noel had married the socialite debutante Tessa Milne in 1960. When he was introduced to me, they were 'camping out' in the substantial servants' quarters attached to the main house in The Boltons, which they intended to refurbish as their permanent home. I was appointed to carry out the architectural alterations and repairs, and to work with Tessa on the interior decorations. Subsequently, over the years, I worked on similar projects with Tessa, as well as with the wives of other clients, whose varying degrees of talent ranged from being skilled at interior decoration to wreaking 'inferior desecration'.

Some while later Noel introduced me to one of his racing and business associates, David, the Earl of Brecknock. I met him and his wife Ginny at their home in Chelsea Square, another one of the most salubrious addresses in London. David, an accomplished polo player, kept his stable of several polo ponies on Lord Cowdrey's estate in Midhurst, Sussex, where he had recently bought a 'polo weekend cottage' which needed extending and refurbishing. Betty and I were invited for Sunday lunch to view the building before watching the polo. When we arrived, David and Ginny were dressed as though they were about to get involved in some heavy work in the garden. After realising we were overdressed, my heart sank further as I drove my white Ford Cortina GTi into Cowdrey Park and had to park alongside the Bentleys, Rolls and Maseratis. Among the spectators sitting on the tier of six wooden plank benches in front of the clubhouse was Her Majesty the Queen. When I went to the bar, I found myself standing next to Prince Phillip who mumbled something to me about the last chukka, took a sip from his pint, and moved on.

The 'cottage' was a 150-year-old large thatched house that was in a fairly dilapidated state. When I inspected the rafters, riddled with death-watch beetle holes, I suggested that the roof only remained intact because all the beetles must be holding hands! Not surprisingly, getting the necessary Listed Buildings and Planning approvals was an easy matter, and eventually the 'cottage' was doubled in size with a massive, new thatched roof.

Two other projects came to me via Noel and David. The first was the redevelopment of a site in Drayton Gardens, South Kensington, where a new petrol filling station with flats on the upper floors was planned. The second was a project for Rocky Stone, one of their racing car engineer friends, who wanted a structural survey report on a semi-detached corner house he intended to buy in Fulham.

I'd collected the keys from the estate agent. He'd said that the house was still furnished, but when I arrived, the place was completely empty. I set up a base camp in one of the bedrooms. Armed with a small jemmy for lifting a floorboard or two, and a tape recorder I was about to get stuck in when I heard police sirens. Through the window, I could see a swarm of policemen surrounding the house. Suddenly, the front door burst open and three cops brandishing truncheons stared up at me standing at the top of the stairs they told me to "come quietly". Reluctantly, they only accepted my story after half an hour of searching through my bag of tools, listening to the tape recordings and a call to the estate agent. It turned out that earlier in the day, thieves had transferred the house contents into a van and left about an hour before I'd arrived. The next door neighbour had reported the theft, but when she had seen me enter the house, she'd assumed that the thieves had returned to the scene of the crime and had called the police again.

Sir Alfred X

After the rebuilding works at St Margaret's Bay had been completed, at some point in the late '60s John Guest invited me to discuss one of his clients who wanted to explore the likelihood of achieving a planning consent to build six private upmarket houses on his parents' two-hectare estate, next to one of the more famous English public schools. His client was the middle-aged son of Sir Alfred and Lady X. Now in their late seventies, the couple still lived in the grand house they had built for themselves fifty years earlier. Although fiercely independent and insisting on looking after themselves, they needed help but their son could never find the right sort of people to look after them. Now, with their increasing infirmity, it was imperative that they should leave the house and move into an adjoining apartment in his home, where the family could give them the full-time care and attention they needed. Fortunately, after much persuasion, they agreed to leave and for the estate to be sold. The family hoped to increase the value of the property with a planning consent to develop the land for a few individual houses.

Arrangements were made for my visit to the property at eleven o'clock one September morning. I drove up the long curving driveway, densely lined with trees, to the pseudo-Victorian Gothic style house. The entangled ivy surrounding the arched stone porch reminded me of scenes from the *Rocky Horror Show* or *Nightmare Abbey*, a nineteenth -century Gothic revival novel by Thomas Love Peacock, a version of which I'd seen on stage when I was eighteen as part of my research on The Romantic Movement and Victorian Architecture. It was a marvellous satire, lampooning the then fashionable Gothic horror melodramas. The comic star was the butler, dressed in a black tailcoat that had turned moss-green with age, who dragged one foot as he crossed the stage to serve drinks.

Had there been thunder and lightning I might have turned back, but breathing in deeply for confidence, I tugged on the bell-pull. The noise set the dogs barking, sounding like a scene from the *Hound of the Baskervilles*. Eventually, when the oak door creaked open, I discovered that the 'hounds' were three yapping Pekinese, now snapping at my ankles. In the dimly lit hallway stood a slightly bent figure with sparkling eyes, dressed in carpet slippers, crumpled grey trousers and a baggy, sailor's blue jersey.

"Sir Alfred?" I asked.

"Yes, indeed, you must be Mr Saunders."

Once inside, there were the sombre and depressing signs of the couple's struggles to take care of themselves, the cats and the dogs. Sprightly and alert, Sir Alfred led the way, although his foot was dragging a little, reminiscent of the Gothic butler. He ushered me to the oak-panelled dining room, crammed with heavily upholstered chairs around a table that was at least six metres long.

"You must meet my wife, Lady X."

Lady X, in a high-backed armchair at the far end of the table, sat with a copy of *The Times* propped in front of her. She was dressed in black, her button-booted feet perched on the fret of the fire, the embers of which were still glowing in the white ash. Her snoring clearly indicated that she was asleep. We stood in the doorway quietly, and when I implored him not to wake her he waved away my plea and moved towards the table telling me that unfortunately his wife was totally deaf.

"She'd never forgive me if she didn't greet you."

The broad table and the jumbled arrangement of unwieldy chairs left very little room for Sir Alfred to walk down the length of the room. Again, I tried to stop him waking her.

"Not a bit of it," he said, waving one hand at me while the other, clenched in a fist, thumped down onto the table. The shock wave of the blow, vibrating through the solid wood, was sufficient to wake his wife. She was startled for a moment, then lowered her newspaper, turned and greeted me with an almost toothless smile and a queen-like wave.

"Good morning, Mr Saunders."

Immediately, she resumed her reading position.

I followed Sir Alfred back through the hall and into the drawing room. An external door had been removed that led into a glazed-in porch which caught the warmth of the sun. I carefully stepped over an old threshold and took a moment to gaze at the serene view of the well kept orchard, across playing fields to the school beyond: I could see why this was Sir Alfred's favourite place to sit.

I sat next to him on an old blanket-covered bench for the next three or four hours, silently enthralled as I listened to his reminiscences. While he spoke in the most lucid, animated and articulate manner about his personal involvement in politics and his slant on British history and the war eras, the dogs lying at his feet were as open-eyed and attentive as me. His voice trembled a little when he talked of his sadness at having to leave the house that had been so precious to him and his family which had been graced by the beautiful and the illustrious for over half a century.

Sir Alfred had designed and built the house for their honeymoon. Some of the fireplaces and other architectural features had been salvaged from the old Café Royale, while the orchard, rock pools, waterfall cascade, Japanese water gardens and artificial lake had been planted and built by him. This brought to mind Sir Winston Churchill, who spent his time building walls at Chartwell when he too was out of politics. Sir Alfred had known Churchill well, and I suspected he was underplaying the importance of his role in the government when I asked him about it.

"Which Ministry?...the Foreign Office?" I asked, because I suppose the appeal of foreign travel would have been my choice.

"God, no!" he said. "The Treasury was the only thing to do if you wanted real power."

Suddenly he jumped up, apologising for being such a bad host. Surely, I must want a cup of coffee or tea?

"Thank you. But please let me help."

I stood up to follow him to the kitchen and quickly sat down again, realising that my offer was almost an insult: he insisted I didn't move. Nervously, I watched him ease himself over the old threshold until he found a firm footing on the other side. The dogs followed him. Sometime later he returned with a tray, dragging one foot and bent over, like the *Nightmare Abbey* butler. I reached out to carry the tray across the threshold, anxiously watching him totter over the step, willing him over it and back into the porch.

Once sitting, he asked me to remind him of my reason for being there.

"Ah, yes...the planning for houses in the orchard."

When I glanced at the tray, I saw to my dismay that there was no hot water. Should I mention it or get it myself? I decided to take swift action. In the half-light I found the way to the kitchen, put the kettle on the range to boil, and quickly returned.

"Ah! There you are." After a few silent minutes, he raised a finger to punctuate his thoughts, stood up and struggled over the threshold to fetch the hot water.

Fortunately, he did not want to hear too much about the purpose of my visit. He was more interested in what I did and, being a young man, what I thought of modern architecture and a range of other topics. Gradually, I could see he was tiring, and although I would have loved to stay much longer I knew it was time to go. I strolled around the estate before I left, through the orchard and water gardens, before returning to the porch. Sir Alfred woke from his nap: I thanked him, and together we walked through to the kitchen.

The dogs, sensing my departure, trotted behind us. As we passed the dining room door I saw Lady X, still propped on one elbow at the table, apparently undisturbed since the morning. The paper was lying flat, otherwise everything else appeared to be exactly as it had been earlier.

"I'll tell my wife you're leaving."

"No…no please don't wake her…she's asleep."

He shuffled into the room. "My dear chap, she'd never forgive me."

Again, in one swift move, he brought his fist firmly down on the end of the table. The vibrations juddered his wife awake and, with a friendly smile, she waved.

"Goodbye, Mr Saunders. So nice to have met you."

I smiled and mimed "goodbye", knowing she had already gone back to sleep.

Later, I reported my planning enquiries to John Guest and his client. Shortly after, Sir Alfred and his wife moved into their son's home and the estate was sold. Regrettably, I never had the opportunity to listen to him again.

Bank, Professional and Commercial Clients

Parallel with the private and residential projects, JLW recommended the practice to some of its major clients such as Price Waterhouse, the stockbrokers Rowe and Pitman, and other international banks, including Chase Manhattan who were about to lease a newly completed redevelopment of a bombsite called Woolgate House.

The Chase Manhattan project was a major coup, especially as the chairman, David Rockefeller, had a passion for modern art and architecture. Chase Manhattan had been responsible for the high design standard for office layouts and interior environments that had transformed 1960s bank design in New York. It was now coming to London.

All the Chase building projects were run from their Property

Department in New York. When three of the senior project managers came to London to interview me in my extremely modest, unsalubrious offices in Cranbrook Road, I got a local architect friend to loan me four of his assistants with their drawing boards and stools, to make the practice appear twice the size. I got the job and which was the beginning of a business relationship that lasted many years, and included major projects in the West End, Bournemouth, as well as various countries in the Middle East.

As the constant inflow of international banks demanded space so Thomas Saunders Associates became the favoured practice, earning a reputation for high quality design, their restoration works, and completing the projects on time and on budget. According to Eric Deane, JLW were pleased to recommend the practice because, he said, I could be depended on to quickly indicate how well a prospective building would provide the space environment and design quality for their client's needs.

Devonshire Row

After six years in Cranbrook Road, the offices moved to Devonshire Row, a narrow street on the fringes of the City opposite Liverpool Street Station between Bishopsgate and Devonshire Square. Shortly afterwards, the business expanded yet again into additional temporary offices in the converted fire station close by. In 1968, I was elected a Fellow of the RIBA.

Derek Amos joined us; and John Cossins, Albert Hayden and Derek Joiner were now running their own teams and keeping pace with the ever more complex building regulations was proving difficult. The inner-city projects involved increasing amounts of building law legislation, such as the Right to Light and Party Wall, so I decided we needed our own in-house building surveyor. Among the few applicants was Delva Patman, currently employed by the Greater London Council (GLC) to deal with building control applications. (At the time, in 1970, it was unusual for women to become qualified building surveyors.) After a second interview, Delva was employed as my PA to handle the amounting complexity of building legislation. It was an excellent appointment: apart from Delva's professional expertise, she became a great ambassador for the practice and had the gift of 'opening doors' to new clients. She had all the necessary qualities to become a future partner.

In addition to the City and West End bank projects, there were other property development companies who used our services, some of which were listed in a brief history of the practice, reported by the freelance writer Michael Hanson in the *Estates Gazette*:

> Tom Saunders is one of the characters of post-war British architecture [and]...between 1968 and 1972 Thomas Saunders and Associates was working for such developers as Compass Securities, Wates Properties, Hammersons, Trafalgar House, Merevale Properties, Regional Properties, Graylaw, Summit, Westminster and City Properties, Chapel Land, Hillgrove and others.

One of these major property development clients, Compass Securities Limited, were specialists in buying disused, semi-derelict, often listed, buildings in the West End, the City and Holborn areas to restore and refurbish as offices. The extensive City and West End property development boom in the late '60s and early '70s demanded the constant need for our own office expansion. A property agent friend suggested that as well as making so much money for our clients, I should devote a little effort to doing the same for myself. (At the time, professional architects were prevented by the RIBA to speculate on property-dealing except for their private investment purposes.)

I took my friend's advice and set out to find an old property that needed restoring, in or near the City, that I could develop for our own permanent freehold office premises. The first deal was a cheap, dilapidated old warehouse that would have been an expensive office to develop and was already too small for the expanding organisation. I sold it on to a property developer. Eventually, in 1971, I was offered a freehold 'on the City fringes' that turned out to be Bethnal Green. Bethnal Green is a relatively little-known 'village' (one of the hamlets of Tower Hamlets) in London's East End, located on the Central Line between Liverpool Street and Mile End stations. The location appealed to my East End roots and is not far from where I was born.

Old Ford Road

A couple of property agent friends came with me to view what they called a 'pile of rubbish'. They smiled, saying I would be brave to buy the property, despite the low asking price of less than £14,000. I ignored their advice, made some quick planning enquiries, and the contract to purchase was swiftly concluded. The *Daily Telegraph* thought that an architect buying 'a pile of rubbish' in Bethnal Green was sufficiently newsworthy to warrant an article and drawing by the artist and art critic Geoffrey Fletcher, a well-known illustrator who also wrote about some of the unfashionable parts of London. (One of his many books, *The London Nobody Knows*, was a popular bestseller.) The original sepia ink drawing that accompanied his article still hangs in our hall.

The listed property, the end house of a Georgian terrace built in 1755 by Anthony Natt as a private dwelling, was in an advanced state of dilapidation. In 1842 it became a refuge for fallen women. From 1924 until 1961 it was occupied by Messrs Monk and Brown, a firm of glass bevellers. Their workshops built in the extensive rear garden area were now a series of tumbledown tin-roofed sheds and converted stables. Then in 1968, attempts to redevelop the whole terrace were thwarted when the GLC registered a preservation order on numbers seventeen to twenty-one.

The house looked as though a bomb had dropped through the roof: most of the tiles had been ripped off and daylight could be seen through parts of the flank wall. The dangerous state of some of the floors, plus all the horrible livestock and dead stock, made it hazardous to go inside. The house and rear workshops had been empty for five years, and standing in the basement, I could see sky through the roof. Before any work could start, the whole house had to be sheeted over and fumigated to get rid of all the bugs and creepy-crawlies.

The approved listed building planning applications allowed the house to be restored and used as a private dwelling and the rear garden area developed for 900m² (9700ft²) of air-conditioned offices with a small, independent unit for a housekeeper. This generous planning consent compensated for the cost and effort of restoring the house to its original splendour. An added bonus was finding intact, throughout the house, the original pine panelling, doors and staircase, albeit covered under thick coats of paint. Although it was a long and costly job for the panelling to be stripped and repaired, it was worth it.

As soon as planning consent was granted, all efforts were concentrated on building the light, spacious, modern air-conditioned offices at the rear for the practice to move in. Next came the restoration building work on the house, and nine months later I set up home in the Georgian house, number 17 Old Ford Road.

The adjacent three terraced houses also had all the original panelling and staircases intact. On the west side was York Hall, the home of East End boxing, with the local swimming pool and Turkish steam baths in the basement. Opposite, on the other side of the road, was another group of early Georgian houses, which stood in front of one side of the Bethnal Green Museum, built for the 1851 Exhibition, and which then specialised in Victorian dolls and toys.

Nearby, east of Spitalfields, where the silk trade had been established by the immigrant Huguenots in the seventeenth and eighteenth centuries, the long dormer windows in the roofs of the lovely terraced houses had been designed to be wide enough to accommodate their silk looms and goods. Originally, Spitalfields was a wholesale fruit and vegetable market where my cousin Lenny worked and Uncle Bill had had a stand. Now, it has become an extension of the Pettycoat Lane market, selling anything and everything. On Sundays, the streets are throbbing with thousands of people bargain hunting. A little further east is the well-known Columbia Road flower market.

Where Bethnal Green extends further eastwards along Old Ford Road, there are delightful small cottages and some of the best Georgian and Victorian terraced houses in London, fronting on to Victoria Park. These houses, and many of the East End blocks of Victorian dwellings, are very well kept, probably because they are still in the hands of charitable trusts. Behind the tall houses is a stretch of part of the Regent's Canal complex that connects to the Limehouse Cut where a couple of narrow boats had been converted into floating restaurants.

Victoria Park, opened in 1851 by Queen Victoria, is as big as Regent's Park, with its own boating lake, well-stocked pond, tennis courts and games pitches, a zoo with a few fallow deer and a couple of rams and some chickens.

All these little treasures are just two kilometres eastward along the Bethnal Green Road from Bishopsgate and the City.

Living in Bethnal Green

Where is Bethnal Green and why did I choose to live there?

These questions were frequently put to me by many of my clients and friends, especially those who lived around Chelsea and Knightsbridge.

To outsiders (non-East Enders), it must have appeared to have been a strange choice forty-two years ago, but the truth is, I didn't choose Bethnal Green: it just *happened* by serendipity.

My house and offices at 17 Old Ford Road were nearer to the centre of London than any place in the West End where to my mind, the inhabitants lived 'out in the sticks'! While the acknowledged 'centre' of London is Charing Cross, which is a halfway point between Marble Arch and Bethnal Green, my house and offices were closer to the 'centre' than Holland Park, the Kings Road, or Harrods. There were many advantages to living in Bethnal Green. I could pop next door to the York Hall baths for a swim at any time of the day, or spend a relaxing hour in the Turkish steam baths; travel to the West End theatres or to visit clients and our sites in the City was quick and easy.

Gang Land Reputation

Many friends believed Bethnal Green to have been a remote and relatively unknown part of London populated by gangsters, latter-day Jack the Rippers and prostitutes. Of course, the East End has always had a reputation for turf warfare and spawning notorious gangs, including that run by the twins Ronnie and Reggie Kray who ruled the East End's underworld. In 1966, Ronnie Kray entered The Blind Beggar pub, casually strolled over to George Cornell, who was sitting on a bar stool, and shot him in the head with his 9mm Mauser. It seemed George had upset Ronnie, calling him "a big fat poof". A few years later a similar murder of Jack 'The Hat' McVitie, added to Bethnal Green's bad land reputation. The truth is, however, that the Krays and other 'successful' East End criminals rarely stayed in their East End 'manors': they moved to the glamour and attractions of the West End as soon as possible. Why else turn to crime? The less successful criminals tended to go thieving in the wealthier areas, knowing Bethnal Green had nothing very much to offer.

(Incidentally, The Blind Beggar is named after the story of Henry de Montford, the son of Simon de Montford, who was wounded in the eyes at the battle of Evesham in 1265. Legend has it that he escaped from the battlefield with his wife and took refuge on Bethnal Green, disguised as a blind beggar. Tower Hamlets' heraldic coat of arms also depicts a blind beggar.)

I never had any fears for my safety living in Bethnal Green. After all, this was my heritage: my parents and their forebears were all cockneys; the East End was an environment I knew and understood. My father, his brothers (except Uncle Tom), and most of my cousins worked in the London wholesale markets and even my third generation cousin Malcolm had a flower stand in the Borough Market.

Soon after moving to Old Ford Road I discovered the joys of its small, closely-knit village society. A few steps along the road was a friendly group of small shops, including the greengrocer who had worked for the same firm that had employed my father in the Borough Market. I felt I had come home.

East Enders tended to eat well, without too much of the 'foreign stuff'. Fish, meat and vegetables were fresh and comparatively cheap, and some of the local delicatessens and Kosher food shops were good. They sold smoked salmon from the nearby ancient oak-smoke holes that also supplied many upmarket West End restaurants: but if I wanted good ground coffee and tasty cheeses I would have to trek to Leadenhall Market in the City.

My new East End friends and neighbours were curious to know why I had chosen to live in Bethnal Green. They usually prefaced their questions with 'not meaning to pry', then, when I answered, quite simply, that I had "come home", my words drew sighs of, "Aah...ain't that loverly." After all, in their eyes, 'I had a few bob', was doing quite well in the 'artistic' business, and presumably, I could live wherever I chose. In other words, if you 'made it' you got out, either 'up West' or 'down Chigwell way' (in Essex), like Jackie, who owned The Camel pub. Those who were successful either kept a low profile (due to the shadiness of their enterprise) or they did their best to disguise their East End roots. East Enders don't have too much to cheer about when it comes to general acclaim and recognition, so when a local man, John H Stacey, won a boxing world title fight, the locals made the most of the occasion with a fanatical reception. 'Big John's' party at the York Hall next door was as rowdy and joyous as the Victory in Europe Day celebrations.

The inhabitants of Bethnal Green in the '70s were over eighty per cent white Caucasian; there weren't too many 'foreigners' (of any colour) and many of the locals were pure cockney natives. My natural cockney twang (polished Bethnal Greenese) helped in my being accepted by the locals who could recognise its genuine derivation. (Clients often asked which part of Australia I came from; the twang was difficult for them to place, and some were snobby enough to be unable to imagine a professional person with East End origins.)

When I lived in Bethnal Green, rhyming slang was still very much in use, its derivation possibly originating centuries ago when the early foreign immigrants established their ghettoes and enclaves in the East End. The immigrants could converse in their own language as well as understanding English but the local cockneys had no equivalent special language. Thus, rhyming slang was evolved enabling them to communicate privately with each other. It was a protective linguistic armour against the immigrants as well as the police and other authorities. These days, Cockney slang, often poorly mimicked, is spoken in a jokey way to please the tourists. It is picked up and dropped by successive generations who have managed to keep the language alive over the years. Cockneys will use words created out of normal English slang and sometimes the word or phrase is two or three times removed. For example, the telephone might be called a 'percy', deriving from a TV gardening personality Percy Thrower. 'Thrower', of course, rhymes with 'blower' which was a slang word for telephone, which in turn originated from the pipe connecting a ship's bridge to the engine room.

Sunday Ritual

Sunday mornings were a quiet, peaceful time in Bethnal Green. Local neighbours, often dressed in their bedroom slippers, would wend their way to the tobacconists for their daily supply of fags, a few sweets, and the *News of the World* or the *Sunday Mirror* (copies of *The Observer* or *Sunday Times* were reserved for the one or two intellectuals, who were thought of as well-meaning eccentrics). A little later, a trickle of well-dressed churchgoers would pop into the greengrocers for some last-minute vegetables for the Sunday roast dinner.

Nearer to lunchtime, the streets became busier with the locals going to the pub for a sedate drink which was more of a social call than an outing for serious binge. Many of the traditional East End pubs served free, bar-counter pots of prawns, cockles and whelks, and later on, the landlord would bring out dishes of roast potatoes to entice the harder-drinking customers to stay until afternoon closing time.

Usually, when the pubs were not crowded, there was enough room in the bars to play shove ha'penny. The exception was The Camel, just a three minute walk from my house, which was packed at all times of the day or night. The young owner, ex-boxer Jackie Rose, employed the most attractive, buxom barmaids who brought in the twenty-something lads who, in turn, attracted the young women drinkers.

It guaranteed that Jackie's bar was always heaving with virile 'yoof'. Good business for many years earned Jackie the classic move to 'a nice house in Chigwell'. (As well as Chigwell, there were other places in Essex that successful law-abiding East Enders turned, including the sought-after arcadia towns of Gidea Park and Upminster. The green fields of Chigwell were favoured by Premiership division footballers where the late East End idol Bobby Moore used to live.)

When the pubs closed after Sunday lunchtime the East End streets were deserted. The customers, with takeaway cans of beer, soft drinks and packets of crisps, had drifted off home for the family Sunday roast before a kip in the afternoon. In the days of big families and long working hours, this was the traditional time for lovemaking. At other times, bed was for sleeping and Mum and Dad were too tired for much else. On Sundays, when the kids were packed off to Sunday school, leisurely reunions could be enjoyed without the fear of waking the children.

Clients and friends enjoyed being entertained at Old Ford Road, although they did have a tendency of getting lost on their way once they'd passed Fleet Street. The eighteenth century pine-panelled dining room in candlelight was the perfect setting, and I played host to some illustrious guests, including Victor Matthews (Baron Matthews of Southgate), David Bailey and his then wife Marie Helvin, the author Trevor Ravenscroft, and Sterling Moss.

Although the house was used for occasional business entertaining, it was also my private haven of peace and tranquillity. One time, a few days before an Easter weekend, I told everyone I would be away for the four days. Instead, I stayed alone in the house with some choice food and drink and listened to hours of music, not once answering the telephone. I remember thinking, as I lay on the sofa in an unusual state of bliss, that this would have been a good time to fade away.

Major changes have taken place in Bethnal Green since 1972: it is now only twenty per cent Caucasian. In the City, the Mermaid Theatre no longer exists and all the big wholesale markets in the City have been relocated: Billingsgate fish market moved to Docklands, Spitalfields has become a permanent extension of the retail markets around Petticoat Lane, and Brick Lane and the Borough are popular 'farmers' markets' with expensive restaurants.

I feel very fortunate to have lived in the village hamlet of Bethnal Green forty years ago, among people with the dignity and character of native East Enders who accepted me as one of the locals.

Hubert Chesshyre

At the time I was buying the house, I met Hubert Chesshyre and his brother, who were under bidders for the property. Four years later, having learned more about the house and locality, I reconnected with Chesshyre who, I discovered, was the College of Arms's Rouge Croix, the oldest of the four Pursuivants in Ordinary. As one of the exalted heralds, he had direct access to all the most interesting information and precious records of the Realm, dating from the time the college was founded by Royal Charter in 1484. I commissioned him to write a book called *The Green: A history of the heart of Bethnal Green and the legend of the Blind Beggar* (ISBN 0 902385 13 5) which included the name of the builder of my house, his family, all the subsequent owners, even copies of their wills that handed the house down through the generations, and much newly researched material on Bethnal Green and the surrounding historic buildings. The book was co-written by AJ Robinson.

Hubert Chesshyre rose from Rouge Croix to become the principal Herald of Arms, and then Commander of the Royal Victorian Order. He was also the Heraldic Consultant for the restoration of St George's Hall after the fire at Windsor Castle.

1972 marked the end of a ten-year cycle in my life. I had got divorced, and two years later had moved the practice from Devonshire Row to its new offices. I had taken up residence in the Georgian house, and Mercedes and Reuben, the cook/housekeeper and chauffeur, were installed in the small house at the rear. The projects kept flowing, the staff continued to expand, and the move to new offices in Old Ford Road, with its in-house lunch facilities to entertain our clients, coincided with our expansion abroad.

7

The Thomas Saunders Partnership

1974–1984

In 1974 I appointed Derek Amos, John Cossins, Derek Joiner and Albert Hayden as full equity partners and renamed the firm The Thomas Saunders Partnership (now known by the acronym TTSP). The ongoing success of the practice was reported in an article published by *Interior Design Magazine*, titled *In the Black:*

> At the time when architects' workloads have reached an all-time low, some practices are doing very nicely thank you. In a recession, clients don't take risks: they tend to choose the practices who have a good track record and/or are specialists in some aspect of design. The Thomas Saunders Partnership does well because it has developed a close understanding of the needs of the banking fraternity and the workings of the City itself. It's not a bad idea to specialise in bank design in these hard times, for as well as a lot of activity by indigenous banks, new foreign banks are constantly opening, wanting a 'presence' in the City... the practice has developed a sensitivity to the specialist needs of the foreign banks, whose requirements include a need to reflect something of their country of origin within the limited space the City has to offer.

TTSP's specialised interior and environmental design and space planning for international bank projects accounted for more than fifty per cent of the workload. It also enjoyed a reputation for producing high quality restoration and conversion works, such as our award-winning City Village scheme in Billingsgate. Commissions for new buildings included the new European headquarters building for American Express. Although, at this time, there were ongoing restrictions on new development in the City and only refurbishment projects were allowed, our reputation for refurbishing and transforming outdated 1960s buildings was recognised by the property media. *The Estates Gazette* asked me to write an article for their *Offices Review*, titled *Turning the Recent into the Modern*.

The following is also an article I was commissioned to write in 1979 for *Interior Design Magazine* titled *Bank Notes*. The editor introduced the piece thus:

> We persuaded leading bank designer Tom Saunders, senior partner of The Thomas Saunders Partnership, to go into print. In this article he describes some of the many changes that have taken place in banking in the City since 1945, and analyses some of the principal factors which influence bank design.

The following are extracts:

> In the early 1960s the City was emerging as the major financial services and banking centre of the world and eventually became the global capital. Before the war, there were a number of international banks such as Chase Manhattan Bank already established in the City, but over a period of less than fifteen years there would be a surge of about 300 foreign banks wanting a presence in the Square Mile to trade in the Euro Dollar which they could only do 'offshore'. Foreign retail commercial banks were not allowed to undertake underwriting and bond market deals. The banks came with the blessings of their own governments which recognised the opportunity to expand their knowledge of London's old-established and sophisticated financial institutions and its reputation for business integrity. Our native English language and geographical location between the money markets of Asia and North America, added to the advantages of establishing a branch here.

> An incoming foreign bank faced three major hurdles. The first was compliance with the Bank of England's requirement that the new premises should have some ground floor space and be located within the 'bank walks'.

For well over a century the documents, bonds, banker's payments, certificates of deposit, letters of credit and cash were moved around the City by messengers on foot. A 'money market' man, dressed in a silk top hat had immediate access to the money trader in the banks. He arrived once in the morning and again just before 3pm, talked briefly about the latest cricket scores or the weather and then asked the dealer "How much would you like today?" (Every bank, every day, had to balance its books by 3pm.) The dealer would say how many thousands of pounds he needed overnight, the money man scribbled the sum into his small notebook and bid him "Good day". Every transaction was done on trust and dealt with by this system of a private delivery service. Despite the electronic revolution, this system is still used to some extent even today.

The second hurdle concerned the confined area of the bank 'walk': this increased pressure on available space within the Square Mile which forced up rents. The pressure, exacerbated by the City Corporation's strict preservation policies that severely curtailed the assembly of large sites for redevelopment, led to the necessity to adapt and refurbish the existing buildings. The Corporation's planning restrictions persisted until the late 1970s when competition from the new offices in Docklands and Canary Wharf brought about a change. Yet another hurdle arose in the 1960s because there was a general shortage of supplies and equipment and to carry out any building work the client's architect had to apply for a building materials permit.

The business in London continued to boom but I had ambitions to establish TTSP as an international practice. When the EEC 1967 Merger Treaty led to full EU membership in 1973, British developers, property agents and entrepreneurs sensed good development prospects in Paris and Brussels. This presented an opportunity to service our UK-based developer clients in Europe and eventually, we employed Denis Prout, an architect from Geneva, to run our first office abroad in Paris.

An Itinerant Architect Prospecting Abroad
Bear in mind that my first foreign travel experience was a package trip to Spain with the family when I was thirty-two years old. Since then

I have travelled to fifty-three different countries, as well as sixteen separate states in the USA and several states in the north and south of India. A few of these journeys were family holidays or for my own private interest rather than exclusively for business, but they proved to be invaluable to our international clients who liked the assurance that TTSP had some personal knowledge of their country, customs and culture. This was particularly so for our American, Japanese, Indian and Middle-Eastern clients.

Following the Banco do Brasil project we built in King Street in the City, I went to Lebanon to discuss a new project with them, but the start was abandoned when the war flared up. I managed to get out through several army checkpoints. Over the years I made many other trips to clients in New York and other parts of North America, Canada, Japan, India, Brazil and Italy. At this time I was also making several trips to Eire for the Allied Irish Investment Bank projects.

When Chase decided to expand into the Middle East, John Freyer, one of their senior premises vice-presidents, was transferred from New York to live permanently in London to coordinate the bank's business. Freyer rented a house in Oakley Gardens, a two-minute walk from my house when I lived in Cheyne Walk. He was our star client and we became good friends, travelling together several times to the projects abroad. Our business and personal relationship led to TTSP completing projects in Egypt, the UAE and Kuwait. David Rockefeller's friend President Sadat formally opened the new Chase/National Bank of Egypt in Cairo and Alexandria. Chase expanded further in Kuwait, where we set up offices in 1975.

At this time we were awarded more projects in the Middle East for Price Waterhouse and other clients. I was pleased to be John's Best Man at his marriage to Elly. Sadly, much later in the 1990s, I was one of the pallbearers at his untimely funeral in New York, by which time TTSP had fallen out of favour with Chase due to certain fee disputes and personality clashes with the partners.

Once our presence had been established in Cairo, Delva, needing new horizons, opened our office in Dubai which served as a staging post for work in Doha, Sharjah, Abu Dhabi and Kuwait. One of our major projects was the Dubai Metropolitan Hotel. Some two years later, Westminster Chamber of Commerce awarded her the distinction of 'Woman of the Year' for her contribution to the commercial ventures of TTSP, and in recognition of her success in establishing the office in Dubai despite the difficulties and prejudices a woman encountered to pioneer new business in an Arab country.

Sadly, and to the detriment of TTSP, the home-grown prejudices of the partners led to a clash when I had made it clear that Delva was an important asset to the practice and that she should be appointed as a partner. For reasons best known to the others (I think it was fear), they would not agree. Delva left TTSP in 1980 to set up her own firm and over the past thirty years it has become one of the most important and successful building surveyors practices in London. She also became the Master of the Surveyors Livery Company in the City of London.

My clash with the partners over Delva sowed one of the seeds that would germinate into thoughts that my own days at TTSP were coming to an end.

The Middle East

During a ten-year period, before the practice had established a thriving office base in Dubai, I began prospecting for business in Middle-Eastern countries. Much of the time was spent following up leads from my Lebanese and Saudi contacts which, on many occasions, took me to Iraq, Iran, Jordan, Dubai, Egypt and Saudi Arabia.

Ordinarily, travelling abroad to business meetings and making presentations for specific projects was relatively stress-free: the clients arranged visas, hotels, air tickets – sometimes even first-class flights – and agents were there on arrival to smooth the way through airports and provide taxi services. Prospecting abroad for new work was a very different matter: it was tiring and frustrating, especially when I was foraging alone. I was only accompanied twice by one of my colleagues on these prospecting excursions.

Eventually, my trips to the Middle East became a once-a-month visit, sometimes lasting four or five weeks at a time. For almost six months of the year I had to be my own secretary, booking agent, telephonist, chauffeur and baggage handler (especially when carrying precious presentations).

Lebanon, Jordan, and countries around the Gulf did have Western satellite systems, telephones and telexes but in some places in the Middle East the communications systems were dire. In Baghdad, instead of telex machines, there was a single cables room in a shack (like an allotment garden shed) with a Morse code tapper like you see in Western movies. This cables outpost served the whole of Baghdad (and probably the rest of Iraq). In Iran, there was a different problem: there, the hotels had efficient banks of telexes and operators, and with a bit of bribery, messages would go out on the same day. But the trouble was that the lines were so busy sending out such high volumes of business telexes, they never kept a machine free to take incoming telexes. I learned to not expect replies.

(At the end of long and often disappointing days, I found writing helped to release the tension. Copies of these letters and diary notes, which I found tucked away in box files, have been a useful source of reference in the writing of this work.)

Venezuela

One of our bank clients, a supporter of the development of a new town and hydroelectric dam on the Rio Caroni, invited the practice to bid for the design for the town planning scheme. Such a prestigious project would be a major coup for TTSP, and British architects in general. I met the developer in his sumptuous villa in Caracas and together we trekked out to the site in the wilderness of lush, uninhabited land.

Everything looked promising, but our preliminary proposals had to be abandoned and the project delayed for the foreseeable future due to organised protests that had been mounted against the hydroelectric dam scheme. The developer then took me to see another site for a hotel on the Isla de Margarita, but that also fell by the wayside. Although it was a disappointing outcome for both TTSP and the American bank, it was an exciting project to work on and gave me the opportunity to visit a country of such a contrasting lifestyles and culture.

Egypt and Saudi Arabia presented the more promising opportunities to explore other prospects, such the El Gezirah Club in Cairo; the restoration work in Adaryajh; and a sports centre in Riyadh.

Egypt

Cairo was a sad city, still trying to recover from Colonel Nasser's fifteen years of misrule, desolation and isolation. My troubles started in 1976 when I arrived there to present our project for the extensive restoration of the El Gezirah Club. It was a prestigious project: the Club had 35000 members, its own racecourse, golf course, mini-

Wimbledon tennis courts, two polo grounds, two swimming pools, squash, bowls and eighteen other sports facilities. At the presentation, all the members (including the chairman, who was the Minister of Tourism for Egypt) gave their unanimous and delighted approval to the scheme. However, they decided to modify the brief, which had called for new restaurants and club rooms, to include additional accommodation to improve the layout.

As the official survey plan proved to be inaccurate enough to warrant a new *avant-projet* anyway, I reluctantly cancelled my flight to Riyadh and decided to stay another few days until the next meeting, when I would finally sit down with the vast committee to finalise the brief.

It wasn't to be that easy. Although the meeting was positive, I was told they needed government authorisation to spend the cash before they could sign a formal letter of appointment. I desperately wanted that letter, especially as I knew there were dozens of other architects queuing up for the job.

His Excellency, the minister, informed me that when the cash was approved we would be awarded the project. I told him that his word, fully endorsed by the other members, was far better than a letter of appointment. It was a lie, of course. There was no way I could trust that his word was his bond; and what if there was another revolution and all the members got shot? One soon learns to be aware of prevarication, evasion, indecision and false promises when doing business in certain parts of the Middle East.

Saudi Arabia

One day in Cairo, when it was taking me an hour and a half to queue up at a Saudi Arabian Airline ticket counter to get a booking for a week later, I wondered why the hell I wanted to go there anyway. The short answer was that the business in London and Europe was well in hand and I wanted the practice to be 'international'.

A week later, standing with my bags on the curb in Kasr El Nil Street, Cairo, I tried to hail a passing taxi to take me to the airport. After ten minutes, one did stop and I jumped aboard. After two other passengers had been dropped off en route, we were less than two kilometres from the terminal, with only a quarter of an hour in hand, when the driver pulled up at the side of the road. He got out of the car, lifted the bonnet, topped up the radiator, and at the same time, with the other hand, undid his flies and relieved himself. When he got back in, the engine wouldn't start.

We were on a slight incline: he tried to push-start the overheated car four times to no avail. It was two in the afternoon and the street temperature must have been well over forty degrees. Finally, when another taxi stopped and began to help push the vehicle, I got out and pulled my case off the roof rack. My driver fought to put it back but I won the battle and waved down the next empty cab, which rapidly reversed back to me. Now there were three drivers, each with a piece of my luggage in their cab, all arguing about the right to take me to the airport, a stretch of road that on a fair day in England I could easily have walked. I ended up paying off the first man, thanking the second, before finishing the journey with the third.

Cairo Diary Note, 1976:

> It is half an hour before take-off, and the flight will be cancelled unless an alternative aircraft can be found to transport a 'member of the Royal Family' to Riyadh who has suddenly been taken ill (a case of alcohol poisoning?).
>
> At nine o'clock, they'd put up the notice saying 'Riyadh'. My luggage was parked some way away, but I had my ticket and passport in my bag. Unfortunately, being the first in line, I was crushed against the counter. Long bony hands waving grubby Saudi flight tickets are thrust under my arms, around my ears (if I had been standing in front of the gap where the luggage is weighed, I think my crotch would have been in peril). They took my ticket but I had to get the luggage. I crawled over the weighing machine to the 'official' side, crawled back further along the line, retrieved the bags and went back the same way. And now, after all that, the plane might not leave!

When a Saudi says 'tomorrow' it can mean anything up to the next six days. They drink coffee and talk business for eighteen hours a day, every day. Life is business, business...and more business and yet real progress is impeded due to their lack of understanding of time. The amount achieved is equivalent to about three hours' work anywhere else in the world. How else does one spend one's days?

On one particular trip, I had arrived in Jeddah from Cairo and had waited three hours for the connection to Riyadh. I had no doubt the hotel in Riyadh had already sold on my room three times over. Telex notes and letters of confirmation count for nought: the men on Reception seem to operate their own private bookings business within the hotel and had probably paid up-front money to buy such a key job.

As expected, my room had indeed been sold on but this time I was invited to share a room with a complete stranger. I got to sleep on a camp bed at three in the morning.

Our client and sponsor was Malik Antabi. Most of my time in Riyadh was spent in his office, waiting for him to return from a meeting. Malik said the Prince who controlled all Saudi sporting projects and activities had approved our scheme for part of the Sports City Project and arrangements were made to meet him at noon. A phone call message cancelled the appointment because the Prince was otherwise engaged. Instead, that afternoon Malic and I revisited Al-Dirah, the original capital city, built of sun-baked earth, to review the scheme we were preparing for a Cultural Centre.

Malik also arranged a meeting with a princess, who was a good friend and client, to discuss residential schemes in Riyadh and Jeddah. This too was suddenly cancelled because her father, an uncle of King Faisal, had had a heart attack earlier that morning. The meeting was delayed until my next trip. Yet another step backwards but later that evening, Malic took me to the house of one of his clients to discuss a new villa job. Discussing business needed endless patience: opportunities kept appearing, but nothing seemed to get done.

Many Saudis had Western university or business management degrees, and some were qualified professional engineers and architects who had grasped elementary technical building terms. The problem was that none of them were actual 'do-ers' – all had become 'percentage fee middle men'. Like Malic, through their connections to the power of the Royal Household, they 'sponsored' other professionals and companies to be awarded contracts. This system was as wasteful of their talents as it was of those they were sponsoring, because there were too many companies striving for just one contract.

After a couple of years my patience drained away.

Iran

Certain Middle-Eastern countries, such as Saudi Arabia, demanded a baptismal certificate with the visa application: their method to ensure you were not a Jew. In Iran, up until the Shah was deposed in 1979, there had been no such ban, whatever one's faith. It was an oil-rich country that attracted Western architects, designers and construction companies to bid for extensive building development projects.

Early in the 1970s I went on a foraging expedition, visiting the great cultural centres of Isfahan, Shiraz and Persepolis. I was keen to see the country for personal reasons too: Russi's family's Parsee roots had originated in Persia over a thousand years ago. I returned to Teheran a few months later to meet a firm of French contractors, a lead from our Paris office, who wanted to work with a firm of UK architects. Unsurprisingly, the British and French could not agree on the tactical bid.

However, there was another project in the offing. Dr Teheranchi, a rich Iranian biscuit manufacturer, selected TTSP from a short list of practices supplied by the RIBA to design his new private residence in Shemiran in the hills above the city of Teheran, where the Shah's palaces were located. He had been encouraged to choose TTSP when he heard that I had some first-hand knowledge of his country. I met him and his wife at their sumptuous house in Teheran to discuss their requirements for a new 'house'. The site was in the vicinity of the Shah's main palace, on a gentle slope overlooking the city in the far distance.

A few months later, on my way to Iran, with the design drawings and a professionally built model packed in a fitted flight case, I stopped over in Beirut to show off the project to other would-be clients, including the Banco do Brasil, who I knew were planning to build a new branch in Lebanon.

Back in Teheran, I presented the Teheranchis with the design drawings and a model of the grand, ultra-modern 3000m² residence, which was more on the scale of a palace. The linear design concept followed the slope of the site with landscaped gardens, courtyards and cooling fountains punctuating the separate quarters for the parents, their children, the grandparents, and the staff, who more than outnumbered the family members. The Teheranchis were delighted with the scheme and gave me instructions to proceed.

I left Teheran triumphant, but the feeling was to be short-lived. When I returned, the design development drawings were approved but, in 1979, just as preliminary work on site was about to start, the Shah was deposed and the Teheranchi household had to flee the country. (Later, we did get the commission to design the interiors for the doctor's extensive apartment close to Hampstead Heath.)

With Iran out of bounds, I made another trip to Beirut, hoping to secure the Banco do Brasil project, but here my luck was no better and this too had to be abandoned due to the threat of civil war. On my departure, I was hurried through several military checkpoints and was lucky to get out before serious fighting started. At the end of this period, the poor arrangements and lack of adequate support for my trips to Teheran and Beirut had left me in such despair that I unleashed a scathing report to the partners and senior staff:

Our expanding business in the UK has, so far, come to us from repeat clients which represent nearly ninety per cent of our workload. Now, we need to develop new clients to increase that last ten per cent of turnover. To be competitive and succeed abroad we must escalate our approach, business efficiency and quality...

Prospecting abroad alone means I have to be my own secretary, telephone operator, and confidante to combat fierce competition from the locals and foreigners who are supported by a two or three man team backed by their organisations with established international reputations.

Travelling on business is fatiguing enough: getting to and from airports, the delays as well as the actual flying time, then using unfamiliar currency, foreign languages, dealing with taxi drivers and others who try to screw everything they can out of you. Added to these are the frustrations with communications, the sense of isolation, trying to make the right contacts, learning local business customs as well as diet changes, long hours waiting for appointments, time changes and different hotels.

The Beirut and Teheran hotel bookings were a fiasco. The necessary changes to my dates were not co-ordinated. On arrival, the Teheran Hilton was overbooked and they expected me the following day. Reception suggested an alternative hotel for the one night. The taxi was expensive. I saw the appallingly dirty rooms, walked out in disgust and returned to the Hilton to sleep on a hard seat in Reception until 4.30am when a room was available. This was an almost sleepless night after a fatiguing flight from Beirut. Our booking staff were sloppy and careless: did they have the impression I was going to Bognor Regis or Torquay rather than Beirut and Teheran?

I cannot express my feelings of anger and frustration at the unnecessary waste of time and money over the fiasco of the documents I needed Tahranchi to sign. The papers had to be sent on by special air delivery because they were not completed before my departure date. Firstly, there are always telex difficulties due to a lack of machines; secondly, the telephone system is always overloaded and it took twelve hours for a free line to London. Eventually I received a telex message four days after transmission from London that gave me the parcel tracking number...

Later that afternoon, Iran Airways telephoned (pure chance that I was in my room at the time) to say the parcel had arrived and gave me another code number to collect their authorisation note from their Teheran offices. The following morning (Saturday), I collected the paper for the airport customs clearance and collection. There, I had to pass security checks showing passport and documents. In the customs hall, a clerk passed me on to a young man who snatched the paper and hurried to another clerk for processing and more signatures. He then ran out of the Hall to another building to search a cupboard for my parcel. I ran with him as I had no idea who he was or how to find him again. The great rush was due to the fact that at 1.30pm everything closed in the main Hall until 3.30, which was my time to meet Teheranchi to sign the papers. In all, thirteen people were involved in recording separate ledgers, counterfoils and carbon copies, while I ran five times from one building to the other, and just before 1.30, the parcel was in my hands.

Then, before being allowed out of the gates, I had to pass three other checkpoints and signatures. Without these documents the visit to Teheran would have been lost.

The presentation of the model, designs and perspectives was a great success and I hope this project will stimulate an appreciation of the work on such projects abroad. So far, our teams have shown inhibited reluctance to produce concepts for projects due to lack of understanding of the nature of such work and that it may not be 'real'. Is it that we lack experience, talent and ability or that we have a generally insular approach to all things beyond the boundaries of Essex?

Hitherto, the business in the UK has come to us without too much prospecting effort because we have established a reputation for producing efficient work which is technically and professionally correct and proper. I feel that our design work has become routine and lacks direction, flair and innovation, and adventurous design opportunities are missed. Our leadership may be delegating too many important design concepts to mediocre designers.

The oil-rich countries wanting to build prestigious projects will only appoint internationally recognised architects and insist the quality design work must be good, adventurous and different. To compete we must nurture imaginative, prestigious design concepts to satisfy the clients' requirements and their egos. We must encourage design 'flair' and clearly define those who are the design strategists as opposed to the technicians. No organisation needs many strategists: we have too few. Quality and uncomplicated presentations are prestigious and even though the project may not hit the right formula the first time, it is the client's initial reaction which engenders confidence in the ability of the practice.

Now we must return to our original speed of reaction and regain the thrusting activities that have achieved success so far.

Iran wasn't all frustration. I did have the opportunity to explore some magical places while I was there. One free afternoon in Teheran, I took a taxi to the foothills above Shemirahn. Where the dirt road ended, I got out and carried on walking along the tracks. I passed groups of teenage schoolgirls and their teachers, all fully clothed in traditional burqa dress with only their eyes exposed. I was astonished to experience how pairs of eyes could silently, eloquently and meaningfully register such a range of expression, from apparent friendliness to a sense of intrusion and surprise at seeing a white foreigner. Undeterred, I continued until I came across a deep, meandering ravine. The 'bridges' were long tree trunks lashed together, crossing the shallow river that lay eight metres below. It felt like I was walking a tightrope.

Further on, I could pick out small buildings perched on the side of the steep embankments, which turned out to be kitchens serving a number of restaurant platforms set in the river, covered with Persian carpets and long-roll cushions. Here, the locals could enjoy an evening dinner sitting in the cool of the ravine. Waiters were already scampering up and down the steep sides, laying out the decks and lighting the fairy lanterns.

(The foothills and mountains above Teheran separated Iran from the Soviet Union. Either Kim Philby or one of the other spies who escaped to Moscow had a framed photograph of the mountains in his flat in Mayfair. Many who knew Teheran were puzzled by the silhouette of the mountains. It looked unfamiliar, of course, because it was taken from the Russian side of the range.)

Review

Prospecting abroad was often fatiguing and frustrating, but it did create opportunities for rest and relaxation, as well as visiting the family in Bombay. In Egypt I climbed into the Great Pyramid twice, sailed up the Nile from Cairo to the Valley of the Kings, visited the Aswan Dam and then on by plane to Abu Simbel. By car I traced Lawrence of Arabia's journey through the deserts, from Cairo to Aqaba, and saw Petra in Jordan. In Lebanon, I visited the magnificent Roman temple of Baalbeck and had a ticket for the annual festival, which, alas, was cancelled when the war started.

In addition to the Nile, I also had the fortune to sail or walk along the banks of other great rivers of the world: the Amazon, the Negro, the Tigris, the Caroni, the Colorado, the Rio Grande, the Mississippi and the St Lawrence. I have also seen the great lakes of North America, the Niagara Falls, and have trekked through vast deserts, rainforests and the Arctic tundra. I have seen some of the great cities and the most wondrous archaeological sites. All these opportunities were extraordinary gifts and blessings.

Prospecting abroad was not all arduous and stressful!

Diary Note, 1976:

My frequent travelling lost many weekends and evenings at home. When I returned and offloaded my reports, I did not resume a normal, regular office-hours routine to compensate for the time spent abroad. This led some of our London-based clients, colleagues, and a few good friends to assume that I had 'retired' to become a lay-about, not taking life seriously and living off the success of the practice. While this negative attitude was resented, I was reluctant to talk about the prospecting abroad until the efforts began to bear fruit.

A few days after I had returned from a particularly arduous and long trip, a friend invited me to lunch that developed into a 'meaningful' monologue. Knowing very little of what I was doing in the Middle East, he suggested that all this travelling around – 'gallivanting', as he put it – seeking pleasures and enjoyment in foreign places wouldn't solve my problems (whatever they were). He suggested I needed something to occupy my mind such as starting up a new business where I could 'have a go' on my own instead of relying on all these people in London to do everything for me. Furthermore, whatever I was seeking, flying about in aeroplanes would not help: having too much time on one's hands can't be good for anyone!

"Bloody sauce!" I thought, but it put me on my guard, especially with my TTSP colleagues and the UK clients! On the other hand, I knew that clients, such as Chase Manhattan, were encouraged to know that I (the practice) had visited and experienced these overseas territories.

Although we completed many overseas projects in the UAE, Egypt and Kuwait, my speculative prospecting abroad resulted in few actual commissions. There were certain vindicating circumstances: the Beirut project for the Banco do Brasil was abandoned when the civil war erupted; the El Gazerah Club project was approved by the committee but in order to avoid the corruption experienced in the Colonel Nasser's military regime, the committee members were changed every six months and the newly appointed members tended to discard what had already been agreed; the schemes in Saudi Arabia were subject to approval by those who based their final appointments on factors other than those concerned with the quality of the design; the approved Teheranchi 'palace' was cancelled when the Shah was deposed; and the new town in Venezuela was dependent on the construction of a new dam on the Rio Caroni, which became a political battleground that ended in stalemate.

Such political volatility is largely unpredictable. When architects are commissioned to carry out a project it can take one or more years before a scheme is developed, finally approved and construction started on site. During the intervening period, a country can change from stability to revolution, as witnessed in the Arab Spring upheavals. On balance, though, I believe my prospecting abroad created positive PR benefits that enhanced TTSP's standing as an experienced, international practice.

Back Home

The projects that continued to flow into the expanding practice created an ever-increasing demand for additional space. We rented the vacant Bethnal Green Fire Station in Cambridge Heath Road and bought a terraced cottage nearby to accommodate Mercedes and her family, in turn converting the small housekeeper's house into the graphics and presentation studio. Jack McCarthy joined the practice on a permanent basis to develop our own art department and workshop, which became an important innovative additional design and installation service.

In 1980, I sold the Old Ford Road freehold to a pension fund, and TTSP leased back the offices. The sale of the property allowed me to fulfil my 1951 prophecy to live in Cheyne Walk where I bought a six-storey Georgian house, that had been built around the same time as 17 Old Ford Road. The latter then became our conference and lunch rooms, as well as the administration department run by Ken Hay. We also set up a building maintenance department to handle all the snagging works and visit the completed projects regularly, to ensure the clients were happy and knew that we still cared! In 1980 we were one of the first firms of architects to install computer aided design (CAD).

17 Cheyne Walk

This house too involved a major building works to restore a derelict wreck. The previous owner had run out of money after she had tried to cure the rot infestation and carry out repairs, which she had done in a piecemeal manner that left the building without a staircase but with some items of furniture and old suitcases still stranded on the fourth floor. The historically listed buildings inspector kept an eagle eye on every detail, although all that remained of the original features were a few lengths of plaster cornices and timber skirting boards. I did what I could to renew whatever original features could be replicated, including finding matching plaster-cast mouldings in a long-established plaster firm in Fulham.

The original, delicate wrought iron work on the front elevation was repaired and the wisteria retrained. The back garden Tudor brick walls were also listed because they formed parts of Henry VIII's manor house. Sections of the wall between my house and next door had to be repaired and needed agreement with my neighbour John Paul Getty, whom I never saw but knew from his driver that he kept a careful watch on all that went on.

Ultimately, the modern interior design was not to the inspector's taste, especially when I built a raised platform in the main bedroom on the second floor so that I could lie in bed and look across the trees to see the lighted Albert Bridge and Battersea Park across the Thames.

I lived in the house for ten years, until 1991. During that time, I founded the Cheyne Walk Society.

Twenty-First Anniversary

1982 marked the start of my next ten-year cycle as well as the twenty-first anniversary of the foundation of the practice, which was celebrated in the Plaisterers' Hall in London Wall.

For me, the founder and senior partner, it was a proud and significant celebration. The practice had expanded with a staff of 130 people. It had completed more than 120 international bank projects for twenty-eight different client nationalities; built many new major developments both in the UK and abroad; and were recognised as experts in the restoration of historically listed buildings.

The success of the practice was largely based upon my leadership, which helped to nurture and foster the talents of the men and women employed there, as well as ensuring that they had the necessary working conditions and environment for those talents to flourish. I took strategic control and led from the front, and although I influenced the design process, I never sat down at a drawing board to impose direct design guidelines. The downside of being the grand strategist is that although you can address concepts, you can never be intimately involved in the tactical work of design detail.

It was my job to pose the pertinent questions to the client to ensure that a full and comprehensive brief was translated into the project design. Occasionally, when asked about the favourite buildings I had designed, I found it difficult to answer because none of our projects were my exclusive creation. But I realise now that I had probably underestimated the influence and effect that I'd had, because so many people, and especially clients, have mentioned that the stamp of the TTSP buildings and interior designs was always recognisable.

The creation and development of the practice was undoubtedly an achievement and yet...I felt unfulfilled – *this is not why I am here!*

Of course, no one knew that, for some time, there had been a compulsion to respond to my quiet inner voice – those gut feelings or intuition, call it what you will – that made me want to embark once more on a journey to...wherever!

The anniversary triggered my decision: I could only follow those unknown paths if I wasn't carrying the baggage of work at TTSP. Several years later, when I read my diary notes of the late 1970s/early 1980s, I realised that I had had vague plans and ambitions to write and explore the esoteric mysteries of architectural design for a fairly long period before that point.

And so it was that after the ceremony I gave the partners my two years' notice. It was no surprise to me either that I had no intention of taking the usual path of a retiring partner becoming a part-time consultant. I wanted to sever all financial and contractual ties. It was only at the partners' request that the name of the practice continued.

Many friends, business associates and clients were somewhat surprised, even shocked by my decision: what could have induced a fifty-year-old man to voluntarily relinquish a secure, substantial income, his status, and a thriving business?

The two-year notice to quit the practice expired in 1984. It was marked by a simple ceremony. As I waited in the studio for the presentation to begin I had a moment of silent elation, knowing the fraught situations and the frustrations of marking time during the past two years were over and my work at TTSP was complete. In that brief moment I reflected on what energies and strength it had taken to create a successful international practice, and how I had made my way in the world, pulling myself up from my early beginnings and environment. I was leaving the thriving business in the hands of competent partners and staff and I am sure it was as much a relief for the partners as it was for me that I left when I did.

Suddenly I was aware of the partners and senior staff presenting me with a Cartier gold watch and receiving other generous gifts from clients, fellow professionals and contractors. I cannot remember who said what about whom, but thirty years on I still have a strong sense of the elation I felt as I walked out of the building for the last time. At that moment I was re-energised and refreshed and ready to set up again as an independent consultant architect.

Coinciding with my notice to retire, Tim Jennings joined the practice. Tim and his brother Alex had lived near us in Nyth Close in Upminster and were school friends with Mark and Christopher and I used to play squash with Tim's dad. Since moving away from Upminster I lost contact with him and his family and had no idea he was interested in architecture and design. Tim is now the MD of TTSP.

8

'Retirement'

1984–2014

So, what prompted a fifty-year-old man to voluntarily give up a thriving, well-paid business? On reflection, there were several strands to the answer.

In the words of the Peter's Principle: I had promoted myself to my level of incompetence and was no longer a hands-on practising architect. Instead, my role had become almost entirely devoted to public relations, writing articles about the practice, being interviewed by the architectural media and prospecting for business, both in the UK and abroad. I resented that so much office time was spent at the partners' meetings discussing (arguing) about niggling administration matters, the partners' and senior staff's expenses wrangles, and which brand of car and accessories they were demanding to reflect their perceived status.

Three men had a great influence on my decision – CG Jung, Robert Townsend and Joseph Campbell. Jung's book *Man and His Symbols* set me on a voyage of discovery towards new horizons. In Townsend's book, *Up the Organisation*, he advocated that all chairmen and chief executives should resign their post after five years in the job, not only because their enthusiasm wanes and needs new challenges, but also because it allows others to develop and rise up in the business. The American philosopher Joseph Campbell said: "The real killer in life is when you find yourself at the top of the ladder and realise it is leaning against the wrong wall." 'The wrong wall' is a sense that this deep of dissatisfaction and lack of fulfilment happens when we feel a gaping black hole in the gut and realise we have devoted our lifetime to acquiring material wealth to overcome our insecurities and fears of our own mortality without taking care of our spiritual self.

Travelling also 'rewired my circuits' and influenced my outlook on life, opening my mind to the interrelatedness of all things and our common bond with nature, art and architecture. This led me to a study of the underlying, esoteric – sacred, if you will – design and structure based on the fundamental principles of harmonic ratios, musical intervals and proportional volumes, which determine the architectural geometry that, in turn, resonates with the same harmonic ratios and proportions in our body. In other words, the quality of an architect – the Master Builder – can be measured as one who designs according to these principles. I will always regret that I was unable to influence and encourage my fellow partners to integrate these perennial principles into our design concepts.

The transformation of my views on architecture and design could be encapsulated in this example of a 5000-year-old Hindu tradition:

> ...the final form of a building had to be sufficiently geometrically accurate (sacred) for the gods to be compelled to be present... [The] architect alone cannot produce a sacred vehicle for the expression of a 'spiritual presence and a space for the heart'... Whenever we approach and enter a building designed according to the universal laws or canon, all the vibrations created by the earth energies, the geometry, the colour and sound will resonate with the whole of our being. Subliminally [we sense] these vibrations and...our psyche will respond to the occult wave patterns. [Then] we will be reminded of our 'common bond' with nature, feel healed and the building...will be a temple of the soul.
>
> *The Boiled Frog Syndrome*, page 246

These experiences and explorations of the outer world drew me to seek other, wider fields of the esoteric world. It became clear that I needed to balance my material world with an endeavour to understand the inner realms, which led me to study Kaballah, meditation, and to experience ten days of intensive, deep meditation at a retreat in France run by the Vipassana organisation.

Of course, at the time I was unaware that my travels to the Amazon and the Arctic, the Atlantic Ocean sailing, and the excursions into the metaphysical world were the classic, archetypal journeys of the mythical hero:

> The hero's/heroine's first step on the path is usually triggered by a sense of longing, boredom, perhaps a desire to rescue someone/

something or an experience of an unusual occurrence...sometimes
known as the call to adventure.

The Authentic Tarot, page 14

Thomas Saunders Management Limited, 1984–1991

Once free from TTSP, I could continue my excursions into the occult
realms as well as take care of my material world, recapturing the
pleasure and exhilaration of working as an independent consultant
architect again.

It wasn't long before several opportunities arose. The Hong Kong
Shanghai Bank Corporation (HSBC) appointed me to act as Client
Representative and Project Director to oversee one of their funded
developments near Tower Bridge that had run into serious difficulties.
Then, I had a chance meeting with Martin Landau, one of TTSP's
clients. He was about to take over a management buy-out of Guinness
Peats' property division and invited me to become a director in his
newly formed City Merchant Developers Limited. I served on the
board for two years until it merged with another company.

As my relationship with HSBC developed, in partnership with
the bank's property division, I began a modest refurbishment of flats
in Chelsea. It was boom time and rents kept on rising, that is, until
1988/9, when the property market crumbled, just as our joint factory
development in Bermondsey was completed. Our business enterprise
ended in disaster. (The building was not sold or let until many years
later.)

I had to give up all my assets, including the house in Cheyne
Walk, to pay off my share of the development costs. Everything and
anything that would fetch a decent price was sold off: my antique
Indian tapestries, various art works, the collection of expensive
crystals that were photographed for an article in the December 1988
issue of *Harpers and Queen*, an Art Nouveau vase I had received as
a retirement present from Trollope and Colls. It all had to go. Every bit
of cash, and the million pounds I had got for the house, melted away
to offset the debt.

The realisation that I was broke came not with a sudden sense of
fear and panic, it was more like a slow darkening of desolation. Money is
an energy force that creates hope and freedom of movement and choice;
without it, it is like being incarcerated without a means of escape. My
heroic journey had ended under the crushing sense of failure.

I had to depend on the charity of good friends to loan me 'street money' and somewhere to live and work. Gradually, I began to rebuild my life.

Miraculously, though, although I had lost everything, it was then that I met Janet and found true love.

Thomas Saunders Consultants Limited, 1991–2014

The management company was closed down, and I set up a new company Thomas Saunders Consultants Limited. As the property market gradually improved, my one-man practice grew. The work included designing buildings based on the Kairos principles of sacred geometry, as well as acting for several years as Project Director in the UK for the American developers Tishman International.

During the mid-nineties, the CDM (Construction and Design Management) regulations came into force. I took a series of week-long seminars to qualify as a Planning Supervisor, which virtually kicked off a new career. Later, I graduated from Oxford Brookes University with an Advanced Certificate in Environmental Design and Crime Prevention. In 2004, when I was elected to the RIBA's newly created level of Client Design Advisor (CDA) a Russian developer selected me from the RIBA's CDA shortlist to go to Moscow to review and advise on the final selection from three schemes by British planners to create a large housing development, located close to the city centre.

After that, I was appointed to coordinate the design and fitting-out of the interiors of the new Hiscox Insurance headquarters building in Number One, Great St Helens, off Bishopsgate. The project was published in *Estates Gazette* in August 1998, titled *Enter the Dragon Man*, referring to the chairman's instructions to design the building according to the principles of Feng Shui.

There have been many other substantial and smaller projects that have kept me gainfully employed over the years. I acted as a mediator on contractual disputes; revamped the Lowell Hotel in New York and designed the sacred geometry for the new headquarters building in West London for the Brahma Kumaris organisation.

Another project came my way when an international American firm of architects invited me to their headquarters in Phoenix Arizona to deliver a two-week seminar to one of their project teams that had been commissioned to design a new building devoted to healing and esoteric teachings. Their client demanded that the design should be based on principles of sacred geometry. As the team had no knowledge of those principles, I was brought in to teach them the fundamentals.

More recently I acted as project co-coordinator on a major redevelopment in Chelsea, as well as a brown field site development for housing in Northamptonshire. I also worked with my good friend and TTSP ex-client Derek Parkes on a Private Finance Initiative scheme and the refurbishment and development of the City Literature properties in Holborn. On one of the sites I dowsed for archaeological remains for the Museum of London, to find early Saxon artifacts.

I have accepted various invitations to lecture. Central St Martins School of Art and Design (now part of the University of the Arts London) appointed me to a part-time post as an Associate Lecturer. I have also been asked to give talks on various aspects of health hazards in buildings. In September 2011 I was invited to deliver a lecture at a conference on Electro Sensitivity, a little-known distressing and often harrowing disability for the many thousands of sufferers in the UK alone.

The culmination of my studies into various aspects of health hazards, as well as my esoteric studies, resulted in the publication of my book: *The Boiled Frog Syndrome – Your Health and the Built Environment* in 2001. (It was translated into Portuguese and published in Brazil in 2004 under the title *Sua Saúde e o Ambiente que Construímos*.) There followed a commission by Elsevier Science Limited to write a peer-reviewed paper entitled *Health Hazards and Electromagnetic Fields in hospital design and equipment*.

My long-standing interest in the meaning of the Tarot, rather than its popular use for fortune-telling, urged me to write about the 'sacred' esoteric codes in the original set of cards. This resulted in the publication of my book *The Authentic Tarot: Discovering Your Inner Self* in 2007.

TTSP sans Thomas Saunders, 1984–?

TTSP's move to its present offices in Goswell Road in 1988 coincided with a recession that necessitated serious contraction, but it continued to flourish and buck the trend, as it has done so during the current 2011 recession. This is due to the underlying strength and expertise of the practice and the careful guiding hand of Mike Carter, and now Tim Jennings. Although the offices in Paris, Dubai, Kuwait and Egypt were closed, new offices were opened in Frankfurt and Prague post 1991.

I never saw or contacted the partners again until I was invited to lunch soon after the practice had moved from Old Ford Road to their new offices in Goswell Road. (This was the last time I saw both Cossins and Joiner, both of whom were relatively young men when they died.)

I went to the Goswell Road offices for the second time when Tim asked me to give a talk about my book, and I met Albert Hayden again when Tim invited me to the retirement party of Mike Carter. Since leaving TTSP, I have maintained contact with Delva Patman and Derek Amos (after he retired from the practice) and they have worked with me on various projects.

Fiftieth Anniversary

On 7th June 2011, at St Luke's deconsecrated church in Old Street (which is now the home and rehearsal centre for the London Philharmonic Orchestra), TTSP invited Janet and me, with about 600 other guests, to celebrate the fiftieth anniversary of the founding of the practice. I was suddenly aware, and surprised, that I had been 'retired' four years longer than the twenty-three years I was in the practice.

We were warmly welcomed and enjoyed the reminiscences of the staff and current partners. How strange it was that the smallest incidents were remembered, such as why I had stopped eating tomatoes when I was in Cairo! It was a pleasure to meet old friends and clients, and particularly satisfying to be greeted by four or five of the young current staff who thanked me for their job! I gave my congratulations and special thanks to Tim and his team for continuing and maintaining TTSP as a thriving and highly regarded practice, and felt the party had drawn this episode in my life to a happy conclusion.

PART III

Travel

9

India

June, 1928–1985

It must have taken great courage for June to go abroad for the first time in her life, to an unknown destination, climate, culture and environment, and to integrate with Russi's family and friends. Although she adored our father and was sad to leave him, I think the thought of getting away from mother compensated for any trepidation she may have felt. Russi returned to Bombay ahead of June. She took the sea route to give herself time to become acclimatised to the changes in her life and to prepare for the impending culture shock.

She arrived in Bombay in 1955 to discover the country was poor and austere, with stringent currency and import restrictions. Like the post-war London she had just left, there were derelict buildings and strict food rationing. The extreme shortages of goods and materials in India demanded a regime of rice-less days and meat-less days and, at one stage, it was an offence to serve food at a party for more than twenty guests. Even through to the late 1970s, there was a seven-year waiting list for a new car, which restricted one's choice to a small Fiat, a BMC Herald or an Ambassador (otherwise known in the UK as a Morris Oxford). Second-hand cars, whatever their condition, changed hands at many times their original cost. The black market undercut everything by half, especially the alcohol, legitimately sold 'off licence'. This Indian form of prohibition, regulated by a permit system, allowed one to buy liquor if it was prescribed by a doctor for 'medicinal purposes', a system that allocated a little more to the elderly, and foreigners too.

Russi's widowed mother and two unmarried aunts, both doctors, were devout Parsis (or Parsees), a group which follows the ancient religion of Zoroasterism, established in the sixth century BC, with its prophet Zoroaster, a fire deity and symbol of divine purity. As Parsis rarely marry outside their faith, there was an initial opposition to Russi marrying June, even though he was a devout agnostic/atheist. The religion does not accept converts. In many ways, it is akin to Judaism: they have a ceremony called a Novjot, somewhat like a Bar Mitzvah, that celebrates a child reaching the age of about eight or nine – a milestone that marks the child's survival into adulthood. Parsis, noted for their thrift and hygiene: they do not bury their dead – corpses are laid out on the 'Towers of Silence' for the vultures to devour. Non-Parsis are not allowed to enter the group's fire temples.

The Parsis of India emigrated from Persia over a thousand years ago to escape Arab invasions. A second migration took place about 200 years later. (Those descendants of the first wave of immigrants are still standoffish with the 'new' arrivals.) They landed in Bombay where they became the established commercial, moneyed traders of India. Farsi is their language.

The Cooper Family

All three brothers, Khatoo, Russi and Burjor, were extremely well educated and cultured. Khatoo, Russi's eldest brother who died several years ago, was considered to be one of India's top lawyers. His wife and two sons were in the same profession. The youngest brother, Burjor, graduated from London's Imperial College with a PhD in aeronautical engineering. Before he was thirty years of age he was the CEO of Willis Jeeps in India. Later, June worked for him when he left the company to set up his own consultancy practice, which advised banks on their industrial and importing projects.

Nothing of a practical nature was beyond the easy-going Burjor who could make spare parts to repair pre-war cars or ancient refrigerators. A fine sportsman and card player, he was also blessed with a brilliant mind, well-versed in the music, literature and culture of East and West. He married Pilloo, a delightful, highly cultured and exceptionally serene Parsi lady of distinction who runs an East-West cultural exchange society. One lunchtime, at her grand house in Bombay, I joined other guests to meet Rostropovich, the internationally renowned Russian cellist, and his wife. That evening we heard him play at the newly built concert hall. Sadly, Burjor died in 2014.

In some ways, Russi shared some of my father's characteristics. Like Burjor, he was a top-class sportsman and card player, also with an easy-going temperament, always ready to share a joke. We have fun lapsing into pigeon 'Indianese' when we are together or speaking on the phone. He has a brilliant academic mind, steeped in the music, literature and culture of East and West, and even in his early eighties he was still being consulted as a marine insurance specialist and expert witness. Like many intellectually clever people, however, changing an electrical plug or light fitting was beyond his capabilities. Everyone in the family was highly amused by his apparent lack of nouse, except June who often found his non-practical, passive nature totally infuriating.

I am deeply fond of Russi, and have always found him to be a tender and loving man. Invariably impartial and non-judgemental, I have never heard him criticise anyone in the family. On 18th January 2012, he was eulogised in a special report in *The Times of India* under the heading:

> Russi Cooper: he gave up Team India dream for LSE. Instead of becoming a test player, he went to England to study marine law and was called to the Bar from Lincoln's Inn in 1947.

Living in Bombay

Russi and June lived in a house in Pedder Road before moving to a spacious seventh-floor apartment in a new residential tower block on Malibar Hill with a sea view over the bay. Abundant strikes and building work corruption delayed the move for two years. Much later, high rise buildings in Bombay sprung up everywhere, many of them built without tower cranes. (The first to be built in India collapsed, and two years later it was still lying where it crashed.) Often, the only mechanical equipment used to build these thirty-storey reinforced concrete buildings was a cement mixer, a vibrator (for industrial use only!) and a hand hoist. The concrete was poured from the shallow pans carried on the heads of women trailed by their kids in a crocodile chain. Scaffolding was dodgy-looking bamboo.

No doubt, the difficulties June encountered in trying to adjust and be accepted into Russi's family ended when she gave birth to Dinaz, who was the first girl child for seven generations. Instantly, June became the beloved daughter-in-law, and her integration into the Cooper family was happily complete.

She became accustomed to a life of ease and relative luxury and, like all middle-class households, she had a cook and a housekeeper who took care of all the housework and shopping, which allowed June to readily assume the role of the Memsahib. She discarded her European clothes – except for visits to London – and wore ever-flattering saris for the rest of her life.

The Cricket Club of India and the Willingdon Club were the centres of social life in Bombay. The club, located in the centre of the city, was founded by a Colonel Willingdon in the days of the Raj to bring together the Indian and British army officers at a time when they were not allowed to meet socially under the same roof. It is an oasis of card rooms, lounges and restaurants, an eighteen-hole golf course, squash and tennis courts, and a swimming pool set in lush gardens. The Willingdon's serene and ordered Edwardian gentility is a haven for the well-to-do of Bombay: the men arrive early in the morning for their leisurely, non-energetic exercise in the pool, before a shave and shower and breakfast; the women arrive later with their families for lunch and afternoon tea around the pool. Here I spent many relaxed and happy hours with June, Dinaz and the family. Without the sanctuary of the Willingdon, life in Bombay would be difficult.

The men's changing room is attended by aged retainers who are always at the ready to help you disrobe and hand you a white wrap and towels, before taking your clothes and reverently hanging them on wooden hangers and placing your valuables in a safe locker. After exercising in the pool and completing their ablutions, the veteran Indian club members, swathed in towels, sit on the rows of polished mahogany benches or wicker chairs while an attendant dusts their feet with Johnson's Baby Powder. Over the years, I could detect no change of routine since my first visit to the club, As ever, there were the jars of Brylcream with the brushes and tortoiseshell combs set out on the mahogany dressing tables for the members who favoured the slicked-back hairstyle of the glamorous film stars and sportsmen of the 1920s and '30s.

During the thirty years June lived in India, I saw her no more than four times in London and about five times in Bombay, including two occasions when I spent Christmas with her and the family. She always seemed to be living a fulfilling and healthy life, which made the news that she had died of a heart attack at the age of fifty-seven all the more shocking. I felt a deep regret that we had spent so few times together. I'd had the same distraught feelings when our father had also died of a heart attack aged fifty-seven.

After June's death in 1985, Russi came to London on business and stayed with me in Cheyne Walk for a few days. The visit cemented the strong bond between us. We enjoyed going out to the theatre and cinema, and we talked about June. All he said was that she had been very happy. I have little doubt that living in India in comfortable circumstances, among her family and friends in tranquil surroundings, had actually prolonged her life.

On several occasions, whenever business trips took me to the Middle East, I called in to Bombay to see Russi. One year we went on holiday together to Turkey and on another occasion when both Janet and I took him with us to Cochin.

Bamboo Banks Guest House

One Christmas I treated him to a four-day trip to the Bamboo Banks wildlife game reserve sanctuary in Tamil Nadu in southern India.

The dawn flight took off at noon, eventually landing at Coimbatore, where Russi had arranged for someone from his Cochin office to drive us to the sanctuary. It turned out to be a seriously hazardous four-hour mountain trek, with the driver ignoring our angry shouting, pleading, and frantic signals to slow down. Russi calmly admitted that he could not speak Tamil and his only means to communicate with the driver was in 'point and grunt' sign language, none of which worked. Despite our screams, and thumping the driver's shoulder, he continued to lurch and weave through the seething mass of people and oncoming traffic. At one point, a bus swerved to avoid a head-on crash, grazing our rear wing. The clash of crunching metal encouraged the driver to proceed with a little more care, but the perilous journey continued unabated, as he dodged deep ruts and recklessly took hairpin bends and blind corners. All the while, lorries sped past us, belching out clouds of pollution. Fear prevented any enjoyment of the magnificent purple-blue mountains, the forests and terraced tea plantations.

Drained of adrenalin, fatigued by the white-knuckle ride, we slowed near a group of women who were washing clothes in a river, then turned into a dusty track which led into the bush-like jungle. There, a sign nailed to a tree read 'Bamboo Banks Guest House'. Through the gates and at the end of a long, well kept driveway was the main building. (Later, we discovered it was the lounge, dining room, kitchen, bar and staff quarters. Nearby were eight guest bungalows.

The estate workers had their quarters in a few farm buildings clustered around a courtyard.)

We dragged our stiff, aching limbs out of the car and slumped into cushioned wicker chairs under the vine-covered wooden terrace. While we were waiting for drinks to be served, Russi admitted that there had been an easier route across the plains to our destination, which we might have taken if we'd been able to fly by Airbus to the airport to the north. Unfortunately for us, Mr Rajiv Gandhi and Benazir Bhutto's historic meeting in Pakistan that week had required two Airbuses for him and his entourage, thereby creating a countrywide domestic fleet shortage. Russi had been forced to go for the Coimbatore airport, trusting that providence would to get us safely to the sanctuary. Unfortunately, providence would have to get us back again, as our driver would be staying at the guest house too, ready for the return trip.

The Bamboo Banks owner, a burly Parsi known as 'CS', was kitted out in regular white hunter-style khaki shorts and shirt. His booming voice kept up a steady stream of satirical, political and religiously cynical repartee. Once the ear adjusted to the volume, his output was highly entertaining and remarkably well-informed, considering that he had spent so much of his life confined to this remote rural quarter. No subject seemed to have eluded his intense study, wit and benign bigotry.

His wife turned out to be an excellent counterbalance to him: she personified tranquillity, knowing feminism, and quiet efficiency. It was she who kept the business flourishing and the delicious food flowing day by day. In CS's mind, all dogs, servants and women were grouped in the same broad category of creatures he was prepared to treat with distant respect provided they served obediently and behaved well. (This is not an unknown attitude of many men who are professionally engaged in hunting, shooting and fishing.) Mrs CS had put up with her husband's deliberately provocative declarations for years and she knew how to rise above his earthy banter. A hardly discernable side-glance from her was usually sufficient to prompt our host raconteur to quickly change his tack. They had spent a lifetime together and noticeably held each other in fond regard.

The day after we arrived, a party turned up in three taxis to celebrate their family Christmas reunion. There was the father, an Indian banker, his American wife and their two children, his parents who lived in Rangoon, his aunt and uncle from Bombay, and his sister and her American partner who also lived in the USA. Both were staunch feminists who had lived together in a loving relationship for ten years or more.

For the next two days, Russi and I watched CS stalk the two women. A hunter who lived close to nature and the wild, he was tuned into instinctive behaviour. If it was necessary to kill or, as he put it, cull animals, it should be carried out with professionalism. You might enjoy the sporting pleasure: it was not the act of killing but the quality of placing the shot that mattered.

Lunch was about to be served when he asked the young American how it could be that such a pretty female had not married. Her girlfriend's chubby cheeks glowed crimson, her urchin-cut hair shivered. The next moment, in what appeared to be casual conversation, CS moved on to discuss his relative who lived in Madras, whose 'naive stupidity' resulted from her vegetarian eating habits. The American girl was instantly indignant, declaring herself and her friend to be vegetarians. Without excusing his 'unintended insult', CS said that his relative from Madras was naive and stupid not only because she was a vegetarian but also because she was a Christian Scientist. Indignation, uproar and anger erupted as the American declared that she too was a Christian Scientist. (As if he had no idea!)

We were saved by the bell calling us to lunch. The two women abruptly decided to eat alone in silent rage on the terrace. After that, there were sporadic skirmishes, but they subsided into an uneasy truce.

If you were to take a body-wrenching elephant ride through the bush it would be possible to penetrate the undergrowth to get closer to the wildlife, but we said that we preferred the forays along overgrown tracks in the noisy, jolting jeep which covered a much wider area. We saw herds of elephant, wild boar, deer, monkeys, snakes and giant squirrels. Disappointingly, tigers, leopards and bears kept out of sight.

Local villagers joined our New Year's Eve barbecue party. A group of musicians played until midnight, after which CS's amplified electronic cassette player had to take over because the band could not play Auld Lang Syne on the sitar. The good food, the pathway flares and candle lanterns created an incongruous festive spirit in the middle of the jungle. Soon after breakfast we departed. Fortunately CS spoke Tamil and gave our driver strict instructions to drive with greater care and caution.

We returned safely to Bombay. The apartment was just as I remembered, except that there was a photograph of June and an ever-burning oil lamp on the sideboard, kept as a permanent shrine to my sister.

Russi has never remarried and has now retired from his post in charge of the port of Bombay. In 2012, he celebrated his ninetieth birthday. He still lives in the same apartment, and frequently spends time in Pune with Dinaz and her husband Hoshang, and their two sons Eruch and Rustum, who are now at university. Dinaz, like Russi, is blessed with a clever mind and an impish sense of humour.

I have visited India many times and have kept in close contact with Russi and the family and have always felt sadness when the time comes to leave them and their comfortable, easy-going way of life. It has always been a pleasure to be with them in Bombay, a place where I can reconnect my spiritual circuits.

We were so happy to see Dinaz and Hoshang when they visited us in France, and every couple of years we have had the pleasure of seeing Burjor and Pilloo when they visited England. We keep in regular touch with the family: Janet and I talk with Russi by phone and Skype and exchange jokey emails with Dinaz and Burjor.

Since my first visit to Bombay in 1967 with Betty and the boys, I have travelled to India a dozen times, covering the north-western region, up to the Punjab, and as far south as Cochin. The first time I felt disorientated, as most people do: it was as if I had landed on a different planet. It is a country that leaves deep impressions, ones that yank me out of my culture-comfort zone.

I am deeply grateful that I have been able to get to know India, and for the joy of being lovingly related to everyone in the Cooper family.

Khajuraho

The ancient Hindu religion was based on reaching spiritual enlightenment through sex and yoga practices found in the book *The Kama Sutra* which encouraged the traditional Hindu to become an erotic, sensual being. It extolled every imaginable sexual pleasure, which can be seen in the temples of Khajuraho. Each level rising above the podium showed the evolution of human beings through the seven stages to reach a spiritual bliss of higher consciousness called *Nirvana*. The deep band covering the largest section of the temple domes was covered with hundreds of erotic carvings, many of which were about a metre or so high, depicting men and women in ecstatic states of excitement, and groups in as many athletic sexual postures as conceived and depicted in *The Kama Sutra*. The exquisitely carved sandstone female figures appeared to be clad in diaphanous saris and there, in the village, were local women dressed the same, as if the statues had come alive.

The Indians created many sensual goodies: the original punka fans were rush mats interwoven with a layer of perfumed material so that the fragrance would waft around the room, and palaces were built incorporating many secretive chambers designed for playing hide-and-seek. Even today, the Jains install a swing as an essential piece of bedroom furniture.

Hindus were fun-loving until Buddha and one or two minor prophets intervened to discourage their hedonistic way of life. To the outside world, modern-day India has leaned to the other extreme, with heavy censorship desexualizing every film, in which even kissing is not permitted.

Christmas Holiday, about 1986/7

The thirteenth-century Mongolian invader Genghis Khan, created a massive empire that included most of India. In 1526, vast tracts of India were controlled by omnipotent Mughal Maharajas, great benefactors who, in the main, took care of and ruled the people of their domain with benevolence. Their palaces, forts and tombs are still fairly well preserved, ancient monuments to a culture based upon a refined elegance, pleasure and abundant wealth. The influence and power of the Maharajas declined when the British Raj took over India in the nineteenth century and finally, they were dispossessed of their land and property after Partition in 1947. The State sequestered their estates and converted the palaces into hotels.

Mitchell Crites, who lives and works in Dehli, Jaipur and London, is an American scholar, art dealer and archaeologist. He speaks seven Indian languages and counts a number of Maharaja families as close friends. One damp, chilly autumn day in England, Mitchell's idea of spending the Christmas holidays in a Maharaja's palace in the gentle December warmth of India was immediately appealing. His idea spread to a few other friends who were well-acquainted with India and soon we were a group of about twenty, ready to commit ourselves to airline bookings and schedules for excursions to other parts of India once Christmas at the palace was over.

Three days before Christmas Eve our group landed in Delhi,

loaded with our individual contributions to the more European-style festivities, taking the risk that Indian customs officials might consider some of these goodies to be illegal contraband. Once everyone else's bags had been cleared from the carousel it became dauntingly clear that mine was lost. By the time I had completed sheets of questionnaires and diagrams to identify the bag it was already halfway to Thailand. Being without clothes for a day or so was annoying but my main concern was the boxes of Belgian chocolates, brandy butter, crystalised fruit and a large truckle of Cheddar also in the bag. To add to my disappointment and anxiety, customs officers laser-beamed their powers of detection on to me: the last, solitary passenger, carrying a bulky piece of hand baggage. I struggled to keep my shoulders level, trying to disguise the weight, hoping they would not want to open the zip. A toilet bag, sweater and camera concealed four litres of vintage champagne, a box of cigars, a side of smoked salmon and a wad of rupees from a previous trip (the Indian Ministry of Finance do not allow you to bring money back into the country). The zealous eyes of the customs officials darted between me and the half-open bag. There appeared to be a pecking order ritual: there was a pause while they seemed to decide who would search me and my belongings for prohibited excess items.

Perhaps it was due to sympathy for my having lost my luggage but they took my word that not all these goodies were for my personal use and that I was simply carrying them for other members of my family who had by now left the airport and were already tucked up and fast asleep at the Imperial Hotel. I escaped unscathed into the misty darkness. Outside, the waiting party discreetly cheered as we piled into a convoy of taxis to take us into Delhi.

Two days later, I retrieved my dusty and battered bag. Everything inside had survived except the boxes of chocolates. The heat of the transit sheds in Bangkok had fused the soft-centred delicacies into brown-and-white coagulated globules.

Samode Palace

On Christmas Eve we jammed ourselves and the luggage into a battered pre-war coach for a five hour journey. It was almost dusk when we arrived at the gates of the walled village of Samode, nestling in a barren, red rock hillside. The locals stared, the young children waved and shouted, cheering us as we inched along the narrow streets designed to accommodate a one-way procession of elephants. The coach squeezed through the ceremonial archway into the outer fortifications of the palace until it could go no further, with just enough room to turn around on the rough cobbles. The village children seemed happy, laughing and well-nourished, trying to practise their few words of English: *Hello, one pen, one pen.* They were not begging for rupees – they wanted our biros for writing and drawing. They scurried away as the palace bearers offloaded the suitcases and holdalls, and the tattered shopping bags filled with packages of Kashmir shawls, saris and precious antique pieces bought in Delhi, wrapped in torn, smeared sheets of the *Hindustan Times*, and tied with an assortment of string.

Mitchell strode up the steep cobbled road which wound along the curved, high, stone ramparts. A troupe of monkeys guarded the banyan trees where the paving broadened out in front of the grand entrance to a courtyard and gardens. In the deepening darkness, flares illuminated the camels and horses, decked out in woven silk and silver bell finery, held steady on parade by small, turbaned boys. Trumpets blared, then firework rockets burst into coloured stars. Two by two we mounted the broad flight of steps that led to the threshold of another archway where a man and two women, perfumed and immaculate in crimson costumes, greeted us with garlands of jasmine and a shower of rose petals, and marked our forehead with the red ochre spot for fortune and grace.

Four musicians beside the fountain played us into the grand quadrangle where we stood in awe, gazing up at the grandeur of the three-storey-high palace with its arabesque-arched arcades and shallow balconies, which projected from the bedrooms with their cedarwood screen-shuttered windows. A narrow spiral staircase opened to a cloistered ceremonial room overlooking the courtyard. The walls were delicately painted in free-flowing blue and white flower patterns, and ceramic and silver mirrored mosaics decorated the domed ceiling, reflecting the glinting candlelight.

Tired and delighted to be there, I flopped down on the opulent, fairy tale turquoise tasselled ottoman, then lounged in the colonial Edwardian wicker basket chairs. My imaginings of being a Maharaja stopped short when an old retainer, bent with arthritis, shuffled into the room. It seemed that I was not going to be bathed and pampered by half a dozen nubile women, flimsily dressed in diaphanous silk. He ushered me into the vast bedroom with a four-poster bed in the middle of a purple carpet. A sofa, chairs and a table stood near the windows;

hooks for the punka fans were still fixed in the ceiling. Just like it was at the Willingdon Club, on the Edwardian dressing table were bristle brushes and Brylcream, set on crocheted doilies. A heavy door opened into a narrow room with an oversized mahogany wardrobe, which led into a cramped bathroom, installed when indoor plumbing was first invented. Mogul palace opulence did not include bathrooms – at least not this one. Unfortunately, this was not the Maharaja's personal quarters and the fantasy of the nubile women quickly disappeared.

The gentle music from the courtyard ended abruptly with a clashing sound of cymbals and trumpets, stirring everyone to get ready for the evening entertainment. Mitchell handed out turban headdresses, we drank champagne with chapattis and smoked salmon, then at ten o'clock we filed through a courtyard and into the grand reception room where we squatted on the cushions behind a long, low table. Bearers, brightly dressed for the occasion, brought in a Christmas Eve feast of Indian sweetmeats, curried rice and bowls of spicy dishes. After the first course, we were entertained by dancers and musicians who, Mitchell assured us, were India's leading exponents of tribal dancing.

After supper we climbed a stone winding stair to another terrace on the palace roof to see more fireworks and the unintended entertainment offered by the antics and agility of the men in the gardens below as they lit the blue touch papers with scant regard for their own safety.

The Christmas Day treat was a lunchtime picnic in the grounds of another old but derelict palace, about three miles from Samode. Six camels hitched to two-wheeled camel carts, which had been designed to carry loads of heavy goods and building materials, waited in the lower courtyard. We climbed aboard, four people to each cart, and discovered that the thin cotton blanket thrown over the rough wooden planks did not transform the hard boards into a comfortable seat. Our legs dangled over the side, our backs pressed against each other for support, and together we moaned and winced with each painful jolt over the ruts in the rocky road. The camels kept in close formation. Our driver, perched on the shaft, calmly smoked thin brown paper cigarettes without any concern for our agony, and unaware that the two people gripping the front of the cart were close to the camel's rear end and in constant fear of being splattered by its frequent defecations. He was also oblivious to the fact that the following camel's high haughty head was streaming saliva, or that, several times, it snapped at the two passengers on the back of the cart with its yellow teeth. The bumping and bruising eased when the camels slowed to a long loping walk, but we envied the cooks and bearers with the picnic lunch who sped past us in the comfort of their cars.

A swarm of school children spotted our camel convoy. They charged across the fields cheering and cajoling us until we arrived at the broken-down entrance to the palace. The waiting bearers shooed away the young boys. Why were there no schoolgirls? Later, I read about this very village receiving much attention from the authorities who were trying to stamp out the common tribal practice that slaughter the girls at birth. The burden of dowries and the traditional lores of rural areas are difficult to overcome.

The palace, built as a summer resort, was crumbling, overgrown and dilapidated, with acres of formal water gardens. Despite the long-term neglect, the original seventeenth-century splendour could be imagined. Cascades and pools created a long vista of fairyland architecture: magnificent terraces, state rooms, bedrooms and inter-communicating courtyards. The picnic lunch, amid the grand noble ruins, soothed away stiff backs, aching bottoms and cramped legs until it was time to return. The camels looked as uncaring as their drivers, so some of us decided to walk back to Samode.

The next day, reverting to a modern means of transport, a taxi took me to Jaipur, known as the Pink City. (I had been there before in 1967.) Waves of humanity thrive and swirl in the streets, and bright red ochre buildings glorify the past few centuries of the Mogul Empire. Even the patina of grime, garish hoardings, painted signboards that euphemistically advertise skin disease clinics, and lines of washing cannot hide the opulent, confident architecture, delicate façades and extravagant interiors.

In government-controlled gem emporiums, precious and semi-precious stones were sold in open trays; garnets, like Smarties, could be run through the fingers. Portly, affluent merchants, white robed, squatting on ottomans, watched over the precious and semi-precious stones and benignly eyed every customer's movement and nuance. Along narrow back streets, every 'shop' was an open workroom where young boys chipped, carved and smoothed blocks of marble. Above were the showrooms of the beautifully crafted sculptures, urns and panels of bas relief.

The exquisite, traditional artisan craft of the Moghul Empire was alive and well-practised. There was an abundance of antique shops, some nothing more than a hole in the wall, others covered an acre or two of open yards and indoor floor space, crammed with modern handmade tourist stuff, crowding out the genuine quality pieces. By now I'd had enough of shopping and sightseeing (I was familiar with the buildings from earlier trips). I was ready to leave Samode.

There was a celebration in the palace grounds the night before we left to go on our own separate journeys. The terrace glowed in the light of two log fires blazing in steel braziers, where chapattis cooked in a stone oven; bowls of rice, salads, fish and curried meats covered the long tables. The celebrations included a group of musicians and dancers. Three scruffy old men squatted on a carpet, tuning up their battered instruments while three dancers strapped bells on their ankles, getting ready to perform.

The leader's gnarled fingers squeezed his Indian-style accordion while the percussionist lisped a song through his toothless lips, apparently berating the men in the audience for trusting the demon drink rather than women. (It was not surprising he held that particular point of view.) The women, dressed in swathes of flimsy sari cotton, turned, twirled and wriggled their ample torsos and abdomen, trying to simulate a belly dance. Perhaps undiscerning Indian males could be erotically aroused by layers of trembling flesh but we were unmoved. After no more than a few twists and turns, one of the dancers sat down on the floor and rubbed the soles of her feet, and the other two also seemed to be in a complaining mood.

Now that the performance had ended, Mitchell admitted that it was a practical joke: the women were professional hookers and the so-called belly dance routine was a cover for them to flash their charms to seduce men who they hoped, would become so besotted after only a couple of turns around the floor that money would change hands. The women would then fulfil their contractual obligations in private while the band continued playing. It was not surprising the women were grumpy and tired – they were not used to being on their feet for more than a quarter of an hour. Mitchell paid them off, and they sloped away to find other more lucrative business elsewhere.

The fires burned low, we said our goodbyes, until the time we should all meet again a week or so later in Delhi Airport for the flight home.

We had all laid our own plans to make our separate explorations or pilgrimages. Some were travelling to Jodhpur to buy carpets and see more Moghul antiquities; others were staying in Rajasthan to visit Agra and Fatipur Sikri. I planned to see the family in Bombay and travel on with Russi to a wildlife centre in south India.

Return Home

I departed for Delhi to meet up with Mitchell and the group. Since going our separate ways a week ago, we all had travel tales of woes and wonderment to share as we queued at the desk, our bulky luggage stuffed with goodies from some of the best bazaars in the world. The announcement of yet another twelve-hour departure delay was received with a serene acceptance of inevitability – this was India. (Even Indians sometimes regret the British Raj is not around in these days of air travel to ensure well kept flight schedules would be as reliable as the train timetables. What price independence and bureaucracy?)

It is remarkable that a country with such diverse cultural and social extremes that over the past seventy years or so, since the 1947 Partition, it has created a major revolution without Communism and foreign interference overrunning their unique democratic political system.

Back in London my purchases were carefully unpacked and the rolls of film rushed to the quick print shop as a means to reminisce the flavour and fantasy world of Christmas in a Maharaja's palace.

10

The Amazon

Preface

In 1973, when the Banco do Brasil appointed the practice to design and build their new bank and offices in King Street in the City, I went to Rio de Janeiro to meet the chairman and board to discuss the project. Fortunately, my trip coincided with Rio's spectacular Carnival and gave me the opportunity to visit Brasilia, the capital.

Flying over the vast territories of Brazil sparked memories of a book I first read when I was twenty-one years old, called *Exploration Fawcett*. The country has held a fascination for me ever since. In the book, a lieutenant-colonel in the Royal Artillery, Percy Fawcett, who was also an explorer and mystic, was commissioned, through his connections with the Royal Geographical Society, to make seven expeditions to plot the boundaries between Brazil and Bolivia. Before his final trip in 1924, he told his wife that he intended to search for a lost city he named 'Z', located in an unexplored region in the Motto Grosso jungle. Fawcett took with him his eldest son Jack and a close friend. The group disappeared, and were presumed dead. Later, their manuscripts and diaries were discovered by Fawcett's youngest son, Brian, and were published in 1953. Since then, several films and documentaries have been made about the various expeditions to discover the remains of Fawcett and his son and what had happened to them. None have been conclusive.

Their manuscripts and diaries tell of the giant anacondas, reported to grow up to thirty metres in length (fifteen metres was the largest held in captivity), and the piranhas, the vultures of the water, that can home in on blood and strip a wounded animal to the bone in less than five minutes with their razor-sharp teeth. They tell of stingrays and electric eels, powerful enough to 'electrocute' a man to death, and the tiny barb-headed fish that bury themselves in the anus of humans and other animals, which have to be cut out for there to be any hope of survival. Then there are the tarantula spiders – even their nests at the base of trees look sinister – and all the hundreds of other insects, animals, fish and plants that possess a vicious armoury of teeth, claws, poison or massive strength. Worst of all are the mosquitoes.

None of the people I met in Rio had heard of Colonel Fawcett, but all were well aware that the Amazon, with its hostile natives and snake-infested swamps of the Motto Grosso, had been the graveyard of thousands of adventurers, from the Conquistadores to the twentieth-century explorers, who hunted for the rich, undiscovered treasures of the Incas, the Mayans, and native Indian tribes. No one I met in Rio had any desire to venture near these areas, which they considered primitive, savage and dangerous. However, someone at the bank offered to help me contact an agent in Manaus who could arrange for a boat and crew to take me into the jungle.

Back in London I suggested to Mark, Christopher and a couple of friends that they might be interested to join me. Eventually, the friends dropped out and neither Mark nor Christopher were enthusiastic (in any case, they were both under age and Betty intended to stop from going). In hindsight, it was such a blessing for me to go on my own: it gave me a chance to come to terms with myself and the aftermath of our separation and divorce.

The following year I landed in Manaus, the capital of Amazonas. It lies some 3500 kilometres (over 2000 miles) from the estuary where the force of the river in full flood drives fresh water ten kilometres (eight miles) into the Atlantic. Manaus was once the world's only centre of rubber tree plantations and production. The rubber barons were enormously rich, sent their weekly laundry to Lisbon by steamer and enjoyed excesses far beyond the later oil sheiks of the Middle East. Their monopoly ended in the early twentieth century when an Englishman smuggled six rubber tree saplings out of Manaus and planted them in Malaya. From these, all the rubber plantations of Asia were grown.

Although the rubber barons, prospectors and gamblers have long gone, the city still retains the atmosphere of a frontier town, despite the magnificent nineteenth-century 700-seater Portuguese Baroque opera house, where both Enrico Caruso and Margot Fonteyn performed, or the Indian Museum, with its vast display of butterflies, some with a wingspan of twenty centimetres, as well as enormous beetles, spiders and other nasties.

Exploration Saunders!

The Boat and Crew

On 29th August, feeling exhausted after travelling for twenty-two hours, I landed in Manaus. The temperature was thirty-five degrees Celsius with high humidity. The air conditioning unit in the rather rundown hotel room was noisy, the windows and door would not close tight, and although I managed to sleep for a couple of hours, when I awoke my body was covered in mosquito bites.

Early the next morning, I arrived at the docks. It seemed incredible to me that such huge cargo boats could sail so far upriver from the Atlantic estuary. The booking agent took me along the quayside to the boat, a smallish, pre-First World War river craft showing patches of rust and looking a bit like a double-decker version of the African Queen. On board, I met the crew, chose one of the four small cabins below deck and discovered there was no shower or bath. All the crew, except Antonio the cook who had a fold-up bed in the galley, slept in hammocks slung under the awning next to the wheelhouse and galley on the upper deck.

These profiles of the crew are drawn from my diary notes and impressions during the following ten days:

The Captain

This quiet, smiling twenty-five-year-old who owned the boat was wearing a sailor's peaked cap, white shirt and shorts when I first stepped aboard. This kit was discarded (apart from the white shorts) as soon as we cast off, only to be seen again several days later when he went aboard the refuelling pontoon. He was in command of the boat, its repairs and anything mechanical. He was not a native jungle Indian.

Bernard – The Bo'sun and Steward

He was a young, cheerful Amazonian Indian who had left his jungle interior village for the bright lights, dancing and fast living of Manaus. He was amusing, fun-loving and constantly played Brazilian pop music on his cassette/radio every time he was at the wheel. No doubt he could take great care of himself and instinctively knew the river.

Judging by the way he served at the table, his stewardship training was somewhat limited. He was interested in languages and we managed to communicate with bits of English, French and the few Portuguese words I had learned. Undoubtedly, Bernard was intelligent: he could read, and I am sure it takes tremendous effort to leave the jungle environment to live in Manaus. Unfortunately, he liked my brand of cigarettes and my supplies were running short.

Laurie – The Interpreter
He had been a librarian in Manaus until two months before I hired him for the trip. He studied in his free time and was pleased to join the boat to improve his English vocabulary. I encouraged him to speak slowly to correct his slurred pronunciation. Laurie was born in the jungle and had all the fearless instincts needed for survival. Like Pedro, the hunter and guide, he walked barefooted through the jungle and was indispensable on every hunting trip to interpret what Pedro was doing or wanted me to do. Once, he skinned a shot caiman. Laurie was an intellectual jungle boy, a keen reader, and even ashore in Manaus he could only sleep in a hammock. I held him in high regard.

Antonio – The Cook
This forty-five-year-old was not a native jungle Indian. Since the trip began, I hardly saw him outside the confines of the galley. He was a gentle guy, cooked very well (usually far too much until he got the message). He had extensive dexterity with a knife, and could skin (except the caiman), butcher and clean whatever we brought back for the table. Everything, apart from the fruit and vegetables, was freshly fished or killed. His cooking was tasty and varied, and he knew what to do with everything we caught.

Pedro – The Hunter and Guide
He was a short, stocky, Sherpa Tensing type. In every sense a man of the jungle; probably hardly a day had gone by when he had not hunted or killed something. His grin flashed a pair of sabre tooth tiger-like eye teeth which, no doubt, came in handy from time to time. He sported a moustache he may have been trying to grow since puberty (Indians have very little body hair). Pedro had instinctive RADAR and alarm systems and an aggressive urge to survive and hunt. He was the real mastermind of the boat and took all the important decisions.

Surprisingly talkative, he wore a wedding ring, laughed a lot and had a poise and balance that was light and completely silent (for instance, when running from fore to aft on the punt when we hunted for caiman).

So much for travelling up the Amazon on my own!

The Amazon Diary, 1973

30th August

10.30am: Cast off. Travelled at about ten kilometres per hour, then stopped for an hour to take on more provisions at a 'hotel' built in the middle of a lake, not far out from Manaus. On the quayside, there were many curious locals and tourists who seemed to be so surprised that we were off to the jungle for thirteen days!

4.30pm: At anchor on a fairly wide stretch of the river. I felt very brave having just taken a swim in the Amazon – there is no shower or bath on this boat – swam ten strokes and thought that was courageous enough. Soaped up and went in again. Coming out the second time (good God, the second time indeed) I tried to pull myself up into the boat and slipped, grazing my right arm. These cuts and grazes I did not want and was very pleased to have my own medical supplies.

Now then, back to this bravery of mine. While writing this piece the captain (who incidentally, has not left the wheel all day!) has been in the water for the past half-hour with Pedro, trying to repair a leak below the stern. They are still there. Well – bravery is in the mind anyway.

We came upriver and through very dense jungle in parts where the waterway is clear at times, otherwise it was only the width of the boat. It appeared that the banks were close too, but these river 'banks' were only floating reeds and through the trees beyond was more water.

I spent the afternoon after lunch on the roof of the wheelhouse: the Sun was very hot – like a sauna. When we had traversed the 'lake' out of Manaus, there were lots of things to photograph. The Amazon is either black or brown. In the foam of the propellers, and when looking at someone swimming, I can see that the water is actually yellow and not sepia. In the big lake were a couple of enormous dolphin-like pink fish which, Laurie says, are man-eaters. The black variety – which the natives never kill – have friendly instincts towards swimmers, much as the Western dolphins do.

Pedro spent most of the day cleaning and assembling the rifles, spears and the rest of the armoury. He also acts as lookout in difficult waters where the passages are narrow or there is a lot of floating driftwood. The engine is slowed to a murmur: everyone aboard senses a certain tenseness and pays attention to what he is doing on the prow. It is amazing how these people seem to know which outlet or tributary to take: it is so dense and it all looks the same. It has, of course, gone through my mind that maybe they don't know and play everything by ear. I will soon know if we land back at Manaus tomorrow.

In tow is a small canoe-like punt for fishing. From the size of fish I have seen, there will hardly be any room for we fishermen. The birds are exotic, beautiful and vividly coloured. Laurie has a fund of folklore stories about how these birds got their feathers and different colours.

6.00pm: On my right, the Sun is setting fast; on my left is a bright Moon. As darkness approaches, the sky is filled with every type of cloud formation. It is clear to see how much the water level has dropped: the Amazon will get lower as the season progresses and even now, the trees lining this particular waterway are at least more than two metres higher. Now it is almost dark when more birds seem to be around.

The Moon gave all the light we needed for dinner. At 8.30 I felt tired and went to bed. We had anchored in a wide stretch of the river as this was supposed to be a mosquito-free area. I did not relish sleeping on deck without a net. They assured me that if I sprayed the aerosol, then all would be well.

It is impossible to convey the sinister darkness of the jungle and the black waters.

31st August
I woke again at midnight to the familiar noises of dive-bombing mosquitoes and the loud din of the jungle. I went up on the deck for about an hour. The Moon was still very bright; there was no movement from the trees; the dew was heavy and the clouds had gone.

Getting up on deck was difficult as I did not want to disturb anyone, especially Pedro. I could imagine his reactions would be swift and self-protecting, even in his sleep.

5.00am: I was awake and back on deck. Within ten minutes everyone had woken and suddenly the boat was shipshape again.

157

One by one, the crew dived in the river and so, without a second thought, I too plunged in.

It is pointless to wear a watch as the Sun dictates all timing and in any case, bedtime at 8.30pm local time and getting up at 4.30am is simply in time with London which is four hours earlier.

This morning, the skies are clear and blue. The river is smooth and unrippled yet the water runs swiftly.

Since 6.00am we have been on the move all day until we anchored in another 'lake' at about 4.00pm.

The highlight of the afternoon was fishing with spinning tackle from the small punt with the outboard motor. From the 'lake', which is only a wide clearing in the river, we made for the tree line and caught three quite big fish. Spinning under the tree line was a most sinister experience – I imagined snakes falling on top of me, and the punt had a bit of a leak in the bow. Also, I lost my bearings but trusted my sense of direction and kept my eye on the Sun.

Once inside the jungle on dry land, the blackness becomes greyer and yet so much more frightening. I suppose it is all in the imagination when the shapes of everything lurking near the black surface of the water seem to be some horrible creature, waiting to strike the most tortuous and stinging blow. Fear can only be relative – Pedro has just gone off into the blackness in the punt. Perhaps a walk in Soho or along parts of Broadway would be just as frightening to him; only I know the relative dangers.

6.00pm: Just had a swim and a soaping down. Apart from Antonio the cook, the others have been trying to re-caulk the stern for about an hour since we dropped anchor. I told them I had a fair supply of chewing gum if all else failed.

I have just taken pictures of the Sun to starboard and the Moon to port. Now, writing by moonlight and above the tree line I can see lightening yet no sound of thunder. Imagine an arc of colour – top and bottom are Prussian blue, the middle a brighter steel blue marking the horizon. The sky and water are the same colour, separated by the band of trees which is doubled in the reflection of the waters. This band is the blackest black I have ever seen. The boat is ringed by the blackness. Even the tree line facing the Moon is so dense that no light is reflected. It is all black.

This afternoon I was stung by a wasp-like insect: at first it was bloody painful but these medical supplies are miraculous. On this particular 'lake' there appear to be no bugs at all. The small awning light is switched on without attracting a single mosquito or insect of any type. The spiders will be hungry tonight – I hope.

The jungle noises are monotonously regular. The big frogs call out with the sound of wild geese overhead and a high-pitched whine, rather than a whistle, is coming from some insect described by Laurie as being 'big'. Occasionally the sloth's drum-like noise simulates Brazilian music.

The night is a most lonely passage as I still cannot sleep longer than five hours at any one time. Last night I felt cruelly cheated when I looked at my watch for the second time to realise it was not 1.20am but one hour earlier. When everyone is asleep I feel a lone traveller in the jungle – not afraid – but alone. Now I simply look forward to the dawn.

The boat is confining and I will be pleased when I can get off and walk. I intended this trip to be one of physical exercise: doing things in a hard, tough manner. Instead, each day presents a mental challenge to overcome the fear of the jungle and the black waters where everything seems hostile and against man. Maybe I have read too much about the nasties but I know they are ever-present here and it is all real. Only the few Indians born in the jungle could survive such hostilities: I am surprised that anything can survive except the vegetation. Then again, I suppose that if the matter were posed to a frog or anaconda or stingray – whatever – it could not understand the survival of men in the First World War or indeed, any other war. If this sounds like an attack of jungle fever, the hostility is very penetrating.

Tomorrow morning, I will go out in the punt to film close-ups of the tree line before we leave for some other place.

I am so looking forward to the dawn.

1st September

5.30am: Went up on deck. The captain and Antonio went out for more fish and came back with two piranhas – rather larger than I had expected – with jaws of razor teeth. They bagged other bigger fish, the same as those we caught last evening. Then I went hunting with Laurie and Bernard to film close-ups of the jungle edge. A flock of pigeon-like birds scattered as we approached; two perched up in the trees. We cut the motor and waited. I shouted to make them get up. Bernard could not understand why I didn't pick off the stationary bird. The gun is a single barrel sixteen bore; I shot one in flight and felt rather pleased.

After the noise of the shot we waited in vain for the birds to return. As we paddled deeper into the jungle I had to restrain myself from telling Bernard that I did not think it was a good idea and was relieved that we only stayed for about five minutes before paddling out again. I forgot that Bernard grew up in the jungle.

Nature certainly seems to balance up the odds: in England, when a bird is shot, a dog retrieves it. Out here, if you want your quarry, then you have to fight for it because the jungle is reluctant to give it up, thus balancing man's supremacy.

Antonio plucked the bird, ready for cooking.

9.30am: The engine is revving up and away we go again.

During breakfast, two old Indians in a punt came alongside. Antonio bought some melons and an upturned young turtle about thirty centimetres across the length of its shell. In exchange, he gave them a cheese sandwich. They told us about the best place to fish (which was not in this area).

It is odd how quickly one becomes acutely aware of tactile contact. While writing, the boat made a slight turn, causing the water tank on deck to slightly overflow. I reacted very fast when the water trickled under my feet. Yesterday, I was standing on the deck over the wheelhouse: it was so hot I had to stand on a towel, the wind ruffled up the edge and fell onto my feet again causing a swift reaction. Whenever I feel something on my skin, in this environment it is a natural to think that it is some hostile creature – and quite often it bloody well is! Noises, movements and when I'm in the punt, even a ripple just below the surface of the water, sends the adrenalin surging through my body.

The enforced exercise of economy of all supplies is interesting. I had to check on things like the consumption of film, booze, fags, and medical supplies knowing that there is nothing until we return to Manaus. I am sure it is good for the soul and wonder how long one retains these senses and feelings once back in the land of shops, money and restaurants. I suppose it needs different survival kits built into the system for London, Paris or wherever else.

This morning, after travelling for about two hours we anchored in a small area about three kilometres across in each direction, then punted off for more fish and birds. The birds are rarely seen and we only caught sight of one – it was reddish brown and quite large. I could have shot it at least three times over but wanted it to fly. Very shrewd was this bird – it jumped (not flew) from one branch to another behind thick leaves and then disappeared. Wanting to shoot it in flight seemed to be contrary to the way they do things here. Pedro was not annoyed but puzzled, especially as it was good foodstuff. Nothing else came in sight. We then had to speed back to the boat when a sudden rainstorm blew up: it only lasted half an hour but there was an awful lot of rain.

After lunch we went out again and just as I was getting into the punt, I noticed that we had the turtle in tow – the poor blighter was on a length of string tied to the stern. They had obviously made a hole in its shell. Apparently, Pedro wants to take it home!

So, we were on the punt looking out for birds and nothing appeared. He stopped the outboard and paddled along the line of trees. Soon he was listening for any tell-tale jungle noises and as we had no luck he decided to go into the trees. Another little battle went on inside me, assuaged somewhat because at least I have the gun. From the water's edge, sitting in a four-metre-long punt, the jungle looks almost impenetrable and it bloody well is almost impenetrable, and very dark.

At the moment the Amazon is still fairly high but as the water recedes so the tree line becomes exposed and reveals the changing shorelines. We paddled in for about 150 metres.

I could not imagine how we were going to pass through the dense trees, especially the young saplings, let alone turning the punt round to get out again. We found the shoreline and stayed silent. Just below the surface were the decaying leaves, dead tree trunks, and everywhere were the contorted shapes which, to me, became snakes and other sinister creatures. Although they were only the twisted branches of trees and vegetation, it still took some time to adjust to the poor light. We saw nothing to shoot, yet the whole place was alive. As we bumped into the trees to thread our way through, so large drops of water fell. A 'curtain' of mosquitoes buzzed and then there were insects like large horse or dragon-flies which travel at about 150 kilometres an hour. The noise they make can easily be described: no doubt one has slept on the first floor of a hotel in the high street at any Spanish resort, or sat in a roadside cafe and been deafened by the locals belting their mopeds up and down. The only difference is that these insects don't appear to leave exhaust trails.

We stayed in the jungle for about half an hour and still did not see a shot. Now this is a slight problem because when we left Manaus we had fresh fish and meat for two days only. We have caught plenty of fish, and apart from the bird I shot, we have no other meat until we go hunting tomorrow. I am told that tomorrow morning we will go walking in the jungle – now there's a thing.

Since the rain came this morning the temperature has dropped about five degrees Celsius. This evening it is quite cool – even chilly – and the sky is heavy with dark grey cloud. There will be no Moon tonight to light up the water.

5.30pm: The turtle has been hauled aboard and I presume it will be fed.

After the rain there appeared clouds of smoke rising above the trees which I assumed to be coming from the reed huts the natives live in and because of the cold they had started fires. However, this part of the jungle is totally uninhabited and the 'smoke' was coming from the jungle.

I have never seen Moon rays before. The moonlight through a break in the clouds is so strong that rays of light appear in the sky. Tonight is damned cold. Nothing here is man-made other than our boat and everything aboard. This occurred to me in the punt when I saw bright red and yellow debris I thought was old potato crisp bags and other litter seen everywhere else in the world except here: even the peelings the cook throws overboard disappear almost immediately – the Amazon swallows everything. All shapes, colours and textures are natural and nothing is man-made. This is a new concept of things to be conscious of – there is no waste, litter or debris. New trees grow on the decaying leaves of old trees. The blackness in the water, caused by the decomposition of vegetation, fertilises the new greenery – just like the blackness of the jungle at night turns to lush green as the Sun rises and turns the colours during the day; I realise this blackness surrounding us tonight is really green and very bright by daylight. So day and night is like the cycle of life and death. It is simply an 'understanding' that the colours are there all the while because the jungle is still green, however it appears at night.

The skies are clearing and a warmer breeze is blowing. Each gust has a temperature different to the next. The Amazon has warm and cold patches one feels when swimming and they change so rapidly from one patch to the next – even the area around the boat.

5.30am: It stayed cold all night. Mist was rising all around the water which was probably no more than six kilometres across. The scene was like old Japanese watercolour drawings – almost monochrome, with watery tones of black and greys. We went fishing in the mist; the water was a black mirror, totally flat; the jungle doubled by reflection.

It was not our morning. I caught the only fish – fortunately it was big, about fifty centimetres long – the shooting was a disaster. I had four shots – three were at birds in flight and the fourth was a sitter that would not get up. I missed that one too. Could it be the gun, the speed of the punt or the sitting posture? It was either a combination of all three or bloody bad shooting. I don't know if God knows but I am positive that Pedro knows. Well, at least I caught the fish for a fresh lunch for all.

Tonight I will see what awaits us at our next anchoring point about five hours away. We should arrive by 4.00pm, leaving an hour or so before sundown. The trouble is that they keep mentioning, through Laurie, how delicious is braised toucan – the sitter I missed.

Now the Sun is shining and the clouds are lifting. It is much warmer, shirts are off and it is time for relaxing.

The scenery doesn't change: although the tree lines get wider or narrower, it all looks the same. So far, we have only had to turn back once – this was yesterday. The book on the Amazon I brought with me describes how the natives 'read' the river, except one cannot 'read' the trees, as the tree and shore lines, and even the main river streams, change frequently. There are no charts either. Every 600 metres or so, the river bends and then divides into two or more channels. Now sceptics could argue that either the captain or Pedro, who are piloting the boat, are on as much of a mystery tour as I am; however, there does appear to be a general sense of purpose on the part of the crew who show no surprise when we arrive at a 'lake'. There are fewer bugs in the middle of the water. When the faint light is switched on for anchorage, Pedro seems to be able to make fairly accurate forecasts as to how good our next stop will be for birds, fish, or whatever.

I have overestimated the maltreatment of the turtle: it has been brought up on deck. Unfortunately, to ensure safe keeping, it has been turned on its back with its legs tied down.

11.30am: For the past hour the landscape has changed; the trees are further back from the water; I can see proper river banks and the jungle is less dense. Every four or five miles there are small villages and cattle searching for food. According to Bernard, quite a few animals are either dead or about to die from starvation. With so much vegetation, I can hardly believe it! Flocks of vulture-like birds are cleaning the carcasses. Laurie said the people are dying of starvation because the hunting and fishing is poor.

Now I must inform the British Museum of a new species I have named Murphia Stukas. They are larger than the British moth and fly, with their legs and broad feet dangling down, hence the reference to the German dive bomber it resembles in appearance, performance, sound and aggressiveness. The Murphia part refers to the IRA: if it ever escalates the war in Northern Ireland, they need look only as far as the Amazon for this armoury for aerial warfare where they will find these creatures already in their own colours – bright ginger. They could be camouflaged in the mops of hair of IRA men and then release them on Belfast. Maybe the British Secret Service or counter-espionage branch would be more interested. Pedro said that the Murphia Stukas has a sting six times that of the nasty which bit me yesterday. At least one can see these coming.

This boat should be renamed the 'Bismark'. A film was made of this epic story of the battle with the German ship and flimsy, pre-war British biplanes carrying torpedoes slung under the fuselage and dive bombers attacking day after day. The planes went in from every angle zooming over the ship, almost touching the funnels. Well – need I say more? As a last word on the matter, it is reasonable to draw such comparison between the relative size of the Gloucester Gladiators and Swordfish biplanes to the Bismark, and the insects to this little boat,

I am conscious that I have made many references to battles, wars and soldiers that the veterans of jungle campaigns would dismiss as romantic hyperbole. In my defence I would argue that as a boy I did experience dodging German nasties and while it is incomparable, one must add the purple patches somewhere and I am finding the journey today a bit tedious. The Sun is not shining. We are on a wide stretch of river and only when we pass little islands and the bird life is there anything to photograph.

5.00pm: Back on board after an hour and half duck shooting. I shot six and felt rather pleased when the captain and Pedro returned with only one duck and one moorhen. The ducks are now being plucked and Pedro has gone off again to find where to hunt tomorrow. Today was good sport and for the first time I felt like the hunter rather than the hunted. We have anchored in a huge expanse of water dotted with islands. Some of the birds are really very big with wing spans of three metres and a variety of exciting colours. Although there were hundreds of ducks, the problem was getting anywhere near them. I only let off thirteen cartridges and three of those were at the same duck. Unfortunately, not every duck was a clean kill and when wounded, they dive under the black water and then bob up metres away. One was wounded slightly; it had plenty of 'go' and I had to wait for him to come up to finish him off. If this sounds very callous – he was done for anyway – and I wished I had killed it first time. Another duck was also wounded so Laurie dived in to retrieve it. With all this blood about and piranhas everywhere, this was not a sensible thing to do. However, he obviously enjoyed the moment.

The thought of piranhas did not occur to me until we got back on board and blood from the ducks being offloaded from the punt was dripping into the water. I decided not to swim this evening and used a bucket douche. After the 'shower' my right arm ached – probably due to the tense and grim exertion of hanging onto the boat while lifting the buckets of water out of the river. The most compelling reason to use buckets of water today is that when we anchored, I noticed a school of pink fish with shark-like fins circling around the boat. When they come up for air they make a strong blowing out noise like an old granddad having a nap with the volume turned up. I saw these on my first day out and remember Laurie saying these were not friendly – unlike the black ones.

Having showered and dressed for the evening (for the first time I have not worn either jeans, jeans shirt or swim knickers) and settling into this bit of writing, I can see those more dolphin-like rather than shark blighters are still there. About the piranha on this lake: I noticed Antonio preparing the duck then throwing the unwanted parts overboard. Disappointed not to see the water 'boil' with blood crazed piranhas stripping the bits off the bones until Laurie said there are no piranhas in this lake – ah, knowledge is bliss! However, none of the crew went for a swim tonight – they too douched from the boat – because of the 'dolphins'. The moral is – follow the natives – never go in first.

3rd September

Last night, my feelings that 'hostilities' had paused were short-lived. As the darkness descended so did the mosquitoes. They were everywhere: even the crew complained. At dinner the table had to be moved into the wheelhouse where we tried to eat there. There were bugs of all kinds and I was dreading the night. As usual, by 8.30pm everyone, except me, is ready to go to sleep. At nine o'clock I started spraying my cabin and for the first time I saw the crew spraying the wheelhouse where Laurie and the captain sleep in hammocks. All night long the crew was slapping away at various parts of their body to beat off the bugs and yet they don't appear to have a bite on them.

I closed the cabin windows and vents and turned off the light to stop attracting any more. At first, I thought of clearing the bottom bunk and dropping a sheet down from the top bunk but in the end settled for an Indian cotton caftan as a shirt, tucked my feet in the sheet, put another caftan over my head and kept my hands well covered.

The heat woke me up at hourly intervals and eventually, I went up on deck for fresh air where at least I could swat the buggers. I opened the windows, sprayed around again and returned to my white shrouds. Although it was uncomfortable, this morning I cannot detect any new bites. It is incredible that in the middle of such a big lake, anchored not 500 metres from the tree line, there are all these bugs and yet inside the almost impenetrable jungle it is bug free because we are on the Rio Negro where it joins the Amazon. The river has no bugs at all because, according to Laurie, the type of vegetation falling into the dense, black water, acts like an insecticide.

6.00am: This morning I struggled to get up and missed seeing the dawn for the first time. The crew was already up and busy.

After breakfast I went shooting with Pedro and Laurie for about three hours. The hunting and the shooting were a disaster. I banged off twenty rounds and shot just one bird! Pedro thought we had bagged enough duck and wanted to go for the big birds with a wingspan of about two metres. Although they are a big target, they frighten very easily and always fly away from the water's edge. We stalked one, it came in range and I shot it. The dead bird fell to rest about two metres up in the branches of trees across twenty metres of water and floating grass vegetation. I could not believe it when Pedro turned the boat into the reeds and got out a duck board to walk on to reach the bird. After ten minutes or so, we could not get nearer than the punt length even though Pedro went over the side to push closer. Our one paddle was not enough leverage to pull the punt through. It took another ten minutes to draw the boat away. Then Pedro stood up in the punt, surveyed the scene, paddled about fifteen metres along the line of reeds and bugger me, he turned into the jungle again!

This stretch of reeds was only nine metres wide before reaching the dense foliage of the shorter trees. Beyond, under the low canopy of leaves, there was a clearing with trees growing out of the water that looked like a cave. This time I bristled with cowardice and told Laurie to tell Pedro that I would rather spend my time shooting than trying to retrieve the irretrievable. Pedro was either deaf or Laurie could not dissuade him. (Later, I learned that this bird is highly priced in the market and is destined for Manaus, not the oven on board.) Again Pedro struggled to push through the reeds with the duck-boards. A quarter of an hour later, we reached the trees and found a way through to the water covered in a green slime and vegetation and under the murky cave. Even many young trees were decaying with rotting branches twisted or bent everywhere and shrouded in brown dried leaves like huge cobwebs. We had to bend double or lie flat in the punt to work our way through to the bird. Here and there were noisy 'plops' in the water – armadillos so Laurie said – dropping to the water because they were afraid. They were afraid! – Jesus Christ – if only they knew.

Crouched in the bow, Pedro pulled through the undergrowth; his back was covered in the cobweb stuff and all sorts of insects and moth-like creatures. Very little sunlight penetrated the gloom and I could see spots of blood where the bugs were biting him. Although I was wearing jeans, I had no shirt either – there seemed little point in taking a shirt for a simple bit of duck shooting on the lake in the early morning! This cocoon of dried, decaying leaves, dark mould and God knows what else covered the whole of my body. Well, the jungle, like the Amazon river, does not give up things easily and (not surprisingly to me) we could not find the bird. However, when eventually we broke through the last bit of the tree line, pleasingly enough there was only a short stretch of reeds, about the length of the punt; then into the sunlight and a fast beat back to the boat to wash away the jungle.

11.30am: It is cloudy and cooler. We are now heading back towards Manaus to refuel; the dock is nearly two days away.

After a duck lunch, I slept until 2.30pm.

We passed the area of the jungle where the Bismark episode took place and this time I am ready to repel the buggers. The bugs that have been a constant nuisance – and with us the whole time – are insects like bluebottles with opaque black wings – the sort of cloak Peter Cushing wears in the Dracula films – and they too suck blood.

Well now folks, this afternoon is walking in the jungle time. Pedro said to cover up everywhere. I put on boots, tucked trousers into socks and wore a thick jeans shirt buttoned up to the top. With a gun, fishing rods and camera, we punted through the tree line to the shore. Laurie sprayed the aerosol over my hands, then I 'bathed' my face with the stuff making my eyes smart but this was preferred to an onslaught of mosquitoes. The spray did the trick for face and hands but when I returned to the boat they had penetrated the jeans shirt in one place on my back. I don't know if it had been the mosquitoes or something else that had taken seven or eight bites, all in diameter of about thirty centimetres of skin.

Black and brown leaves in various stages of decay carpeted the jungle floor. Every step on the fallen, big palm leaves made a crunching noise. The afternoon Sun was bright outside but inside the jungle it was twilight and too dark to film unless I pointed the camera at the sky. Pedro picked his way through, breaking young fern-leafed saplings. Whenever he paused, he stood on one foot with the other tucked behind his ankle and silently pointed up into the trees at monkeys which I could not see. All I could hear were the buzzing of the mosquitoes and the jungle cracking away the whole time. When Pedro stopped, the jungle sounds suddenly stopped too except for the incessant cracking noise: I then realised that Pedro was using these young saplings as signposts to retrace our steps. I followed Pedro, treading exactly where he trod – step by step – with Laurie behind me. He pointed to the burrows of armadillos and tracks where wild boar had been. Here and there were patches of red earth where a tall tree had fallen; in this dense jungle I wondered how a dying tree could fall and land in a horizontal position...

Two hours later, to get back to the punt we had to walk through a curtain of bugs: the buzzing of the mosquitoes ceased where their territory ends at the shore line. I could breathe once again as we paddled along the tree line for about half a kilometre, then into the trees to fish for piranha. The technique is to use a bamboo stick with a metre length of steel trace and hook tied to a nylon line to the end of the rod. As the bait of raw meat on the hook is lowered into the water the end of the rod is used to violently agitate the surface. The piranha sense that an animal, wounded in a fight, has fallen in the water. The splashing in the water attracts them and there you have piranha fishing.

We returned to the boat in a rain storm.

5.00pm: While Laurie and I went for a swim, shampoo and a soaking to clean off the jungle debris for the second time today, Pedro set off again in the punt.

Later, writing this afternoon's events and as darkness closed in, I heard the outboard motor. It was Pedro towing the captain and Bernard in the spare punt. It seems that when we returned, he saw that they had gone fishing without the other gun and their paddle. The engine had broken down in the rain storm and they tried paddling back with their hands. How did he know they needed help? How did he find them? How did he know which direction to take and why he went in the first place is a mystery? Survival instincts and heightened senses are difficult to comprehend.

Sadly, the turtle is now being made into soup and the stupid cook threw away the shell!

7.30pm: Heavy rain clouds. We ate early in the claustrophobic wheelhouse. I am writing by the single light on deck and only the occasional mosquito becomes troublesome. Tonight I told Laurie that after refuelling tomorrow, another four or five days will be enough. Apart from the 'walk' this afternoon, it is difficult to get any exercise – at least the type which is relaxing and without tension. Now, I am getting ready to return to my 'jungle'.

This afternoon I recognised that physically, I am neither strong nor aggressive. I let two piranha off the hook because I did not strike when I felt them on the line. This morning I shot badly because I lacked the aggression one needs to 'push' the gun at the quarry to kill and to do other things like cocking the gun. When swimming, I have had difficulty hauling myself back on board. Most of the time I relax too easily and readily and am not aware of the strength needed: instead, I only use mental strength when I really need to exercise power. Probably, this is why I like to know in advance what is about to happen because generally, I handle surprise situations badly and have to resort to 'pulling rank' to get back to where I am in control and return to a state of being at ease.

This morning, I had not prepared myself for the trip into the jungle and tried to stop Pedro from his tenacious drive to retrieve the bird. There was also fear of what might be lurking in the reeds, the enormous insects buzzing around and the sense that anything and everything could attack in such a dark tunnel we were about to enter. Whereas, this afternoon, I was ready to go into the jungle for the walk and although it was far more unpleasant in terms of bugs and eeriness than this morning, I was prepared for it. Maybe this is why I am a long-term planner.

I want to go out with Pedro at night for the caimans and have a go at spear fishing.

Tonight the sky and the water were pitch black – dark clouds covered the Moon. I was on deck finishing off the last little piece of egocentric writing when I saw Pedro about to leave in the punt to look for alligator caiman. I decided immediately that I wanted to go, so Laurie came too. Armed with harpoon, gun and torch we set off in the overpowering darkness. Since starting this Amazon trip, I knew that at some time we would go out for caiman and my conscience has been troubled, knowing this would not be hunting food. However, the natives do eat alligator meat. And so, forgetting I was in my 'relaxing on the deck after dinner' clothes – not my jungle jeans – I jumped into the punt and headed for the black silhouetted tree line. The technique is to flash the torch at low level into the water where the trees grow out of the river and the caimans' eyes show up as pairs of bright red lights. We traversed the tree line for a few hundred metres, stopping the outboard then paddling through the tree line into the murky jungle when the dozens of glowing red eyes appeared. As we got nearer to the array of unblinking eyes, Laurie whispered that we have to get in very close and to shoot if the caiman is big; if it is smallish then use the harpoon and if it is a young one, don't do anything. Right, but how do we know how big the thing is? His answer was that you don't know until you are close enough to see! This I found somewhat disturbing because I knew the 'daddy' ones are bloody big and again, sensed I was the hunted rather than the hunter.

Every time we approached the red lights they vanished under the water – except, before one caiman had completely submerged, I did get in a shot. To retrieve it, we had to go another four or five metres further into the depths of the jungle – we were already in about six metres or more – then heave it into the punt. There were no more caiman to be seen.

Back on board, the light was out and the others were fast asleep in their hammocks. We lifted the caiman on board; it measured about two metres long from head to tail. Later, the Moon shone through a gap in the clouds and stayed bright for the rest of the night.

The jungle at night was not as frightening and awesome as the earlier trek in the daylight. Strangely, the caiman hunt in the dark was totally absorbing; even the mosquitoes were brushed aside with mild annoyance, and did not feel like a mental endurance test. No doubt, hunting for a quarry such as wild boar, focuses the mind and blots out the anxiety of treading on a snake or being attacked by big nasties, and the overall hostile, sinister atmosphere. On reflection, I would be ready to go out after caiman again, face the black jungle at night and the possibility of only wounding a big one that could retaliate and easily turn over the punt, yet in daylight I would need a great deal of prior notice to summon up the courage before going into the jungle to retrieve the wounded bird in the swamp.

Even returning to the safe haven of the boat has not been uneventful: back in my cabin, I sprayed the aerosol particularly at three buzzing mosquitoes. After many direct hits they still persisted; at least if their eyes smarted as much as mine did they might have to get some fresh air at some time. I gave up trying to knock them out and went through the same ritual of wrapping sheets around myself, wearing one caftan and covering the other one over my head then carefully tucking it around my neck. Just before the final touches, I opened the big window, jumped on to the bunk and thrust arms under the sheet. Immediately, their buzzing around my head starts and it goes on all night.

4th September

It was fairly cool up on deck for air about one o'clock this morning. After five or ten minutes I went back to the bunk and repeated the process of shroud wrapping. Three hours later I felt a hot pain in the heel of my foot and hobbled back up on deck again. In the half-light of the oncoming dawn I searched for the cause of the pain: was it some nasty bug that had crawled under the sheet, or while out in the boat last night something could have fallen into the punt and bitten me? After the jungle walk, when we got into the punt to cast off from the shore line, something stung my arse: it was a bloody big ant that had bitten through my jeans!

It seemed like hours had passed, waiting for the crew to wake up. In daylight Pedro could see two problems: the first was a black thorn stuck into my heel (maybe I brought it back on the sole of my boots and in bare feet had stepped on it in the cabin); the second problem was a festering wound under the skin. My holdall, stowed under the lower bunk, had one of the metal handles left open and two or three nights ago, when I jumped down from the bunk my heel caught the sharp handle: it was night-time and I should have used the antibiotic cream.

Pedro turned me round, lifted my ankle between his legs – the same stance horses are shod – then went below and came back with a Gillette razor blade and a bottle of jungle juice medication. He slit the skin to release the pus, cut out the black thorn, then sloshed on the juice – and that was that. I felt no pain from the blade work and of course once the thorn was out, the pain disappeared. The other cut still hurts. Time will tell!

There seemed little point to suggest that the blade should be sterilized – he would probably argue that it was new and clean already! Instead of using my own medical treatment, I thought his juice might be more potent. Again – we shall see.

8.30am: For two hours the boat squeezed through the narrowest of passages and two or three times it had to 'jump' over the shallow waters. Laurie says Pedro comes out here in a canoe in the drier season and mentally plots the course of twists and turns. Along the journey there seem to be dozens of options which appear to be open to us but according to Pedro, they only lead to dead ends. Suddenly we came to a vast, open stretch of water, at least five kilometres wide, and now the boat is carried along on the fast current down to Manaus. We have been out of the jungle for about twelve hours and for the first time for six days, in the distance I saw buildings other than the few village huts. This does not fill me with excitement in the least and after the fuel stop I will be pleased to return to the jungle. Perhaps I would not be so enthusiastic to return if it were not that the Rio Negro is without mosquitoes. For the first time this morning I did not bathe in the river: maybe it has some soothing properties or else it was just the bad attacks of bites I had yesterday. My skin feels afire despite using the cream ointment which on previous days has been soothing. In any case, last night I decided that three or four days more will be enough on the Rio Negro.

After refuelling in Manaus we are heading for the Rio Negro. The sky is overcast and for the past three hours the bugs have stayed away – probably because it is dull and cooler.

3.15pm: I saw the swirling convergence of the Amazon and the Rio Negro. Here, not far above Manaus, the yellow Amazon and the black Rio Negro retain their separate colours for many kilometres: the river of sepia water colour mixes with another river of black Indian ink and at first it seemed like a trick in the sunlight creating a camouflage pattern of a thick oil slick on muddy-coloured water. The different densities of the two rivers eventually merge a long way downriver. Anyhow the photos will do a better job and it really is fascinating to see. The power, energy, vastness and aggressiveness of the Amazon river and the jungle are indescribable and incredible. Unless one were born here, thus acquiring instinctively all that is necessary to survive and not be swallowed up (metaphorically and literally), it is exhausting to be on constant alert.

We landed for two hours at the Lake 'hotel' for provisions, refuelling, and I managed to arrange a return to Manaus on 9th September and fly on to Rio Negro on the 10th.

A woman came on board who needed a lift back to Manaus where she was acting as a courier around the city for a BBC film producer called Robert Saunders. She said very few tourists take trips into the jungle and rarely stay even for just one night; even fewer go alone other than with a crew. I felt rather pleased about that.

As we waved her goodbye on the quayside and headed into the Sun setting in the western sky and the unknown, I felt elated and impatient to get onto the Negro and bathe in the water there.

8.00pm: An hour and half after dinner, we anchored in the mouth of one of the tributaries of the Rio Negro. The lights of Manaus can be seen in the far distance. Close by is the jungle with all its familiar noises and, miraculously, without the buzz and torment of the mosquito. Everywhere I have bites and do want not go through that again. Tonight, even Pedro said that he had not experienced the severity of the attacks we had yesterday. So far so good – we are without mosquitoes and now wondering what alternative nasties may be present. After all, there must be some reason why so few people (in fact, I am told there are none) live in this region and yet, according to Pedro, although the hunting was good for caiman, ocelot, boar and so on, it can only be done at night.

Everyone is tired after the long twelve-hour journey. I am ready to relax and enjoy the moment because by comparison, everything here seems to be rather more hospitable (but only by comparison). I have never seen so many stars. In the darkness this jungle is different, the trees are much taller and there appears to be a definite demarcation between land and water with even a low cliff-like terrain. It will be interesting to see it in the morning light.

5th September

Where we are anchored is about 100 metres off the shoreline of a stony beach of cliff rocks about 150 metres long. As usual, I woke at midnight, went up on deck for a couple of hours to see what was happening, looked at the Moon then back to my bunk, still suffering from the mosquito bites from the night before, and longed for the dawn when I could bathe in the water.

My 'problems' have been caused by sheer carelessness on my part – the jungle never lets you off the hook. First, I should have checked that mosquito nets would be on board. Second, when I stepped on to the holdall on the floor, half under the lower bunk, I should have used the cream medicament on the wound. Third, I did not cover up when hunting for the caiman.

Today, my feet are one big, joined-up mosquito bite. My heel is still painful and my body is covered in bites because of the lack of a net. If I can avoid scratching the bites they tend to stay below the skin surface and eventually disappear. The river water does tend to soothe whereas the medicaments do nothing for this lot.

6.00am: After bathing, we were under weigh again. By 3.30pm we had anchored for the night. Here, the hunting is only at night-time and without the bugs – we should be okay.

It is incredible that it is totally bug, mosquito and fly free (thinks! – why didn't we just drop anchor around these parts for ten days?). There are, of course, the big horseflies, beetles and other things that come and go rather than making direct attacks. Apart from the absence of nasties, the jungle does look much the same except the waters are a deep rich black/brown colour – like an oil sump.

The Sun has been shining all day; tall white clouds ring the horizons. This is perfect for nursing the wounds and recharging the adrenalin yet I am constantly conscious of the menace and treachery of the river and the jungle. In fact, because there are no mosquitoes along the Rio Negro, it provides an environment for other creatures big and small to exist in abundance and, in particular, the caiman alligators and animals of the cat family.

The anchorage is in a little tributary out of the main stream for me to bathe in the refreshing water to 'cool' the bites. Here the Rio Negro is well over two kilometres wide between the shorelines where only the tops of the trees can be seen in the water that grow to a depth of at least 100 metres. How deep the water is around the line of trees is difficult to estimate.

Since we arrived here, five or six local native boats and one-man canoes have passed by, which is strange because I am told this region is almost uninhabited. Maybe they were hunters. Where we have been for the past six days, there were, in parts, more signs of life – I suppose the people prefer the mosquitoes because they seem to be unaffected by them.

The crew is a happy lot who occasionally joke with each other. Last night, Pedro must have gone out hunting after I had gone to bed. This morning, he jumped on to the punt and pulled out a young metre-long caiman from the hatch where the quarries are stowed, which he caught last night with his bare hands. He held up the vicious-looking creature to show us on deck. Just as the captain dived into the water, Pedro threw the caiman close to where he was swimming. The captain 'sprang' back aboard: the caiman surfaced with only his eyes and snout above the surface. I think it was out for revenge, staying menacingly close to the boat until we left the anchorage. Everyone found it highly amusing – my contribution to the laughter must have sounded rather more of a hysterical shriek and hope this sort of practical joke is reserved for close, long-standing friends.

This afternoon, Pedro said we will drop anchor at about six this evening and later tonight we will go out for caiman. Tomorrow, we will hunt for the big animals (whatever that means) – he reckons there are plenty about. (With luck we will find them before they find us!) Pedro is jungle man personified and I am pleased to be on his side.

And now the bad news: it is about 4.00pm and the bugs are buzzing. These, I am told, are a different sort of mosquito and the good news is that I am assured they do not attack at night. I shall wait and see!

5.00pm: We have come out from under the shelter of the tree line and making way to the other side. Here the river, about twelve kilometres wide, is like the open sea, fast running with fairly big waves. We have battened down – this boat was never built for this type of water!

We have been travelling for nearly eleven hours. I am on deck alternating between using the camera, reading a book, writing this diary and bathing the bites.

The boat makes about twenty kilometres an hour in open water, so we have sailed 200 to 250 kilometres north-west up the Rio Negro. There has been no sign of life other than the jumping fish.

6.30pm: We have dropped anchor in a 'lake' and the punts and outboards are being prepared. After a swim and dinner, we will be off.

Pedro, Laurie and I set off in the punt. There was no Moon, the stars were shining and the jungle, only about 150 metres from the boat, looked very black. My eyes became accustomed to the darkness as we slowly cruised along the shoreline, flashing the torch into the dense trees. After about three kilometres, Pedro stopped the engine and paddled from the prow of the punt. (When he walks along the punt it is like a gymnast on the beam: he can leap from one punt to the other carrying heavy weights, like an outboard motor, and still keep a perfect poise.)

Pedro paddled straight through into the undergrowth. Silently, he propelled us along with just one hand, using the other to flash the torch on and off, piercing the darkness and the big trees, looking for animal scratch marks; then along the line where the surface of the glass-like water met the thicker parts of the low reeds, and then he looked for track signs in the shallow water as we approached the steep shoreline of dry land.

We had penetrated 300 metres into the jungle, pushing through narrow gaps in the low-lying trees, thickets, twisted vines, branches of trees and foliage, when suddenly there appeared an inner lake where the trees were thick and tall, like a high cave with a black mirror floor. Pedro pressed on under the canopy to the other side of the lake and again shoved our way through the dense jungle where tall trees were still growing in the water and the lower vegetation struggles to fight for an existence.

In absolute silence, I could not even see a wake from the paddle, and for what seemed like hours, we punted in the darkness along different parts of the shoreline waiting for animals to come down to water. All natural light was blanked out. Pedro's pale green shirt looked odd for hunting gear, but when he was not flashing the torch it was impossible to see any light reflected from his shirt and he was crouching in front of me. The darkness was total.

Loud noises surrounded us. The buzzing sounded like overhead high-tension cables; frogs constantly croaked to each other; and intermittently there was a strange 'ping' noise like the asdic sound-effects in wartime submarine films, except this sounded like the whole of the British fleet homing in on one sardine tin. A clacking sound added to the cacophony – it reminded me of waiting for luggage to come on a carousel in Terminal 1 among hordes of holidaymakers wearing straw sombreros, newly returning from Benidorm with their unruly kids clutching a bull doll or Toledo sword, clacking a pair of souvenir castanets. Naturally, everyone except their parents is conscious of the ceaseless clacking. This is the same clacking noise in the jungle; at first, I thought it might be a few hundred armadillos having an orgy.

Pedro was annoyed that we saw nothing to shoot, and it was time to go. We had been in the jungle for more than two hours. The trip was exciting and although not a shot was fired, I was pleased to be out of the way of the bat-like creatures zooming around us every time the torch was flashed. Whenever I come up on the deck – the longest period I have slept has been for about four hours – there at the stern end of the boat is Pedro, fast asleep in his hammock and still slapping away his bare skin where little bugs are bothering him. Each morning, on the deck under his hammock there is a graveyard of numerous dead bugs he has emptied from the hammock when he climbs out. Even in his sleep he is able to kill off the opposition. Pedro decided to leave this particular stretch for a better place to hunt. Here, they could be heard but not seen.

10.30pm: Back on board after hunting the lights were out, except when Bernard had sprayed my cabin he left the light on. Luckily, still no mosquitoes but a variety of other bugs and in particular a moth-like insect with a bright neon light glowing bright green like a beacon. I tried to clear them out, sprayed again and climbed into the bunk.

The heavy rain woke me. I went up on the foredeck to shower in the downpour to cool and ease the bites. The clacking was still going on. I assumed the armadillos were still making love. If so, whatever the foodstuff consumed by the armadillos or the armadillos themselves would have been well sought-after. The second time I went up on deck, noises joined in the main jungle chorus, sounding like various species of barking, howling dogs and lots of whistle calls and hoots. Swimming around the boat was another school of pink dolphins, puffing and blowing as they surfaced.

6th September

7.30am: We cast off about an hour ago. It will take another two hours to reach our next anchorage where Pedro says we will go walking in the jungle.

I dressed to cover up as best I could and steeled myself for the trek. We beached the punt and walked for three hours. In comparison to the other jungle walks, the absence of mosquitoes made it pleasant enough with time to see the beauty of the jungle, the growth, the greens, browns and the denseness under the canopy of trees. We came across a little waterfall and for about two kilometres, made our way deeper. All was dark, the floor a cemetery of decaying trees and leaves, the hollow-sounding ground felt like a continuous bed of rotting vegetation – moss greens and, predominantly, blacks and browns. At the base of some trees were the beehive-like tarantula nests. Everywhere insects crept and crawled.

I was armed with gun and camera. Pedro carried his own gun and used his machete to cut, point and probe the ground and vegetation. Every few paces he stopped, resting on one foot, keeping absolutely motionless. Suddenly, he pointed into the trees – a quarry had been spotted. I was looking for the spots of an ocelot or an animal of some kind. Pedro kept his gun trained on the target, whispering to Laurie what he could see and telling me to shoot. All I could see were leaves and trees. In the end Pedro fired and down came a magnificent eagle-type hawk with a wingspan of nearly two metres. Pedro then cut some young creeper vine and tied up the bird to make the carrying easier for Laurie. The last thing I was looking for was a bird and in any case, I did not particularly want to shoot one.

After trussing it up we walked on and then Pedro and I spotted something at the same time. If I had not seen it move as it went up the tree I would never have picked it out from the foliage. It was an animal about the size of a large squirrel. I killed it, retrieved it, and then made our way back to the punt. This biggish rodent, used by the Indians for medicaments, is apparently rarely caught and well sought-after. We traced our tracks back to the punt and, paddling our way back to the boat, Bernard and the captain came alongside in their punt. They had been fishing with a rifle. Bernard held up a green snake about four metres long he had killed just as it was about to catch a small rodent creature on the tree line edge. When the animal dropped into the water for defence, Bernard shot the snake.

So ended the morning's hunt. Pedro plucked and butchered the bird, saving all the plumage intact for Laurie. I went swimming while Antonio cooked lunch. He said the eagle is good eating – maybe for them but not for me.

This afternoon it rained for an hour. Now the rainclouds have passed, everything is quiet again waiting for the weather to settle before deciding what to do next. It is likely we shall remain here in this backwater and wait for some night-time hunting. Pedro has gone off on his daily reconnaissance. I am sure he is not as aware as I am as to the total extent he has my survival in his hands. Inside the jungle, especially at night, whether on foot or in the punt, I lose all sense of direction. Never before have I experienced such complete reliance on any other man.

After lunch and a siesta, I went out in the punt with Pedro and Laurie to get the 'SP' for tonight. We went upriver about five kilometres. I took the gun and camera and apart from small birds, saw nothing. Pedro, however, seemed to be interested in all sorts of places that were likely hunting grounds later. It was a leisurely 'cruise' along the tree line – this I established before we left and only wore jeans, no footwear or shirt.

We seemed to be going a long way from the boat. Pedro was absorbed and we might have gone even further until the engine started to give trouble. By the time it restarted, storm clouds had gathered and down came the rain. It was gentle at first, then suddenly there was the most fierce fork lightning and thunder and the temperature dropped by about twenty degrees. We shivered in the cold and the force of the rain stung our bare skin. So, violence – sudden violence – erupted.

This part of the river was about 200 metres wide, with no inlets, just many interminable bends. We arrived back about six o'clock, very cold and wet. There will be no hunting tonight. The storm continues to rage and the noise of the rain makes it impossible to talk at normal volume.

I don't know if it was because of the impending storm but when our engine stopped, the jungle was silent apart from the occasional bird whistle. Even this morning, when we were trekking in the jungle, it was very quiet – almost silent. Only at night is the deafening noise unending until dawn breaks.

At about 8.00pm there was a lull in the storm. Pedro flashed the torchlight along the tree line. Soon after he had decided to go out hunting later, the rains returned and certainly, I shall be staying aboard. It rained most of the night.

7th September

8.00am: It is cool and dawn was hardly noticed. Out in the punt we found a little tributary, discovered a short stretch of shallow rapids and pushed the punt up and over the rocks. Further inland we searched for the cascade we could hear in the distance. Here was the most claustrophobic, dense jungle I have been in so far – no wonder absolutely nobody lives here. We must be the only people for hundreds of kilometres. Pedro sharpened his machete on a stone at the water's edge, then hacked a way through the steep, slippery, dense undergrowth. Slowly, I edged forward with the camera slung over my shoulder and the gun gripped in one hand. Yet another facet of the jungle came to light in the form of various types, sizes and lengths of spines. The big spines, protecting the stems of a palm-like tree, are easily seen and avoided but when we reached the cascade, my hands were covered in whisker-like spines – some had pierced my thumb. Pedro studied the wound and attempted a bit of instant surgery with his machete. (Although I got out the thorn when we returned to the boat, I could not clean out the dirt inside Pedro's incisions. I hope the antibiotic cream is effective!)

Today is Independence Day which accounts for the crew being in a festive mood. Laurie wanted to return to the cascade to take photos so we went back to the boat to get his camera and Bernhard and Antonio wanted to come too. After the photo shoot, we set off for another spot in the jungle we saw yesterday. Today, it had changed.

We got in fairly close, then we had to get out to pull the punt over trees that had fallen in the water across our route. Antonio and I balanced on one end of the trunk while Pedro, Laurie and Bernard heaved it over. Bernard fell in and shot up back into the punt damn quick (this was a favourite spot for electric eels). With all this effort, the waterfall was still about fifty metres away. Laurie and I took our pictures. While the others were searching for sharpening stones at the cascade, I stood still in the jungle, watching the huge butterflies that glow with iridescent blues, greens, reds and yellows. Apart from these, I saw no bird or animal.

It was a good fun time – almost like a picnic.

Later this morning we cast off again. The Sun came out for about an hour before the clouds came back again. Perhaps it will not rain any more today and, depending on the weather, will make our way back to Manaus, hoping to stop somewhere for hunting this afternoon or tonight.

Heading down the Rio Negro for about two hours, we then turned into a 'tributary' which was hardly visible – to me anyway – and just wide enough for the boat before anchoring in a 'lake'. This is the most beautiful place I have seen so far and sadly, it is the last port of call.

This afternoon, with gun, camera and piranha lines, Pedro and I went out to get the 'SP' for tonight's hunting. Paddling silently, we saw a troop of monkeys. Apparently, they always leave one on guard to warn the 'pack' and if he fails in his duty, they have a bit of a punch-up. I missed two or three shots at birds and the fishing was totally without a nibble even though we moved from one dark spot to another until, three hours later, the Sun had dropped below the tree line. On our way back to the boat we were raided by these large wasp-like Hells Angels swarming around and through us. Their nests, high up in the trees, are like 'bowls' about the size of footballs made of mud and leaves. If these insects are disturbed, they will attack, even through the water. Pedro reckoned that when I tried to shoot a bird, I nearly scored a direct hit on one of the nests that are everywhere, hanging like giant conkers on the branches.

The jungle noises are getting louder. The buzzing insects have gone and everything is still. There was a 'plopping' sound in the water and between the dark patches in the trees there was a fairy lights display by the firefly beetles.

8th September

Tonight was the last night to hunt in the jungle. There was no Moon, not even a star to light up the deep darkness. After dinner, Pedro, Laurie and I set off and saw lots of caiman eyes but I was after different game. We paddled through the tree line and stayed inside the jungle for two or three hours. It was so dark that only very occasionally could I see Pedro's shirt. Most of the time he silently paddled with one hand, gliding the punt through the undergrowth and overgrowth for about ten metres off the shoreline that twisted and turned. Every so often, Pedro bellowed a sound as if somebody had kicked him in the groin – he hoped to get a corresponding call from our prey.

Here I was, posing as the great white hunter, this time complete with jungle boots, cartridges in my thick jeans top pocket and a gun at the ready. Two hours later, Pedro whispered that he had spotted a 'pakka'. Now this animal is the largest rodent in the world, about as big as a medium-sized dog. Pedro, crouched in the bow, beamed the torch on a small area of tree to give me the line of shot. It moved, then froze, clinging to the trunk. I fired and saw the animal drop. Pedro got up from his crouching position mumbling something – Laurie answered back as we paddled towards the shoreline. What was the argument about? Pedro said I had missed it, Laurie said he saw it on the tree and saw it drop.

Pedro stepped out of the punt, walked about five metres to the tree, picked up something and carried on searching. What the great white hunter had done was that he had shot a creature described as a jungle rat – it was indeed about the size of a rat with a bigger head. This was on the tree trunk just above the position where the pakka was standing. When I shot, I was standing up, Pedro was lying down and in a fairly limited field of light, the angle gave me a different view. We collapsed in laughter. I was pleased for the pakka and paddled our way out of the jungle to make our way back to the boat.

I reflected that I would prefer to go back to the clay pigeons – at least they move whereas here, with the exception of the duck, everything freezes.

9th September

Early this morning everyone was busy and within five minutes we were under way for the long trip back to Manaus. Last night, well after midnight, I spent over an hour on deck. The Moon was up and the jungle still very noisy.

Today is sunny with a cooling breeze. I have packed all my things, pleased to be leaving and on my way back to Rio and on to London.

Postscript

Of course, there isn't an anaconda curled up in every tree and in fact, I only saw one type of poisonous snake. The real 'nasties' were the ever-present beetle bugs and mosquitoes. The enforced daily swimming to keep clean was more of a quick dip in and out wearing tight-fitting swim trunks – the thought of the anus boring fish was always uppermost in my mind!

In the Amazon, everything is set for attack or defence and most things seem destined for a violent death, except the trees which die slowly of strangulation by the creepers as their wrecked hulks are broken down to a powder by the humidity and beetles. The only creatures that defy the camouflage greens and blacks of the Amazon are the beautiful, colourful birds and butterflies.

At the end of this journey, I understood why the Amazon had such fascination for me, with my almost obsessive need to experience it myself. I am also ever-grateful that through a series of circumstances, I had the good fortune to make the journey alone.

Sometime in the early 1990s, Janet and I met Fawcett's nephew at Baroness de Pauli's home in Hampstead. He too had searched, and found no further evidence to shed light on the mysterious circumstances of his uncle's last expedition.

One of the classic films of the 1980s, showing extraordinary scenes of the Amazon and the Manaus opera house, was Werner Herzog's *Fitzcarraldo*. It was based on the true story of Brian Sweeney Fitzgerald – the natives called him Fitzcarraldo – a mad Irishman, obsessed with building an opera house in the Peruvian rainforest upstream, similar to the existing magnificent Portuguese Baroque opera house in Manaus. His girlfriend, who ran the local bordello, pressed her rich rubber baron clients to fund the building. They refused, but told Fitzcarraldo that there was a vast area of rubber trees waiting to be tapped where he could make his own fortune. The problem was that the plantation was inaccessible due to upstream rapids. Undaunted, he restored an old rotting steamer and, with a team of natives, hauled the boat up and over a small mountain to get to the trees.

Another classic of the 1980s was Herzog's factual documentary film of the making of *Fitzcarraldo* and the heroic actual scenes of the natives manhandling the steamer up the mountainside. Unforgettable!

11

France

The Romance

Scenes of the liberation of France on Pathé newsreels in the cinemas
of 1944 were the beginnings of my love affair with the country. The
spate of brilliant films in the 1950s – *Manon* starring Cécile Aubry,
Rififi, *Monsieur Hulot's Holiday* and especially *La Ronde* starring
Simone Signoret – were only shown at the original Curzon 'art'
cinema in Curzon Street. (I had to save for weeks to pay for a Pullman
seat costing one pound; the normal cinema price was less than two
shillings or twenty pence in new money.)

The fantasy of speaking fluent French was on my special wish-
list. Undoubtedly, not being taught a foreign language at school was
one of several anxieties and resentments I'd nursed during puberty.
(Languages weren't taught at secondary moderns in the 1940s; only
the public schools, state grammar or county high schools included
French, German and Latin in the curriculum.)

It wasn't until the early 1970s that my inability to speak French
presented any real obstacle. Most French people we'd met on family
holidays, driving to Brittany and Paris in the 1960s, were bilingual,
and there had been no hiccups due to the language when I worked in
Amiens for one of our house-builder clients from Folkstone. When the
British property developers decided there were riches to be mined on
the Continent everything changed and the practice took on projects
in Paris and Brussels. We recruited Ahmed, a Tunisian who taught
French and English at the French Lycée in Kensington, to come to the
offices twice a week to teach me and others working on the continental
projects. Sometimes, business meetings could not be programmed to
suit Ahmed's schedules, which disrupted the teaching. Some progress
was made – albeit soon forgotten!

Letter Written in Paris to My Office, About 1972:

I have been here for a week and for the first time (10.30pm Monday) I am alone with a bottle of burgundy and feel fresh enough to write.

Paris is a city for walking the streets among the exciting buzz of life. I have discovered that it is quicker to walk than going by taxi or metro. The weather has varied from dank autumnal cold to hot summer-like sunshine: the weekend was particularly good. Saturday's stroll along the river bank led me to sensational boutiques selling gorgeous goodies: this is the place for Xmas shopping and for the first time I had the opportunity to see what Paris is like beyond either side of Les Champs Elysées.

The so-called economic crisis has only hit France in the past few weeks. Here, there is a sense that they will overcome their problems easier and quicker than other countries – certainly more so than Britain. Probably, the expensive luxury of living in Paris creates a boost and confidence.

One could write a novel every day describing all the bizarre happenings, non-happenings, anomalies and frustrations when doing business in say Riyadh, Cairo or other Middle-Eastern cities, whereas in Paris, being far more civilised and used to 'our ways', the day-to-day business routine is tame and unexciting. Although good new business may be about to happen, the real interest is sustained by getting to grips with the language.

Generally, the meetings in the office are in French (even though the visitors may speak a better English than my French, I can insist because it is my bat and my ball). Usually, at meetings in other people's offices, English is spoken, as many business folk are English who have lived in Paris for three or four years. Noticeably, they hardly ever miss the opportunity to show off their French to order coffee or take a telephone call. However, once the natives can see that you are making a bit of an effort, they like to switch into their English (to likewise impress their secretaries or whoever else may be around). When two people meet, after speaking just one or two phrases, each can immediately ascertain precisely who has the better command of the other's language. The sensitivity is uncannily accurate. Daily meetings are not such hard work – it is the language that's so tiring. If I am fairly certain that someone, such as a taxi driver, does not speak English, I try out the little phrases picked up from Ahmed's lessons to get the ego massaged.

The practice needs to find a little studio flat to call 'home': we can then start making the best of Paris and ease the travelling between here and London.

Eventually, in 1974 we established an office, with Denis Prout in charge, and a rented pièd á terre. A couple of years or so later, we followed the many English developer clients and agents who did not strike gold, and retreated to the shores of Dover. (A re-enactment of Dunkirk comes to mind!) At about this time, my personal love affair with France also went into decline when, sailing in the bay of Toulon, my boat was bombarded with low velocity shells by la Marine Nationale. (See Chapter 12, Sailing.)

Villefranche-Sur-Mer

The frequent travelling to our office in Paris had rekindled my desire to learn the language, and to progress further than the barely remembered rudimentary phrases from Ahmed's lessons. I had hardly moved beyond the 'bonjour' bit, and only spoke passable 'restaurant' French (provided the waiter was an understanding person who was familiar with the struggle *les Anglais* have with foreign languages). The frustration stimulated my resolve to sign up for a four-week course at an Institut de Francais. Our Paris office made enquiries and found a school based in Villefranche-sur-Mer where, only a year earlier, my friends Len, Bonny and I had sailed into the bay off Cap Ferrat. I remembered the ancient port, with its quaint arched-over streets and cave-like alleys, and was delighted when the office booked me on the next course. A studio flat in the port was rented through a local agency.

On the 1st August, I drove my Mini Cooper from London to the sleeper train at Bologne. After twelve hours in a couchette compartment (which only reinforced my abhorrence of caravans and camping), I drove in the glorious sunshine from Avignon to Villefranche-sur-Mer on the Côte d'Azur.

It was late morning before I located the agency to collect the keys for the flat. Since leaving the train in Avignon, I had been rehearsing all my 'restaurant' chat, searching for phrases like: *"Acceptez-vous le card credit?"* or *"J'ai commande deja l'addition"*, or *"apportez moi..."*

As it turned out, the woman's English at the agency was worse than my French. She tried to speak 'restaurant' Anglais, then quickly reverted to her native tongue (the French always overvalue their sense of superiority). I worked in a few phrases about my name, my office in Paris (*mon* or *ma bureau*? – God knows), and asked her to take me to the flat '*tout suite*'! I hoped she would only respond with a simple "*Oui*" or "*Non*", without the usual expansive and polite replies to elementary statements and requests. She seemed to grasp that I was in a hurry.

I followed her car down a winding road from the town to the old harbour, crammed with sailing boats and expensive motor cruisers, past the University of Paris for Oceanography, and into the new port, where we parked outside a white block of flats called Les Galets d'Or. The flat was a most delightful, bright studio on the second floor, elegantly furnished by the American owner. (He had something to do with show business promotions, and the agent said Shirley MacLaine, Rex Harrison and other 'well-knowns' had stayed at the flat.) Off the bedroom, which was on the mezzanine floor over the main living area, there was a balcony garden planted with aromatic herbs.

The school, perched high above the village centre, had once been a grand, private villa with spectacular views across terraced gardens and the Mediterranean. It was well past lunchtime when I arrived, only to remember belatedly that on the first day, students were supposed to be at the school at ten o'clock for grading tests. At two o'clock, some four hours late, I joined the other hundred or so other students who had gathered to listen to the introduction to the 'system', the 'do's and don'ts', delivered by Monsieur Colbert, le Directeur de Institut, who spoke perfect English with an American accent. Obviously annoyed at my late arrival, he ushered me to the last empty chair at the front.

Monsieur le Directeur liked the drone of his own voice. His expert use of English idioms and colloquialisms was a challenge for the non-English-speaking students who had to listen intently to the whispered simultaneous translations. The majority of the students were American; the Germans, who spoke good English, were the next largest contingent. There were a few English students, most of whom were connected with the Corps Diplomatic or aimed to become members of the European Parliament. There was also a number of staff from Sotheby's, which intended to open a branch in Monaco.

Monsieur Colbert seemed unable to grasp that we were intelligent, responsible people who understood that when he said that he did not want cars parked in a certain place because the delivery vans found it difficult to unload, we would indeed accept his good judgement. We did not need twenty minutes about the history of traffic patterns over the past four years. Similarly, that if he said it was against the law in France to make a noise after ten o'clock at night, we were quite able to accept it as a statement of fact. And so it went on...

He then came to the teaching system. First he told us that above all were 'Les Verbs'. He wrote these two words on the blackboard behind him and then turned, knelt on one knee and crossed himself in religious fashion. He proceeded to tell us about the programme of events, lectures and teaching methods. We were urged to refresh ourselves weekly by reading the 'short' pamphlet, which reiterated, almost word for word, the *Institut's* irrefutable logic of how to teach French. After that, he reverted once more to 'Les Verbs', telling us, as he searched for an ashtray on one of the tables, to forget nouns: we did *not* need to know the names of things. He picked up the ashtray (probably the same one used every month for new intakes) and brandished it at arm's length, emphasising that we did not need to know the French name for an ashtray, *but* we did need to know how to say:

"Where can I buy one?"

"How much is it?"

"Who gave this to me?"

"Can I pass this to you?"

"Have you seen it?"

"What are you looking for?"

And so on...hammering home the point to exhaustion with even more verbs.

Still brandishing the ashtray, the *Directeur* paused to survey the cowed audience and, putting it back on the table, asked if there were any questions. In a split second, like one of those uncanny experiences of deja-vu that suddenly flash into your head, I blurted out, "Yes, I have a question. What's the French word for ashtray?"

The hoots of laughter did not simmer down until sometime after he had gestured and mouthed "*doucement*". He regained composure, smiled, and mildly delivered the threat that as I had not yet taken the grading tests it was not necessarily certain that my application for the course would be accepted.

Finally he informed us that henceforth, when inside the school precincts, we must only speak French. This felt extremely daunting to us beginners, particularly when he went on to say that any transgression would cost both the speaker and the listener ten francs each (about one pound sterling). The only time the rule was relaxed was if we received a telephone call from the outside world, when we could revert to our native language (this was before the advent of mobile phones). Any fines collected would swell the kitty for the end-of-course party.

Generally, everyone obeyed the rule, but students would occasionally sneak behind bushes in the gardens to speak in their own language (often married couples or friends talking about what they needed to buy for supper), hoping that they were out of earshot. Often they weren't.

The next morning's grading tests placed me in the debutants third grade (the lowest). You were graded according to your level of grammar, comprehension and conversation. There were eight grades: the first three were for absolute debutants, then four intermediate grades for those who knew some French, and one for the few advanced students. I discovered later that the grading system was anything but precise.

In the grade above me there was a fifty-five-year-old Yugoslav who had a remarkable command of the language, but his problem was that he had learned all his French from the peasant resistance workers during the war. Although his fluency should have been a help in his newfound profession in the embassy service, unfortunately he spoke with such an appallingly rustic accent that much of his teachers' time was spent correcting his pronunciation. Also in his class was an American who had very good comprehension and grammar but could not put two words together; he had no ear for French pronunciation, and sounded the final syllable of every word.

The classes were mostly question-and-answer sessions. In one session, the teacher asked an American in my class, who had been studying French for years and had already taken five one-month courses at the school, whether he had drunk wine or beer in the bar the previous evening. She repeated the question two or three times, and each time he muttered, "...*la biere*??"

Eventually, he said, "Je ne comprendre pas la biere."

At that, the teacher made a drinking gesture. Eureka: "Ha. You mean LAAR BEE AIR."

The words 'you mean', said in English, cost him ten francs!

The days settled into a regular pattern: up at 7.30am, a squeezed fruit juice, then a twenty-minute climb up the narrow steps from the harbour followed by ten minutes of cooling off in the school gardens before going to the lunch room for the continental breakfast. Classes started at 9am.

First, the teacher would ask what we had done the night before. (Whenever it came to Ali the Iranian, the only variation to his standard answer 'casino' would be whether he had won or lost.) Then we looked at film strips and repeated the recorded dialogue. The tape recorder was rewound again and again until we could comprehend and pronounce the phrases. (Usually it was the pronouns that caused confusion.) After that, we had to make up sentences to describe the scenes in the film without the taped dialogue. Often, this was hilariously funny until we had to concentrate on the questions and answers using different tenses illustrated in the film's dialogue, such as:

"...the mother of Pierre has just given him a birthday present because today he is ten years old."

Individually, we had to respond in the past tense negative to the teacher's question: "Was it his birthday yesterday?"

This technique became complex when one member of the class was asked if he had given a present yesterday to another member of the class; then the teacher would swiftly point to someone else to demand if the first person had or had not given that present to the second person.

This unreal interrogation ended at eleven o'clock. Then we had a half-hour break before meeting back in the classroom where we prepared for the laboratory in the afternoon and made a note of the homework requirements for that evening.

Lunch was served at noon. Each table seated seven students, as well as a teacher or one of the office staff who would vigorously promote conversation, firing questions and correcting every response that was not delivered in accurate French. Sustaining the pressure of constant alertness rather diminished the pleasure of the good food.

After lunch, each class was directed to either a garden patio or one of the drawing rooms. The next hour's session was devoted to more reposeful activities: listening to traditional French songs and trying to understand the lyrics; or to poetry, especially that of Jacques Prévert, which was recited delightfully, first by the teacher, then by one of the students until, eventually, comprehension would dawn on us. Sometimes we played games like Twenty Questions, when every question had to be correctly phrased and the 'victim' had to answer using a complete sentence: "No, I am not an object made of metal…"

At two o'clock, we filed into the laboratory and plugged in the headphones and microphone. This daily one-hour session was a most intensive and arduous exercise, constantly monitored by the teacher. At the end of this 'torture', the headphones were ripped off and groans of relief were audible. Even the advanced students felt the pressure of the laboratory work. Then, a well needed half-hour break to recover before we headed back to the classroom for the last session, which was either the correcting of the previous evening's homework or having to tell one's short life story.

Classes ended at five o'clock. Many of us congregated in the lunch room for tea and biscuits, tired and still casting around for the right French phase or particular verb. Usually, I hurried down the steps to the flat, where I changed for a swim in the bay, before going shopping for the evening's dinner.

The only time it could be said that I 'won' happened just prior to an afternoon session in the salon. I asked our teacher if he could read some poems from *Mots d'heures: Gousses Rames*, a book I had brought from London. On the blackboard I wrote the following (as well as another couple of 'French' nursery rhymes):

Lit-elle messe moffette.
Satan ne to fete.
Et digne somme coeurs et nouez
A longe qutaime est-ce pailles d'Eire
Etre Satan bile ailleurs
Et ne fredome messe Moffette, ah ouais.

It was totally incomprehensible to the teacher, who imagined it was from ancient classical French. When he read it in his impeccable French accent, the twenty or so English-speaking students fell about, convulsed in laughter. The teacher was totally confused.

One evening in a bar while I was drinking with three other American students from our debutant class, I discovered they too were interested in sailing. Next day we met in front of the *Directeur's* office, struggling in our best French to decide which one of us would make enquiries to hire a boat for the coming weekend. One of the Americans, despite years of learning French, always floundered, using lots of '*la... las*' in a bid to hold his listener's waning attention. Suddenly, Monsieur Colbert came out of his office, listened to our mumblings and joined in our 'conversation', correcting every mistake. Then, for practice, he asked the American to say how much sailing and navigation he had done and whether he had checked the weekend's weather forecast. The American fumbled for answers, then leapt through the open main door next to the office, bounded up the three or four steps and through the gate, and stood in the roadway with his arms outstretched, shouting: "I don't know the fucking word for weather!" (The road way was 'neutral territory' which avoided his being fined ten francs.) Then he leapt back into the lobby to share the brunt of Colbert's testing interrogation once more.

It was sad to be leaving the idyllic flat, the school's routine, the hard work, the camaraderie and the month-long fun and amusement. The last day was exam time for all the students in the morning, then more lectures on French slang. At five o'clock everyone assembled to receive their '*certificat*', their end of term report and drink a farewell glass or two of champagne.

The intensive course certainly got me off the 'P and G' (point and grunt) stage. I envied those whose jobs in Monaco, Paris or Brussels meant that they would continue to be totally immersed in the language every day.

I drove back to our office in Paris where, with Denis Prout, I made three presentations in halting French.

The intermittent visits to Paris ended when the office was closed down. Thereafter, only my trips to the Vipassana centre in Auxerre, to the boat in Marine de Cogolin, or to the two Kairos seminars at Chartres Cathedral presented opportunities to speak French. (About fifteen years later, Janet and I took a short holiday to St Tropez, making our 'pilgrimage' to Chartres Cathedral en route, where we shared a profound spiritual experience as we traversed the labyrinth.) It would always take the first two or three days to attune my ear to the language, but I would struggle in vain to regain the reasonable fluency I had acquired at Villefranche: if you don't use it, you lose it!

Unfortunately, almost all that I had learned in Villefranche continued to elude me, and it didn't help that all our friends who were French-speaking natives insisted on practising their English on us.

In desperation, I returned to the *Institut de Francais* school in 2011 for another one-month intensive course. This time, I was not put in the lowest debutant class! Monsieur Colbert was still *Directeur*, and the successful teaching system and curriculum were exactly the same. Slowly, modest progress was made.

Living in France

In 2006, Janet and I toured around the Mediterranean, along the coasts of Italy and France to look for a small permanent holiday home on the Côte d'Azur. Our *Plan A* was to downsize in London from our three-storey house in Highgate, where we had lived for ten years. A year later we rented an apartment in Villeneuve Loubet for two weeks as a base camp to explore the property market. A few days later, after discovering that the French authorities impose restrictions upon flat-owners on the times when a piano and other music can be played, *Plan A* changed to *Plan B*. We set out to find a detached villa where Janet would be able to play her piano whenever she wanted.

An agent took us to view a villa in a domain of twenty-four houses called Les Jardins de Pomone, next to the Fernand Léger Museum, close to the Medieval village of Biot. The village is internationally known for its glass blowing and was once the headquarters of the Knights Templars. The beaches of Antibes were just five minutes from the domain.

Unusually, the villas were not Provençal – they were two-storey Bauhaus-style buildings surrounded by trees and gardens with a vast swimming pool and tennis court. The marble-floored rooms, bathed in light, with floor-to-ceiling sliding windows, provided the space and flexibility we needed, including a music studio for Janet's work. So, in 2008, the villa Margarite became our permanent residence.

The Norwegian Fougner family – Erik, Nina and their three young daughters – sold the villa to us and moved to a larger one on the opposite side of the road. The other immediate neighbours were French, Russian, Danish, Belgian and Dutch. (Only one other couple in the domain was English, but they spent little time in Pomone.) The generosity of spirit of all our kind, helpful and friendly neighbours became, and continue to be our long-standing friends.

The slower, measured pace of life compared to London soon revealed itself. The distinct seasons were clearly defined by the snows on the mountain tops, the yellow flowering mimosa trees in February that announced the start of Spring, and the garden and roadside blossoms that marked the changes throughout the year. Living in these idyllic surroundings of lush gardens, almost constant sunshine, fresh sea air, lack of noise from aircraft and traffic, and constant birdsong, induced a period of uninterrupted creativity in both of us.

We never bought an apartment in London as planned: the property market had suddenly gone sour, and when, eventually, the house in Highgate was sold, we couldn't afford to buy a pièd á terre. As a result, we travelled back and forth to London quite a bit over the next six years. Eventually, and for a number of reasons, including the burden of looking after such a large house and garden; the frequent travelling; the rising cost of living; the French socialist taxation and bureaucracy, we decided to sell the villa and return to England to be nearer our family and UK friends and to be back in the buzz and energy of London. There was also the added complication of avoiding permanent residency.

In 2013 we returned to Highgate. In the week before we left, our immediate neighbours organised a Sunday picnic lunch around the pool and presented us with a beautiful piece of hand-blown glass by one of the artists of Biot. There were tears, sad farewells and offers of a bed whenever we wanted to return for a holiday. We shall miss the close camaraderie, the enjoyment around the pool, the long evening suppers on Olivier and Catherine's terrace, and the pleasure of being greeted with a smile and a *"bonjour"* by everyone – the young and old, friend or stranger.

12

Oceans of Pleasure

Offshore Shelling

The outstanding feature of my first offshore cruising experience was being shelled by the French navy in Toulon Bay.

My dinghy racing days ended in 1972 when Betty and I divorced. I never returned to Stone but kept in contact with Len and Bonny and talked about finding a cheap boat for hire to sail along the South of France coast.

A friend introduced me to an American bit-part film actor living in London who rented out his boat, which was berthed in a marina in La Ciotat, about thirty kilometres east of Marseille. The photographs looked enticing and the cost was reasonable enough, so Len, Bonny and I decided to set off for a couple of weeks on what should have been a gentle Mediterranean cruise.

Standing on the quayside in the marina we looked at the boat: it was painfully obvious that it had not been particularly well kept. The halyards, sheets and lines were a tangled heap of ropes lying in the saloon. Fortunately, the sails appeared to be in good order and the galley looked serviceable, but we then discovered there was no on-board shower room or toilet which meant, in sailing parlance, we would have to 'bucket and chuck it'. (Rough camping on land – let alone on water – has never appealed to me.) My first reaction was to go back home or find another boat, but after the initial disappointment, we could see it was seaworthy enough and set about making it shipshape.

After an almost sleepless night, we came to terms with the boat's idiosyncrasies and fairly limited capabilities. Next morning we set sail. Leisurely – or should I say 'sluggishly'? – we cruised along the coast for nine days, stopping overnight in marinas as far as Villefranche-sur-Mer, some 200 kilometres from La Ciotat. Here we spent an afternoon and evening sightseeing to relax us before making the return journey.

Before dawn, we chugged out of the little port in the old part of the town into the open water and hoisted the sails, which filled with a fair easterly breeze. Encouraged by the following wind we decided to make as much headway as possible along the coast and eventually arrived at Cavalaire-sur-Mer, just west of Saint Tropez – the halfway mark on our route back to La Ciotat.

The next morning, with time to spare, we sailed the short distance to the group of Port-Cros islands and dropped anchor on the leeside of the island. By late afternoon, as a stiffening wind veered to the south-west, blowing directly up our stern, we hurriedly left the anchorage and dashed for shelter in the mainland port of Hyères. The wind developed into a strong Mistral (which can last from two days to a week depending on the time of year, although the strength usually slackens from evening time to early morning). Time was running short to return the boat to La Ciotat.

Before dawn, we slipped our mooring, motored out of the harbour into a relatively calm sea and made our way to the headland, Golfe de Giens, that marks the eastern point of the Gulf of Toulon, the home of the French fleet. As we rounded the point, the wind strengthened, building up the waves. There was no point in hoisting the sails – the boat was not capable of tacking into the wind. I was at the helm, struggling to steer into the waves that were pounding against the port bow, pushing us further into the bay, when Len spotted a mysterious, bright, multi-coloured buoy. He grabbed the binoculars and, in disbelief, saw armed men in assault craft preparing to attack the harbour cliffs. Next came a booming bang and suddenly a huge splash erupted from the water about 150 metres astern. We had run into a NATO exercise, and this shot across the stern was, in marine parlance, telling us to clear off.

Len, a wartime fighter pilot, looked around the boat as if trying to find something with which to shoot back. The French navy never forgave the British for sinking the French fleet in Toulon in 1942 to prevent the ships falling into German hands – they say they scuttled the boats themselves – and now it seemed this was retaliation. Low velocity shells continued to be lobbed in our direction, this time from the shore battery's gunnery officer who was taking advantage of the situation to use our boat as target practice. We could see the puffs of smoke, followed by loud bangs, then the plumes of water that seemed to be creeping closer.

We were doing our best to conform but the head-on, gale-force wind prevented speedy progress. The boat shuddered with the waves, each one buffeting us closer to the cliffs: strenuously, I struggled to steer to the far side of the bay. Even more worrying was the rescue helicopter hovering overhead, perhaps expecting us to be shipwrecked. We were now running perilously close to the rocks and with little sea room to spare, we managed to steer round the Cap Sicié point and turn with the wind behind us.

Somehow we were able to avoid a broach-to catastrophe, and with a following wind we arrived in Bandol. The next morning, the boat was restored into fair shipshape for the last leg to La Ciotat.

My romance with France had been temporarily suspended!

Big Boat Sailing

Over the years, experience has taught me a number of things I didn't know then. I realise now that before I had made the turn out of the headwind, I should have tied together all the spare lines, sheets and ropes to make a sea anchor, which I could have cast astern to slow the boat down. I have also learned since about the hazards of broaching to: when the turn is made in a following wind and heavy seas it speeds up the boat, and the next wave can drag it astern under the next oncoming wave, with a likely capsize.

Undeterred by what might have been a disaster I went on to charter other boats: the first in 1976, when I sailed around the Aegean Sea to Piraeus and through the Corinth Canal with Mark and Christopher; the second, a year later, we sailed from Corfu to Cephalonia with six other friends. Sometime later, David King, his then wife Babbs and I chartered a catamaran run by the skipper and his wife. We sailed from Calvi in Corsica through the Maddelena Islands and on to Porto Cervo in Sardinia where Raymond Maggar joined us for a couple of days down to Olbia.

Azulea

These sailing excursions were an enjoyable *avant-goût* that increased my appetite for a boat of my own. In the late 1970s, I was paying a punitive eighty-three per cent income tax and knew that if I started a new company business I could reclaim the past three years of tax.

The local tax inspector agreed that a boat-chartering business in the Mediterranean and the Caribbean would qualify for a tax rebate.

The ideal boat for my purposes was a fifteen-metre Trintella ketch, built to my specification in s-Hertogenbosch in Holland. I named the boat Azulea.

Sir Francis Chichester said a boat should be one foot in length for every year of your age, but when he circumnavigated the world single-handed, he was sixty-seven and Gypsy Moth IV was only fifty-two feet (sixteen metres) long. Before he set sail, a reporter suggested to him that he was not a strong young man. He agreed but said he now had a lot of low cunning!

As a dinghy sailor, I learned sail craft and very little else about the technicalities of offshore cruising. So, while I impatiently waited for Azulea to be built, I arranged private lessons at my house with Commander MJ (Joe) Rantzen (Esther Rantzen's uncle), the author of several books on using a sextant, meteorology, astro and coastal navigation, and many others written for The Little Ship Club. I then qualified as a radio telegrapher, took a RADAR course on the Solent and attended the Perkins factory in Coventry to learn how to strip down and repair a marine engine. At the end of each day on the course I always ended up with bits of engine left over, a worrying habit if I ever had to face an emergency at sea!

All this studying had to be tested. Joe Rantzen believed that anyone who could con a boat from Southampton, cross the English Channel (one of the world's busiest shipping lanes), master the Alderney sixteen-knot race of tide between the Channel Islands, then navigate the rock-strewn waters around Saint-Malo on the Brittany coast, they would find the rest of the world comparatively easy. He suggested I should charter a fifteen-metre boat with an experienced skipper and crew, a team from one of the Royal Yachting Association's training courses, to test my sailing skills.

Taking the helm from Southampton across the English Channel in daylight was within my comfort zone: but when it got dark it was another matter to identify the various lighthouse beacons around the Channel Islands and along the French coast. Every lighthouse is marked on the charts with a specific number of occulting intervals. To discover which lighthouse beam sweep is in view, you have to count the seconds between the phased occlusions and flashes.

I managed to hold the helm steady as we were caught up in the

Alderney Race and made for an overnight (early hours of the morning) port in Guernsey. I thought navigating the waters around the Channel Islands was tricky enough until the next day when I had to pick a way through the rocks and the buoys marking out a number of deep water channels, to approach the port of Saint-Malo. And as if that wasn't enough, there was a twelve metre (forty feet) range between high and low tide, as well as the difficulty of getting the boat through the locks to the harbour.

I was quietly confident by the time I was conning the boat back to Southampton. I felt ready to take charge of my own boat, and knew the sea to be totally unforgiving and demanding of respect at all times.

The year before Azulea was completed, all the 'yachties' around the world were shocked to hear about the Fastnet race disaster. (Fastnet is held in the relatively shallow waters of the Irish Sea, just south of Bantry Bay.) The 303 boats were caught in a sudden gale-force seven storm: sixty-nine yachts finished the course, fifteen people died, twenty-four boats were abandoned, and yet only five sank. The first lesson that can be learned from this is never to abandon your boat; the second lesson is to learn how to open and use a life raft (most, if not all, offshore boats keep a life raft canister on board but very few yachties know how it works and what to do when it inflates); the third lesson, rarely heeded, is to stay sober – you always need your wits about you at sea. (Generally, if the skipper and crew of the majority of boats that go to sea were to be breathalysed, they would be confined to port.)

After Fastnet, there was no hesitation: I booked a place on the next survival training session at the Nautical Training College in Green Hithe, on the Thames. The morning session was run by a captain who had commanded a wartime Arctic convoy escort destroyer on the bitterly cold and deadly sea route to Murmansk, during which all his toes had been lost to frostbite. With twenty others, I learned about survival in extremes of cold and hot weather and what to pack in our survival kits on board.

The afternoon session dealt with how to break out a life raft, and what went wrong on the Fastnet disaster. Then we had to change into swimwear, put on an old coat, trousers and lifejacket, jump off a fifteen-metre board, swim across the thirty-metre pool then scramble into a life raft. While we waited our turn to climb up to the diving board we were hosed down with cold water. This was, indeed, a realistic 'abandon ship' experience.

In 1980, I enjoyed one of the happiest days of my life, taking Azulea's helm, sailing through the canals and into the open sea at Rotterdam, then on to Southampton where the final fit-out was completed. To avoid UK tax penalties, the boat had to leave UK waters as soon as the fit-out work was done.

I hired an experienced skipper, an engineer, and a deckhand for the maiden voyage from the Southampton boatyard to the berth I had bought in the Marine de Cogolin, near St. Tropez. (Later, it was a pleasant surprise to find Azulea's berth was next to Herbert von Karajan's unnamed racing boat – the only clue that he was the owner was the treble clef sign on the stern counter.)

Sailing across the Bay of Biscay in a February blizzard for a week was difficult and fatiguing. The snow eased but the wind hardened as we passed Finisterre, before dashing for shelter to a harbour close to Porto. Two days later it was still bad weather when we cast off. Then, as we headed out to the open sea, the deckhand fell seasick. He had to be strapped in the cockpit, wrapped in duvets and waterproof sheets. He did not move for five days, except to pee over the side, and only recovered once we called into the Algarve port of Lagos to re-provision. The weather improved from Cape Trafalgar to Gibraltar, where we went ashore to take few hours' break and to try and sort out the inevitable maiden voyage teething troubles.

It had always been my intention to berth the boat in Marine de Cogolin myself, but now, with the bad weather delays, time had run out. As I had to be back in London the following day, I decided to fly back and leave the crew to sail the boat on to the Côte d'Azur. It was then that I discovered there were only two flights a week; the next one not until five days later. The only answer was to sail on to Malaga in Spain but, by the time we got back to the harbour after a fish and chip supper, a sudden gale had blown up. Risking a near mutiny by the engineer and deckhand, we set off in a dreadful rainstorm. The crew stayed below.

As soon as we rounded Europa Point at the southern tip of Gibraltar, the skies brightened in the moonlight and, with a following wind, I had one of the most exhilarating spinnaker sails ever. At dawn we landed in a little marina not far off Malaga. I searched for a taxi to take me to the airport while the crew set off for the berth in France. The local policeman and customs officer allowed me to leave only after I had managed to convince them that I was not a smuggler.

Back in England, the crew was paid off and I hired a bo'sun to look after the boat while I was not aboard. There was no charter work to be had on the Côte d'Azur because the French – as ever – never miss an opportunity to impose taxes. So I enjoyed cruising around the Mediterranean whenever the chance arose, and prepared the boat to sail to Antigua the following October, to arrive in time for the Caribbean charter season. The bo'sun moved on to another boat. In his place I hired a married Scots couple who were experienced in charter work.

Atlantic Crossings

Every October and November dozens of deckhands, cooks and skippers collect in the South of France ports, hoping to find a boat for the charter season so they could work their passage to the Caribbean. We interviewed several before settling on two young sailors to help with working the boat and the cooking – also, with an uneven number, the twenty-four-hour-a-day watches can be alternated. Once they accepted that Azulea was a 'dry' boat and not try smuggling booze aboard, we agreed the terms. (It is dangerous to cross the Atlantic with crews who are constantly the worse for drink, and those hoping to hitch a lift should be alert to the dangers of working their passage across in a boozy boat.)

The first leg of the voyage to Antigua entailed sailing to the port of Las Palmas in Gran Canaria, where we finally provisioned the boat before crossing the Atlantic. After that, the voyage was simple: we sailed due south until the Cape Verde islands were below the horizon; then, when the puffy white clouds drifting in a clear blue sky signalled the trade winds, we turned to starboard (sharp right), hoisted every bit of sail available and headed west for about eighteen days until a tiny speck appeared on the horizon. This was the ultimate test of my navigation skills!

Among the many the pleasures of long-distance sailing is being lulled to sleep by the gentle rhythm and motion of boat and the sound of the clinking halyards and stretched creaks of the rigging. Even in a deep sleep, I was subconsciously alert to any slight wind shift or weather change, like a parent being constantly aware of a baby's movement in its cot.

One night I awoke, sensing the sound of strain on the rigging. The stiffening breeze had turned into a howling wind and, just as I got out on deck, the spinnaker blew out and the halyard slipped under the keel, wrapping itself around the propeller. When daylight arrived, one of the crew had to fix up three snorkel tubes so that he could breathe underwater while he cut away the tangle of rope wrapped around the propeller shaft. Meanwhile, I was winched eighteen metres up the main mast in a bo'sun's chair to unravel the jammed reeving and re-fix the satellite and radio aerials and the anemometer wind vane that were dangling on wires at the peak.

The damaged satellite aerial could have been a problem had I not had my sextant aboard. Joe Rantzen's teachings on astronavigation had demonstrated how sextant readings could be taken from particular heavenly lights. All I needed to plot my position were good sunshine and two reliable clocks – one for Progressive Estimated Local Time and the other for Greenwich Mean Time – to establish longitude. Each day, at precisely noon, a Sun reading would plot my position. I don't know if, in these days of sophisticated satellites, the Royal Navy continues the tradition of reporting 'the evening star, sir' (Venus) to the bridge. Venus, the brightest planet in the sky, is the first to be visible at dusk which is necessary when taking a sextant reading to bring the starlight down to the horizon to plot the boat's position.

There were wondrous, constantly changing seascape scenes, the most amazing dawn and evening skies and illuminated, starry night times when satellites whizzed overhead. Dolphins played in the bow waves for hours. Sometimes, we passed close to a school of surfing whales and once, a whale, at least thirteen metres long, leapt completely out of the water seven times. I didn't know whether I should stay on deck to watch or dash below for my camera. On its final leap, all I got on film was a big splash. Strangely, and it was not my imagination, I could be on watch, with the autopilot steering while I read, I could 'hear' when whales or dolphins were nearby. Was it a sixth sense that tuned into their subsonic calls?

Daily, the lure trailing astern, occasionally caught a tuna or a large mackerel-like fish. Nothing, not even another boat, came into view or disturbed the broad horizon for nearly three weeks, until a tiny speck, topped with a halo of cloud, appeared in the far distance. Had my navigation proved correct? Yes – indeed, it was Antigua! We dropped anchor in English Harbour. It took me the whole of the first day on land to steady my sea legs and stop swaying.

Every year the so-called 'Dragons' from North America, Canada and the UK meet in the restored buildings originally built by Nelson at the dockyard at English Harbour, to inspect the boats for the season's charters. Before recommending a boat to their clients, they interrogate the owner and crew and inspect every locker and berth, including the galley for tell-tale signs that the cook will have cordon bleu cooking skills, and they'll even lift the floorboards to check the bilges are dry.

I flew back to London once the Dragons had returned to their respective dens, and was pleased to find that they had arranged a few charter bookings for the boat. I returned in May, to join in the annual, boozy Antigua Race week to celebrate the end of the season, before sailing the boat back to Europe.

By the end of May, when the Caribbean is prone to hurricanes, there is a mass exodus of boats heading north-east to Bermuda, on their way to their stop-off on the Azores, before the last leg across to Europe. Even at this time of the year, the North Atlantic weather can be rough, and sailing into headwinds means the voyage time is unpredictable.

The storms worsened between Bermuda and the Azores. Battered by heavy seas, we were pleased to shelter there with dozens of other boats, also struggling to get back to Europe. In the harbour there was nothing to do except add the name of the boat to the other graffiti names on the harbour wall, drink in the steamy, humid café and try to look interested at the other *yachties*' banter and oft-repeated tales of their confined lives at sea. (Even Royal Navy and merchant seamen talk of all the far-off places they have seen but, in reality, most of the sailors hardly venture outside the gates of the ports.)

After five days and a break in the weather, we joined in the mass exodus of yachts leaving the harbour, heading east.

Within a few hours, a new storm front blew up. Each watch was cut to just two hours; it was hard to endure longer than that, strapped into the cockpit port and starboard, gripping the wheel to ride the mountainous seas. Some days, the peak of the mast was level with the top crest of the waves: it was a continuous fight against the headwinds. The saloon was awash, and the cabins were strewn with damp clothing and other belongings that had been catapulted out of lockers and stowed storage. The safest place, and the one most comfortable to ride out the incessant pounding, pitching and being tossed from side to side, was one's bunk. Lee cloths – a canvas curtain attached to the edge of the bunk and strapped to the ceiling beam – and a bagged sail restricted the lurching from port to starboard.

Eventually, after several days, the bilges could be pumped dry and the debris cleared, while the storm slackened as we approached the calmer waters of the Straits of Gibraltar and the Mediterranean. Fortunately, I have never been seasick or afraid of the sea, but this had been an endurance test for all of us on board.

Hard times and hazards are always soon forgotten, and in the calmer summer times, I sailed along the coasts of Corsica, Sardinia and France. Eventually, I prepared the boat to sail Azulea back to Antigua for one last charter season. The following May, I sailed up the coast of North America to Nantucket Island and Martha's Vineyard where Azulea was bought by a New Yorker.

Owning a boat is like standing on a prow, drenched in spray and chucking five pound notes into the wind. As any boat-owning yachtie will confirm, the second happiest day of your life is when you sell the bloody thing! It had been a wonderful and fulfilling experience, but I was pleased to be relieved of the financial burden.

Cruising

Ten years elapsed until I sailed again, and that was with Janet on holiday in St Lucia. Cruising around Rodney Bay in a four-metre dinghy was the first time Janet had experienced sailing, and she quickly learned to handle the helm. Fortunately, one morning in a gusting wind, she gibed the sail and the boat capsized (I say 'fortunately' because once you have capsized a boat, managed to turn it upright, climbed back in and carried on sailing, all fear is dispelled!).

A few years later, friends invited us to race their boat in Cowes Week on the Isle of Wight. Another time, we enjoyed sailing the Solent with a different group of friends, and one year, while moored off Portsmouth, we were close to the Tall Ships celebrations. On our last offshore trip, we chartered a gulet to sail from Marmaris in Turkey with our friends Jill and Tony Paxford. Sadly, the weather was not kind and on the return leg we ran into an uncomfortable headwind that somewhat marred the holiday.

I am always most comfortable living at sea level. In France, we lived not more than fifteen minutes away from Port Vauban in Antibes, reputedly the largest yacht centre in Europe, where Abramovitch berths at least one of his monster boats. We were invited to sail with Raymond Maggar on his motor yacht, and with other friends on their day boats. It is always a pleasure to be around boats, and strolling along the Bord de Mer watching the kids in their sailing class flotillas and seeing the big boat races in the bay is hugely enjoyable. Sometimes it helps me to relax if I recall the movement through the waves that rocked me to sleep on the long voyages.

Out of curiosity, I totted up the distances I had sailed over the years, including the Amazon and the Nile: it amounted to about 13000 miles (20000 kilometres). That is more than enough for an amateur yachtie in one lifetime.

The Arctic

On a business trip to Toronto, I met Ian, a forty-something banker whose passion was fishing. He was a member of an elite group of a dozen fishermen who chartered a boat on an organised two-week trip to the Arctic every year in late August and early September to fish for Arctic char, a reddish-pink salmon. At this time of the year the char migrate in vast shoals from the rivers to their warmer feeding grounds in the open sea.

Fellow all-weather yachting folk who have sailed the Atlantic, the Baltic Sea, the North Sea, around the British Isles or the Bay of Biscay will have experienced, at some time, the icy cold and blustery gales that blow down from the Arctic. Whenever I feel a biting wind, it triggers memories of reefing down the mainsail, breaking out the red storm gib foresail, casting sea anchors astern, and being harnessed into both sides of the cockpit to keep the boat as steady as possible, while, wet and cold, you wait patiently for the storm to blow over.

Ian's invitation to join the next fishing trip to the Arctic presented me with a once-in-a-lifetime, unmissable opportunity to experience, first hand, the region where all that bloody awful weather comes from. It would make an appealing contrast with the Amazon and the arid deserts of the Middle East as well.

The following August, with all my old ski clothes, snow boots, silk long johns, waterproofs, sweaters and a heavy-duty sleeping bag, I met up with Ian and his group in Toronto. They knew my interest wasn't really the fishing – I just wanted to be there – but in case I might want to join in, Ian loaned me a spare rod and told me where I could buy a couple of spinning lures and a cool box.

A commercial, three-hour flight from Toronto landed in a remote airport somewhere in northern Canada where the twelve of us and the two men who organised and ran the expedition, plus our sleeping bags, clothes, fishing equipment, tents, food, and fuel for heat and cooking, were transferred to a private twenty-seat, twin-propeller plane.

Because everything we needed for the two weeks had to be air-lifted, the plane was so overloaded that even the aisle was stuffed with camping equipment and cool boxes. An hour later we bumped down on a stony beach about 800 kilometres north of the Arctic Circle. I had no idea where we had landed, other than that it was somewhere in Canada's Northwest Territories above the northern tip of Baffin Island (probably across Lancaster Sound, near Devon Island). First, we needed time to adjust to breathing in the cold dry air after the heat of Toronto. We took it slowly, unpacking the plane gradually, pitching the big tent, setting up the camp and cutting up wood. After the plane had roared away, only the crackle of the open fire broke the silent darkness.

The two organisers were older men who prepared and cooked, kept the fire burning and the tent tidy and clean. Ian and the other fishermen were fit, forty-something business folk. They had split into groups of three, each team keeping to their chosen stretch of riverbank where they pitched their fishing tackle, rods and cool boxes. Soon after breakfast, they would set off to spend most of the day casting their spinning lures. Everyone was allowed a maximum quota of Arctic char that they could take back to Toronto but the sportsmen kept on fishing nonetheless, putting the excess fish back in the river once they'd landed them. I joined Ian and his friends on a few occasions to try my hand at lure fishing, but without much luck, even though there was a continuous abundance of fish running in shoals in the clear waters. Ian added my quota to his, doubling his allowance.

Back at the tent, wet clothing was draped around the perimeter, and after supper we crawled into our sleeping bags with our feet nearest the fire.

I was the outsider, the non-fishing intruder, and although everyone was friendly enough, I found a greater rapport with the half-dozen Inuit Indian families who were camped close to the beach landing strip. They always travelled north in the summer, from their settlement centres in the south, to enjoy and keep contact with their culture and natural habitat. Since the Cold War, many of these native people (Inuit means 'real people') were employed at the strategic defence system sites scattered across the Northern Territories of Canada and Alaska.

Although I joined in the banter with Ian and the other fishermen,

I preferred talking with the Inuits, who spoke their own indigenous language as well as a form of North-American English. Both the young and their parents wore a permanent grin that creased up their weather-beaten, leathery skin and half-closed Asian-like eyes.

Many of the older men were sculptors who carved the dense, sage-green volcanic stone into highly sought-after works of art, the kind often found in galleries throughout the world. Apparently, the prized stone, which came from some far-off area further north, was difficult to quarry. The men used diamond blades and rudimentary rasps and saws to cut it. I bought a beautiful piece – a father, mother and child on a sled – from one artist. It still adorns a table in our sitting room.

The father of one of the Inuit families, who had a canoe with outboard motor, took me with him on several fishing jaunts close to the lake shoreline. On one trip he had to rev up the engine and sharply veer away to avoid the danger of the sudden upward rush of water as a polar bear emerged from the deep. Another time, the skies were crystal clear when we set out to paddle along the beach, but then, without warning, the light faded and we found ourselves a long way from the campsite in a blinding blizzard. The weather was so unpredictable, even for the Inuits.

I learned to keep a careful watch on my position when out walking alone and spent most days wandering along the river and the shores of the nearby lake. Strolling through this treeless, mosquito-free wilderness of multi-coloured tundra, white and grey rocks, coarse grasses and tiny flowers struggling to feel the weak sunlight, outcrops of moss-covered stones along the water's edges, was like a mini meditation. In this extreme silence, I felt I could hear the world turning. I wish I could have ventured further afield to see more of this desolate, beautiful landscape that so perfectly matched my own sense of solitude and isolation at that time in my life.

I had gone to the Arctic to experience for myself the source of some of the most appalling weather conditions ever experienced on land or at sea. Now, as if to reinforce the power of nature, at the end of our two weeks the weather closed in and we had to wait another five days before the plane could fly in to land. Then, just as it was about to arrive, we were told to leave behind whatever we could to lighten the load, including the main tent and other equipment, because the pilot was worried about landing on the pebble beach. He flew in three times at speed to test touching down before he was satisfied it was safe to land, and only then on the proviso that we bundled ourselves and the luggage into the plane while he kept the engines running. This was real flying by the seat of the pilot's pants!

In spite of the anxiety we felt as the plane took off, as well as the incidents with the bear and the blizzard, and the feeling of being cold most of the time except when huddled around the fire with the rest of the blokes, this trip was one of the two most tranquil and memorable times of my life. The other was being in the cockpit, on watch alone, in the open sea.

I am always happiest when at sea level.

PART IV

Metaphysics

13

Occult Explorations

'Occult' is a word often associated with the paranormal, or something dark or sinister, but the word simply means 'hidden'. In the teaching traditions of Mystery Schools, profound occult wisdom was only revealed to the initiates as they gradually progressed to a deeper understanding of the mystical levels and universal phenomena and greater inner self-knowledge.

Preface

My Prologue mentions the somewhat arcane astrological patterns and the seven and ten yearly cycles of significant events that became evident as I delved into the letters, diaries and general research for this book. When I began setting out the material for this chapter, only later did it occur to me that my excursions into the occult have followed yet another pattern of events described below in my book, *The Authentic Tarot*, in the chapter *The Mythical Journey of the Hero/Heroine*:

> Although there are variations to the symbolism, the Tarot's twenty-one steps on the path of initiation are the foundation of many classical myths and, fundamentally, follow the same underlying themes. Before twentieth-century psychotherapy, archetypal characters in the classical myths and fairy tales were the source for self-awareness and our spiritual journey. These traditional archetypes, depicting some of the sub-personalities hidden in the shadows of our mind, are similar to the characters in the Tarot's rite of passage to fulfil our quest for self-knowledge. They are symbolic expressions of the primal nature of human beings which direct us towards what CG Jung called 'individuation' – our destiny to become self-realised. At the mystical level, the stories are

a portrayal of soul experiences and universal spiritual truths. The journey ends in a happy-ever-after marriage – the wedding being the integration of the masculine and feminine principles that can transform our life.

The mythical journey of the Hero/Heroine runs in three segments: *Separation*, *Initiation*, and the *Return*. It is a rite of passage from unconscious naivety to fulfilment.

Separation, the first step on the path, is usually triggered by a sense of longing, of boredom, or an unusual experience known as *the call to adventure*. We can either retreat into the eternal round of material gratification and ego trips or set out on our quest to satisfy our inner yearnings to become whole and to transcend the unconscious human condition. What deters us is *fear*.

The *Initiation* of the Hero or Heroine involves those ordeals that arise from our facing the *shadow* (our complexes that hold us in thrall), as we begin to understand that we have to discover our own innate wisdom and knowledge.

The *Return* marks the journey's end when the Hero or Heroine emerges from darkness of the cave or forest into the light (of consciousness). This rebirth or resurrection carries with it the prospect of self-healing, and the mastery of ourselves in body, mind and spirit.

The Occult Quest

One of the best series of TV interviews I've ever watched, *Face to Face*, was broadcast in 1959 in black and white. Each opening sequence began with an excerpt of Berlioz's *Les Francs-Juges* with a Felix Topolski charcoal sketch of the person about to be interviewed by John Freeman. The interviewer's gentle voice drew out some of the most poignant insights in the life of his guests, one of whom was the renowned psychoanalyst Carl Gustav Jung. It was one of the rare occasions when Jung appeared on television, and when Freeman asked him about his thoughts on religion and if he believed in God, Jung paused, smiled and said, "I don't need to believe – I know."

Later, I understood that his view transcended orthodox religious dogma and went to the heart of spiritual mysticism. For me, this was not a Kabalistic 'lightning flash' moment – it was more a feeling that a low pilot light had been ignited. I have no recollection of any special awareness of the flame during the next seven or eight years, a period which was overshadowed by my setting up and establishing my practice, but then came two significant events, which occurred when I embarked on an intensive quest of exploration.

The first event to have a profound influence on my life was a family trip to India in 1967 to stay with my sister June and her family. I was prompted to evaluate and reflect on the shortcomings of certain aspects of my life, and even their futility, as well as where I stood in relation to where I had been, and where I needed to change course. India always seems to reconnect one's circuits, however hard-wired we think we are.

The second event happened on a beach in Portugal in 1969, while I was waiting to meet a client to investigate the development potential of the unfashionable areas to the east of Faro Airport on the Algarve (more popularly known as the *Algrave*). I started to read CG Jung's book, *Man and His Symbols*, which began the slow burn of delving into the esoteric aspects of design, the perennial teachings of the ancient Mystery Schools, the natural laws, sacred knowledge, spiritual teachings, and the universal interrelationships of mind, body and spirit.

Three years later Betty and I divorced: my one and only relationship, which had endured twenty-six years, had come to an end. Was this a classic case of mid-life crisis demanding sexual freedom and the search for reassurance that one is not losing one's masculine powers? Much later, I discovered that perhaps the real mid-life crisis was more to do with a growing awareness of one's mortality: "Who am I?", "Why am I here?", and "What is my destiny?"

In the year following my divorce, the chaotic mess of my life became slightly more settled once I had returned from the solitary three-week trip to the Amazon jungle. For the first time in my experience, at the age of forty-two, I had put my life in the hands of complete strangers. In terms of the Tarot, I had acted out an archetypal 'rite of passage'. I had taken only one book with me on that trip, *The Teachings of Don Juan*, by Carlos Castaneda, who says that when we set out on a quest for self-discovery, we have no clear perception of the objectives, nor the hardships it will entail. It is a journey into the unknown to explore the 'occult' or hidden mysteries and to seek answers to life's perennial questions.

Separation

The *call to adventure* was certainly triggered by the unusual experience of the Amazon trip and the constant state of *longing* for a loving and fulfilling relationship.

I believed that if only I could get my relationships right, then most if not all the problems in my life would be resolved. I clung staunchly to this view until I came, reluctantly, to the awful realisation that maybe – at first only 'maybe' – the root cause of my problems, especially in relationships, could be ME! What was I to do?

Eventually I started therapy and was advised to join a week-long seminar in London by an American group called Insight. They had been brought over from California by author and broadcaster Bernard Levin and Arianna Stasinopoulos, who later married Michael Huffington and followed a political career. I got to know them well and attended other Insight seminars in America and Canada.

The Initiation

1977 marked the beginning of the next seven-year cycle. It was to become a major life-changing period of chaos and release, which began when I went to Champney's health farm for a week with my friend Ted Brian and two of his mates to relax and play cards. There, I met Mary. We married and unsurprisingly, in hindsight, divorced after three years.

Don Juan, a Mexican shaman, speaks about the 'enemies' we will encounter before we can become 'a man [or woman] of knowledge':

> The first enemy we will encounter is Fear, [and] if we turn away our life can become harmless and ineffective. Dispelling the fear leads to the second enemy – Clarity of Mind – through which we may become assured and courageous. But if this newly acquired sense turns into a feeling of invincibility, it will block our pathway to further learning and understanding.
>
> Having attained clarity of mind, we will then meet our third enemy – Power, which can blind us and divert us from pursuing our quest for learning. At this point, the danger is that we may come to the end of our life without ever understanding ourselves and the world about us.
>
> By defeating these three enemies, we have no more fears; our clarity of mind and the self-control over power mean that we are almost at the end of our quest, but we must now confront the last enemy – Old Age. This is a battle we can and must fight while knowing we can never win...if we give in to tiredness or yearn to rest we will become feeble and lose our clarity, power

and knowledge. But...if he lives his fate...he can be called a man of knowledge, if only for a brief moment when he succeeds in fighting off his last invincible enemy. That moment of clarity, power and knowledge is enough.

The Authentic Tarot, page 20-21

To my cost and stress, I encountered *Power* and a dangerous feeling of invincibility when I returned from an Insight seminar. I was convinced that despite all the extraordinary upheaval and pain of my second marriage, that I had the power to forgive and forget, and exercise love and kindness to overcome the difficulties. How wrong and naive could I have been? The symbol of the dangers arising through egotistical invincibility is expressed in the Tarot card number sixteen: the *Tower of Destruction*. It was a hard lesson to learn: one called Hubris!

Participants of Insight and similar 'spiritual therapies' are induced (seduced?) to believe that whatever the problem, all can be overcome and resolved with compassion and understanding: the acceptance that everyone is essentially honest, sincere and speaks from the heart. In other words, love can conquer all. We come away from these seminars convinced that there should be no boundaries and lose sight of the dangers in naively applying such concepts. After that, I tried to heal the wounds with self-exploration, and so desperate was I to not repeat the same relationship patterns, I spent many long periods as a celibate monk!

Insight started a chain reaction that took me from the purely material, exoteric world into the realms of the mesoteric (psychological) and esoteric (spiritual, divine) worlds. It began with healing, dowsing and Kairos, and then took me to the College of Psychic Studies where I attended transpersonal psychology courses, exploring the archetypes embedded in us all.

Learning to decode the profound psychological meanings and purpose within legends and fairy tales, and the symbolism of the archetypal gods and goddesses in myth, was a far easier way to grasp the essence of my own psychological traits. Later, my explorations led me to the ancient Mystery School teachings and those initiations and heroic journeys we are all taking on our individual path as we travel from naivety to wisdom.

This personal study, which is never ending in its nature, led me to a wide range of seminars, conferences and lectures in the UK, France,

India, America and Canada, and a serious review of my life so far.

The remainder of this chapter describes some of the paths I have taken in my quest, in the hope that eventually I may discover the inner light.

The Tarot

By the late 1970s, having been drawn to explore the ever-recurrent archetypal characters found in the world's myths and fairy tales, I was led towards the Tarot. The deck of cards is like an encyclopaedia of seventy-eight encoded pictographs and numbers that hold the mystical keys to a profound understanding of the full spectrum of human nature and the characteristics that mark the milestones along our transformational journey from naivety to self-knowledge.

After having studied the cards for several years it became clear that the Tarot, in its authentic format, is a divination tool that can connect ourselves to our own innate 'knowingness', revealing where we are on our path through life, as well as the next step forward towards self-realisation and fulfilment. It is simply a process of insight and intuition.

> The intellect has little to do on the road to discovery. There comes a leap in consciousness, call it intuition or what you will, when the solution comes to you and you don't know how or why.
>
> Albert Einstein

I gave many talks and demonstrations on the Tarot on Pete Murray's show on London's LBC (London Broadcasting Company) radio channel. Then, in 1992, the *Marie Claire European Magazine Limited* commissioned me to write a feature to publicise the *Marie Claire* Tarot Line and to launch Tom Saunders as their Tarot reader. The editorial strapline read:

> The sages believe that if you can unravel the secrets of the Tarot, you will understand the universe and the complexities of human nature; it is an oracle for complete self-knowledge. Tom Saunders, the Marie Claire Tarot reader, explains the meanings of the cards and how correct interpretation of the pack can give you great insights into your life.

The magazine carried the Tarot Line for three years or so. Since then I have given readings, lectures and practical seminars in the UK, and in Santa Fe and Albuquerque in America, and more recently in France.

Using the Tarot for prediction and fairground fortune-telling is a debasement of the cards: no wonder there is the popular conception that they are a sinister tool for evil and 'the work of the devil'. The erroneous misuse of the cards and the plethora of new deck designs that make no attempt to express the symbolic language of the pictographs and numbers, prompted me to write *The Authentic Tarot: Discovering Your Inner Self*, published by Watkins in 2007.

Healing

At a Mind, Body, Spirit conference in 1976, I met Olive Broadbent and her husband who were the leading lights in the National Federation of Spiritual Healers (now called The Healing Trust). It was, and still is, a well-regarded healing organisation, one that is recognised by the NHS. They encouraged me to take their two-year probation course to qualify as a full member of the Federation. Twice a week I drove a few miles outside central London to one of their healing clinics in Bromley, where every week there were eight healers, two probationers and about forty 'clients'. First I worked with Olive or one of the other experienced healers, then after a year I was allowed to work alone on three or four of the clients. Towards the end of my probation, I needed three written 'testimonials' about the healing work I had done for these clients and how they had responded, before I could be elected to full membership and be registered as a practising healer.

The essence of this form of healing, which has been the foundation of esoteric teachings throughout the world, is based on the ancient concept that the physical body is enveloped in subtle energy fields:

> Statues, paintings and drawings of the saints and other luminaries...are depicted with the whole body or just the head shrouded in an aura or halo of shimmering energy – the light of a divine person. We lesser mortals also have a sheath of subtle energy fields... In keeping with the ancient dictum 'as above, so below', a human being is not just skin and bone, muscles and organs; nor is the planet Earth just a mass of physical material. At a macrocosmic level, the extremity of the Earth's gross or solid body is the crust of soil and rock... Surrounding this physical

matter is the atmosphere, the stratosphere, the ozone layer... which are the 'subtle bodies' of the Earth. Together, the gross body and subtle body form an integral, unified holistic system that is essential to sustain life.

At the microcosmic level, the extremity of [our] gross or material body is our skin. This is enveloped in a spectrum of energy fields called the etheric, auric and astral subtle bodies. The etheric body, extending a few centimetres from the skin, is a protective sheath that can be felt by sensitive hands as if a soft balloon or cushion. When a person (or animal or plant) is in a state of disease the sheath feels jagged or broken, allowing the body's life force to 'drain' away. Beyond the etheric body is an aura or halo of colour... The varying 'pulses' and bands of colour [indicate] a person's physical and psychological state. Beyond the aura is the astral body [where] our thought patterns reside. All living organisms are a holistic, integrated combination of the gross and subtle bodies.

The Boiled Frog Syndrome, page 154

With this form of healing, apart from lightly placing the hands on the person's shoulders to tune into their breathing patterns, they are not touched: the healer's hands work in the person's etheric body and sense the energy fields of the spine. In other words, the healer is 'dowsing' the subtle bodies. This practice of healing led me to dowsing and the Earth energy fields.

I also worked on sick animals and, through a mutual friend at the BBC, the radio presenter Pete Murray came to me with his dog Peppi, with whom he had a most strange psychic rapport. He had taken Peppi to a veterinary clinic in Cambridgeshire where the dog had been diagnosed with a large tumour on its liver. They told Pete that it was best if Peppi was put out of his misery within the next ten days. After three healing sessions with me, Pete took the dog back to the clinic where they discovered that the tumour had disappeared. (Peppi went on to live a very energetic life for another seven years until he was savaged by another dog.)

At the time, Pete's successful daily programme on LBC radio attracted several million listeners: the show covered a wide area of what might be called 'the more occult aspects of life'. Pete invited me to talk about the healing work, extra-sensory perception, the Tarot, dowsing and sensing the positive vibrations in buildings. Over the next three years, I featured on his show every month or so.

My interest in the healing power of crystals prompted the freelance journalist Amanda Cochrane to write a lengthy piece in the December 1988 issue of *Harpers and Queen*. She reported:

> Within minutes of stepping inside Tom Saunders's stunning Georgian Chelsea house, one starts to succumb to an atmosphere so serene it is nearly narcotic... The self-assured founder of a firm of architects responsible for designing over a quarter of the banks in the City...[also] devotes time to working as a healer, dowser and writer.

The magazine *Healing Today* (August 2006) invited me to write an article about Feng Shui and other world cultures that have similar traditions, such as the Celtic practices in Europe. The piece was titled Masters of Geomancy and included some of the material from *The Boiled Frog Syndrome*. The same magazine asked me to write a piece titled Money and Spirituality – Are They Compatible? The editor's strapline read:

> Some healers express a 'conscientious objection' to accepting money for their services – even refusing resolutely those charitable donations freely offered to the Federation [The National Federation of Spiritual Healers]. In this article Tom Saunders, FRIBA and Healer member, hits out at what he sees as the negative attitude to the use of money as a purposeful energy for furthering spiritual aspirations.

> (Date of publication unknown)

I continued to work as a registered healer from my home, making hospital visits when requested, and continued to do so even when living in France, including acting as a NFSH mentor for probationer members.

Dowsing

I first became interested in dowsing on a family holiday to India in 1967 when we went to the Rajasthan 'ghost town' of Fatehpur Sikri. The town took fifteen years to build (it was begun in 1570), only to be abandoned fourteen years later when the drilled wells ran out of water. Although the sixteenth-century dowsers had miscalculated the quantity of the source, it did bring home to me that until we had piped water, architects and builders would always have had to dowse a prospective site to find a subterranean supply of water.

The National Federation of Spiritual Healers introduced me to Colin Bloy, an acknowledged inspirational healer, dowser, author, and successful businessman. In 1976, he invited me to his home in Brighton and after a brief talk and a cup of tea, he cut up a pair of wire coat hangers to make two L-shaped rods. We drove to a chalk pit on the South Downs for my first lesson in finding the buried archaeological remains of a settlement that he had discovered a year earlier. (Eventually the local archaeological society verified the accuracy of his dowsing when they began excavations.) We moved on to dowse the Earth's energy lines, as well as a stream running under a nearby church.

Bloy's healing work was also celebrated in Portugal and Spain, where he was a regular broadcaster on the subject. His research into the Cathars Templars led him to suspect that there was a cave holding important relics in the region of Andorra, in an area that was difficult to explore. He asked Bill Lewis, the equally renowned healer and map dowser, to try to identify the exact location. Bill map-dowsed the several chambers and eventually the cave was discovered and explored. In it, a stone carved with a Templar cross was found.

In 1981, Bloy founded the Fountain Project in Brighton, which became the focal point for healing communities. (Similar projects called the TONGO group are still running; see www.fountain-international.org.)

Eager to learn more, I joined the British Society of Dowsers and attended many weekend courses at various country retreats, including Stonehenge. Sadly, Colin died in 2004.

Map Dowsing (remote viewing)

Bill Lewis, one of the finest map dowsers, enjoyed an international reputation for his work in finding remote oil fields and buried archaeological sites, as well as being an experienced healer. Fortunately, I got to meet him in 1983 at a fiftieth anniversary celebration weekend conference of the British Society of Dowsers, at St Catherine's College, Oxford. Bill knew of my connection to Keith Critchlow (a friend who is mentioned below) and agreed to give me a half-day teaching course in map dowsing at his home in Ebbw Vale in South Wales. I was delighted with the invitation, especially as it would give me the opportunity to visit the town where I was evacuated in 1939. (I discovered that Ebbw Vale had changed: forty-five years on, I could see nothing that resembled my childhood memory of barren countryside and the sparse groups of miners' cottages dotted on the hillside.)

Bill lived in a modest cottage in the town. We started in the garden, where he tested my field dowsing to find three or four articles he had buried; then we moved inside, and I followed him upstairs to the landing where he opened the door to a deep, narrow 'cupboard'. Inside was a three-metre-long table along the wall, allowing just enough width for Bill to sit on a wheeled chair. Above it, stretching the full length of the wall, was a dyeline photocopy diagram of the complete electromagnetic spectrum of the universe.

I squeezed into a chair, wedging the door open. Bill had asked me to bring a small-scale map of anywhere of my choice. It showed a group of houses in Cheyne Walk, Chelsea, one of which was mine. Bill laid out the map, told me to not cross my arms or legs otherwise the energies would be restricted, closed his eyes, and twirled his well-worn chestnut-brown wooden pendulum patina in his right hand over the map. Holding a pencil in his left, he began tracing across the map, making marks each time he paused. His marked-up points on the map, in the back garden of my house and in the street behind, seemed to indicate the traces of old foundations. He then pinpointed a spot on the roof of the house next door to mine, opened his eyes, licked his forefinger and ran it along the diagram on the wall. His finger 'stuck' about a third of the way along. Bill decided that his mark on the roof must indicate the presence of a high-frequency radio transmitter.

The houses and back gardens in Cheyne Walk were built over Henry VIII's manor house, and it certainly seemed as if Bill's pencil markings revealed the archaeological remains of that building. I knew already that the rear and part of the side walls to my garden were a historically protected Tudor brickwork structure. However, the question of whether or not the foundation outlines were accurate paled into insignificance when Bill's astonishing dowsing managed to locate the aerial mast of the high-powered radio used by my neighbour, John Paul Getty, a recluse whose way of keeping in contact with the outside world was as a 'radio ham'.

Bill could not have known that I would ask him to dowse that particular area of Chelsea, yet with astonishing accuracy he marked up several other locations in the street that I could verify.

After Bill Lewis's training, I found it easier to map dowse before going to a site in order to locate the precise position of whatever it was I was looking for. When a firm of building contractors asked me to dowse their thirty-six-acre site in Glasgow for a new shopping mall, British Coal said that they knew there were five mine shafts under the site, although their records did not show their exact position. The contractors needed to know where to construct extra reinforced floor slabs to bridge the shafts. An A3-sized drawing of the site was posted to me with the instruction to map dowse from London.

When I visited the site it was a muddy quagmire. I was delighted that I did not have to trudge up and down the whole thirty-six acres with a pair of plastic rods. My map dowsing indicated the locations to within a metre or so, allowing the contractors to test with confidence before reinforcing the slabs effectively. It was certainly cheaper than using a JCB to excavate the whole site area.

Dowsing Thomas

In November 1985, I received a phone call from Deidre Rust, the secretary of the British Society of Dowsers, who invited me to give the society's annual lecture at the Royal Academy in Piccadilly, scheduled for the following April. I was surprised and flattered to be asked.

I accepted Deirdre's invitation, trusting that she knew more about what an audience would want to hear from me than I knew what to say. The theme was entirely my choice, provided it had something to do with dowsing, but although I had three months to prepare the lecture she needed a title for the programme now. Three days later I recalled the previous night's dream: the title would be 'Dowsing Thomas' and the theme would be the dowser's trust of innate intuition.

In Aramaic language, the name 'Thomas' means 'twin', and refers also to being a builder. According to the *Dictionary of Names* it means 'Twice Blessed'. However, many people's response to the name will always be, "Ah…Doubting Thomas." The term probably originated with Thomas the Apostle who did not believe Jesus had been resurrected until he had sufficient proof. I do not regard myself as a doubter or sceptic, but I do like to verify the truth of something personally, through touch and feel, and to be guided by intuition.

Members of the British Society of Dowsers come from a wide-ranging spectrum of so-called 'ordinary folk': farmers, builders, scientists, business people, military personnel, academics, professional architects, many of whom hold high-ranking positions in the outside world. Very few make it well-known that they are practising dowsers, especially those who feel they may be ridiculed or treated as a crank, but it is true that many professional dowsers enjoy the reputation, acclaim, credibility and respect of private employers, businesses, oil companies, and even governments.

The word 'dowsing' is a bastardisation of the French word 'source', meaning 'spring or water course'. The practice is often viewed in the West as the work of tricksters in magic or witchcraft, and the Christian Church still associates it with sorcery and the sinister work of the Devil. In other parts of the world, dowsing is an accepted practice: for example, it is still a part of the curriculum for student architects in Russia. (The Empress Katerina II of Russia included a pair of dowsing twigs in her coat of arms.)

Two thousand years ago, Vitruvius wrote detailed instructions on the various methods he used for dowsing a site for water, and until utility companies began installing piped water, architects, builders and developers would almost always engage the services of a dowser. Unfortunately, today's architects have lost contact with Nature and Earth energy fields; instead, in London for example, they call up Thames Water to locate the nearest pipeline.

Dowsers depend entirely upon intuition, backed by experience and experimentation. Intuition belongs to Jung's 'feminine principle', and generally, women are more readily inclined to be guided by their intuitive thought processes. The 'masculine principle' of *logos*, or logic and rationality, inclines men to trust reason and deduction as their basis for operation. While many male dowsers, artists, theoretical physicists and entrepreneurs are aware that they work in both modes, few businessmen actually acknowledge that they use intuition as well as logic, although it is invariably the mix of the two that will bring them success. Some will admit to having a gut feeling, or attribute their success to luck, coincidence or serendipity, but they will persist in refusing to acknowledge their own innate intuitive power. (Most will ask for 'proof' that intuition does actually exist.)

Albert Einstein said his theory of relativity came to him in a dream. He could have tried to use logic, working on a whiteboard for a million years, without ever discovering an answer, but it was his intuitive dream that he was riding across the universe on a *curved* beam of light that inspired his formula: $E=MC^2$.

Many healers use dowsing and kinesiology techniques to diagnose the cause of a person's illness. Dowsers can discover and plot the Earth's subterranean energies and use various methods to 'correct' the adverse black lines that cause diseases in any given location. Other dowsers, working on ancient monuments, earthworks and standing stones, have helped to reveal the secrets of their origins, as well as contributing to their preservation.

It is sometimes said that some dowsers become too dependent on whatever piece of equipment or appliance they use, to the extent that before they can respond to a simple question or request they have to 'ask' their pendulum or other device for an answer. In 1983, I witnessed such an event en masse at the fiftieth anniversary conference at St Catherine's College, Oxford. The chairman and master of ceremonies was Michael Bentine, the well-known comedian who had been one of the stars of The Goons. It was not so well-known to the general public that Bentine was also a highly regarded healer and dowser.

In the steeply raked chairs of the auditorium, that day I experienced one of the most dynamic expressions of 'reaction' (an automatic response to a stimulus) I have ever encountered. I had seen some of the participants dowsing during their coffee or lunchtime breaks, using rods, pendulums and other devices to detect and measure the energy fields of the trees, weeds and grass in the grounds of the college. Now I was about to have the chance to see the devices in action inside the auditorium. As I returned to my seat after a coffee break, the American woman who had a seat next to me was hunting for the cushion she used to support her back (she had spine problems). She called to the chairman, asking if anyone could see it. It was an amazing sight to witness the automatic response to her question: almost without exception, all the three hundred participants whipped out their rods, pendulums, Pasquini springs, wire coat hangers and hazel twigs which simultaneously pointed in the direction of a lone figure engrossed in his book. He raised his head, suddenly aware of the laser-like energy beaming towards him, and when he stood, he and everyone else could see that he had been sitting on the American woman's cushion.

Everyone can experience a hands-on experience of finding, say, a buried water pipe, something which can verify ('prove', if you will) that their natural intuitive ability can be demonstrated and repeated. Dowsing can be an important balancing agent, countering the predominance of logic and reasoning, and restoring a greater dependency on intuition in all walks of life. I believe it could even lead to our major lifework: the healing of the planet.

My work in field and map dowsing continued over the years for building contractors. The work included: discovering the source of flooding in the basement of one of the German Embassy buildings in Chelsea; dowsing for energy fields in Spain, where a group of healers intended to convert a farmhouse into a clinic; and map dowsing for the Museum of London, who wanted to look for Saxon archaeological remains at a site in Keeley Street, Holborn, and needed a dowser to indicate where to dig on the cleared site. More recently, in France, I saved a friend from the trauma of having to admit that he had lost his new white-gold wedding ring under an extensive area of terracing where he had been laying the paving tiles. I dowsed the whole terrace and marked one of the tiles, where, to his relief, he recovered the ring buried in the soft sand bedding. (In France, Janet and I also ran dowsing courses for the locals.)

Kairos

Sometime in the early 1980s, I joined the Research into Lost Knowledge Organisation (RILKO), which promotes a range of subjects on occult mysteries, and over the years I have delivered several lectures to its members. Later, I was elected to be a member of The Scientific and Medical Network. It was through these two connections that I joined Professor Dr Keith Critchlow's internationally renowned organisation, KAIROS. Its mission statement in every *Kairos Newsletter* reads:

> Kairos was founded to promote the recovery of traditional (perennial) values in the arts and sciences. This has deep and complex implications yet can be simplified into a view which is focused on the Unity of Being and the fundamental interrelatedness of all things. For the ancient Greeks, the word mathema originally meant 'study', so the four mathematical arts/sciences we know as the Quadrivium can be understood as uniting the nature of inner perception by which we 'study', and the nature of the source of our impressions of the outer world.

The basis of the Kairos teachings is Plato's *Seven Liberal Arts*: firstly the four immutable languages of the Quadrivium: Arithmetic, Geometry, Music (or Harmony) and Cosmology (or Astrology, the logic of the stars); secondly Grammar, Rhetoric and Dialectic, which form the Trivium. In Dialectics, two or more people stand side by side in true communication with each other, using perception and intuition in combination with logic and thinking-power, as they search for the truth of the matter. They are not on opposite sides, trying to win or score points in argument.

A group of healers in Wiltshire invited Keith to design a new timber-framed building for their healing clinic. As always, before designing a building he needed the site to be dowsed to plot the Earth energy fields and to place the building in the most auspicious location. Usually Keith used Bill Lewis, the map dowser, but as he was unavailable this time, Keith asked me to go with him to the first site visit to dowse the land and work on the project.

Every year or so, Kairos would run two-week seminars. These were intensive programmes for architects, designers and others who wanted to study and practice Plato's Seven Liberal Arts and find out about esoteric aspects of 'sacred' architecture. In 1985, I went to the Colorado seminar in Lindisfarne, which is sited on sacred Indian land close to a disused goldmine high up in the mountains. The forty or so participants were invited to bring illustrations of their current project for discussion.

One of the participants was a senior lecturer in architecture at one of the major universities in America, who, with his wife, spent their holiday periods travelling to a village in Jordan to research the archaeological remains for their joint PhD thesis. This ancient site had been overbuilt by the Greeks, the Romans, the Early Christians, and so on, up to the present day. The lecturer produced a plan of the small town, showing scattered dwellings and various buildings around a public square, as well as the position of known archaeological remains. He said that it was difficult to carry out any intensive excavation works, and that he really needed to know more about the siting of the ancient walls, the original flow of the river, and most importantly, the location of the underground tunnels.

Keith suggested that the lecturer should ask me to dowse the map to identify the locations. I asked him to prepare a list of questions, and the next afternoon he spread out his map on a table under the shade of a tree in the heat of the Colorado summer. With my eyes closed, a pendulum in my right hand and a pencil in the other, I began dowsing to answer his many questions. He sat beside me taking notes while, still with my eyes closed, I marked up the map.

When the dowsing ended, the lecturer talked about the tunnels. He told me that the previous year he had discovered what appeared to be an entrance to underground caves in the old remains of the temple of Dionysus. (In most fortified villages, in case of siege, there was a secret way in and out under the walls.) My map dowsing marked up a line of caves at the entrance to the temple (a section of which were man-made) that led into a group of large cisterns, no longer water-filled, which then continued as natural caves, eventually becoming man-made excavations once more, before the tunnel emerged outside the walls on the opposite side of the village to the temple.

After the session, when we were alone, the lecturer pulled me to one side and looked around him to make sure he wasn't being overheard. He then whispered to me that during the three or four years he and his wife had been visiting the village, they had got to know more about it. He said, very confidentially, that he did know about some underground caves that were used by the Jordanian Intelligence Service, but that he had never suspected that they were located in the ancient escape exit tunnels. He was a little concerned that his enquiries might have been interpreted as a subversive act of espionage against the Jordanian government!

The Kairos seminars widened my interest in the allied subjects of healing and dowsing, and the significant effects that light, colour, spaces (based on the harmonic ratios inherent in our body), and music can have on our mind, body and spirit. It became evident from reports in the media, as well as through my own investigations and studies, that both the architectural design and the materials and equipment installed in many modern buildings were a major source of discomfort, and even serious illness, for many occupants. It was clear too that through its location, design and interior, one building could be responsible for unease or distress where another could give comfort and be uplifting to the spirit.

Over the years my concern grew that the teaching and practice of architecture is, and always has been, inadequate. Throughout my five years of full-time study there were neither environmental lectures nor exercises in designing for how people live, work or play inside buildings. Even in the history of art and architecture lectures, the fundamental human aspects of design and the more esoteric teachings used by the master builders for millennia were simply ignored. Nothing has changed today: architectural education is still focused on the treatment of façades. Wherever possible, I had encouraged TTSP to integrate the range of esoteric studies, research and findings I had unearthed during the period I'd spent working with Kairos and Keith Critchlow, but without much success. It was only when I 'retired' to work again on my own as a consultant architect that I had the opportunity to put those teachings into practice.

Some fifteen years later, these explorations and studies culminated in my writing *The Boiled Frog Syndrome – Your Health and the Built Environment*. I hoped it would serve to illuminate some of the health hazards, pitfalls and adverse effects on the psyche that the buildings we live and work in throw up, and how the risks can be reduced or eliminated by exercising prudent avoidance. The book pointed a way forward for practitioners to create healthy buildings that enhance the spirit and show respect for the holistic, multi-dimensional nature of humankind.

The need to write *The Boiled Frog Syndrome* was triggered when I read Vitruvius's *The Ten Books of Architecture*, written two thousand years ago, which eventually became the 'bible' of the Renaissance, lasting as an obligatory course book in Western schools of architecture until the early twentieth century when it was cast aside as being anachronistic and having no relevance or value in our modern world of today.

The *Ten Books* was addressed directly to Augustus Caesar, the Emperor of Rome, advising him, as the principal client and patron, as to the best criteria for his choice of architects and engineers. The book stated that he should only appoint those who were master builders with an understanding and knowledge of certain esoteric teachings (perennial wisdom), and that it should be in the power of the client to demand that the professional in question should be of a certain quality. The patron should also be able to influence the standards of training and education of these professional craftspeople.

When I first came into contact with Professor Keith Critchlow and the Kairos organisation, which taught this perennial wisdom (the foundation of design throughout the ages), I felt I had come home. It had become increasingly distressing to witness the majority of architects suffering a downgrading of their role, something which happened in the latter part of the twentieth and early twenty-first centuries, making them anything but 'master builders'. It is to our great loss that the teaching of these perennial values were abandoned in the 'brave new world' of the late nineteenth century, and that they continue to be ignored today.

I attended many Kairos lectures and week-long courses in the UK, France, America and India on the subjects of Sacred Geometry and Architecture and discovered that vestiges of the ancient Mystery School teachings still exist in the West. Occasionally I delivered lectures myself and became a trustee for twenty years until I moved to France. Soon after, when Keith was in his seventies, he decided to close down the organisation and focus on collating his extraordinary experience, original research and wisdom into printed form.

Vipassana

Dawn Note, 27th October 1985:

> For several years now, my regular morning ritual has been to get out of bed, light a candle, have a pee and then sit down to meditate for twenty minutes or so. There have been many periods in my recent life, particularly when going through the difficulties of marriages and divorces, I know I could not have survived the harshness and trauma without the solitude and a centredness, taking stock of my thoughts, feelings, anger, resentment and hurt. Meditation helped me to process these without becoming locked up in the gut and lower chakras. It has been a process I have had to go through for my own salvation and without it I doubt I would have ever taken that first step forward. These traumas were a timely shock, otherwise I could have stayed stuck in my life, taking the apparently easy way out for a quiet life.
>
> Had the jolt been too overpowering, I might have succumbed to a serious illness or unable to survive the searing fire. Through meditation I maintained a balance and awareness to restore my life, spirit and soul.

These lessons had to be learned by personal experience, hence my name Thomas – Doubting Thomas. (It is not that we are sceptical or cynical, it simply means that until we have tasted it – whatever the 'it' is – we cannot speak of that taste.)

Soon after writing this *Dawn Note*, a friend returned to London from Bombay where he had been recuperating from an 'overdose of spirituality': he had been conducting research for a film about the gurus and ashrams of India and had, for several months, been trekking the wilderness. His Indian host in Bombay had suggested that before returning to Europe he should seek out one SN Goenka, a master who taught the Vipassana technique of meditation in the many Vipassana centres in India, Nepal, Australia, New Zealand, North America, Japan, and Europe. My friend tracked one down near Bombay, feeling in need of solitude and inner peace, and joined the group.

As I listened to him speak of his extraordinary ten days of meditation and transformation, the experience clearly showed itself in his face and body expressions. (I discovered that the Vipassana meditation is a discipline of contemplative insight or *mindfulness*.) Hearing him, I was eager to experience for the first time an intensive and prolonged discipline, such as he described. I had practised meditation on a fairly regular basis, since becoming a registered healer, and now I wanted to take it further.

The Vipassana office in Liverpool informed me that Goenka would be present later that month at a course in Auxerre, in the Bourgogne region of France. I reserved a place and studied the pamphlets that came with the application form. The rules stated that during the whole ten-day period, total silence would be maintained (speaking was only allowed if you needed to ask an assistant teacher for clarification on the technique or to discuss any material matters). Books and writing materials were not permitted, the sexes were completely segregated, and no one was allowed to go beyond the confines of the grounds.

We would have a twelve-hour programme of meditation every day. At first glance this was daunting – I had practised meditation for ten years now but had never experienced any form of spiritual discipline for more than a few hours at a time. Still, the Vipassana technique was enticing:

> Suppose you had the opportunity to free yourself of all worldly responsibilities for ten days, with a quiet, secluded place in which to live, protected from disturbances. In this place the basic requirements of room and board are provided and helpers on hand to see that you were reasonably comfortable. In return you would be expected only to avoid contact with others and, apart from essential activities, to spend all your waking hours with eyes closed, keeping your mind

on a chosen object of attention. Would you accept the offer?

Suppose such an opportunity existed, and that people like yourself were not only willing but eager to spend their free time in this way. How would you describe their activity? Navel-gazing or contemplation; escapism or spiritual retreat; self-intoxication or self-searching; introversion or introspection? The common impression is that it is a withdrawal from the world but meditation need not be an escape. It can be a means to encounter the world in order to understand it and ourselves.

The pamphlet added that in accordance with Vipassana tradition, everything is free, but after the completion of the ten-day course and without any obligation, a student is allowed to make a donation according to means and inclination. (All Vipassana centres are financed by student donations.)

According to Goenka, Vipassana meditation is based on the original teachings of the Buddha 2500 years ago. There are many derivative forms of meditation which use mantras, visualisations and other techniques to focus or transport the mind, but Vipassana is a process of self-observation within the body, leading to a direct experience of the universal truths of impermanence and constant change – something which we can understand intellectually yet rarely know, feel, sense or recognise as a reality. It is not an intellectual or philosophical pastime, nor is the ten-day course akin to a spiritual health spa to escape the cares or misery of everyday life. It is claimed that the technique can eradicate suffering, develop equanimity, calmness, balance and achieve a sharpened awareness of the mind.

One Sunday afternoon in July, after spending a day at Chartres Cathedral, I drove about 150 kilometres through the closed-up, empty villages in the remote countryside south of Paris and arrived at the dilapidated and disused railway line of Auxerre. From there, I drove through a dark cavern of trees and on to a rough dirt track surrounded by vast open fields and woodlands. At the end of the track stood a gaunt single-storey building. An inscribed tile, inset in the apex gable end, indicated that originally the building had been a holiday centre for the disadvantaged children of the nineteenth arrondissement of Paris.

An attendant directed me to park on the far side of the meadow alongside an assortment of well kept Citroens, Mercedes and Volkswagens. (This was unusual: generally, people attending spiritual gatherings show little regard for material possessions and their means of transport often expresses a disdain for worldly goods.) I locked the car and disappeared from the 'real' world for ten days.

There was a large dormitory where groups of six beds were separated by white sheets suspended from wires. At the end of the corridor were the toilets and showers. While I unpacked my toilet bag, wooden meditation stool, cushion, a couple of Kashmiri blankets, a change of T-shirt, sweater, jeans, underwear, towels and a sleeping bag, some of the 'old students' (those who had previously taken a course) were also setting out their things.

The Meditation Hall, a temporary building with wooden-framed sides and a stretched plasticised canvas roof, stood in the middle of an acre-sized field. Strands of coloured rope marked out the separate entrances and boundaries segregating the sexes. Screens in the food serving area also prevented close visual contact.

There were about 100 women and sixty men, with an average age of between thirty and thirty-five. Apart from an old disabled Frenchman, who leaned heavily on a crutch, the majority appeared to be fit and healthy. Only a few appeared to be lacking in material success. We were a cross section of middle-class Europeans with varied careers, and there was no distinguishing characteristic to indicate that we were on a spiritual quest seeking the Dhamma path of self-realisation.

For the induction talk, we were grouped according to our language; there were fifteen different nationalities. Afterwards, everyone gathered around the tea urns until we heard the soft sound of a Tibetan bell indicating that from now on total silence would be observed. There would be no communication in speech, gestures, sign language or written notes. The bell also sounded the segregation of the sexes, and several couples and small groups of friends made their farewell embraces before proceeding to the Meditation Hall. The women filed in from one end, the men from the other.

Laid out on the floor, close together, were Caribbean-blue canvas padded squares about seventy centimetres wide. An usher directed the 'old' students to the front, the 'new' students behind them, and those like me who needed to sit on high stools or prop themselves against the wall to the back. Everyone had their assortment of cushions, wads of rubber padding for knee supports, blankets, low wood stools and hinged boxes to kneel or sit on. Two French couples on holiday, looking for a few days of peace and harmony, had come across the centre by chance and had decided to join in, never having experienced meditation before. They looked surprised! Otherwise it seemed that everyone else practised some form of meditation on a fairly regular basis.

Quietly, we nestled into the cushions, wedging up our posteriors and settling into our varied positions, which ranged from a full lotus to sitting upright in a chair borrowed from the dining room. Thin shawls draped our shoulders and backs so that only our bare heads felt the chill evening air. Complete stillness, silence and tranquillity descended. The fading light measured our private inner journeys as we sat oblivious of anyone else or the world outside.

An hour passed before the middle door opened and a quiet rustling signalled that others were entering the Hall. Then a soft deep honey-rich voice began to chant. After several minutes the key changed, the chant ended, and the old students, who were obviously familiar with the music ritual, chanted in reply: "*Sardu, sardu, sardu.*" (By the next day, the new students recognised the cue to join in the chorus.) This was not blind devotion but an acknowledgement of the spiritual quality of the work being undertaken, and the moment when cramped legs could be eased and the body relaxed.

I opened my eyes. In the centre of the long wall, seated on white cushions, were Mr SN Goenka and his wife, three male and three female assistant teachers on either side. When Goenka Ji spoke (in India, 'Ji' denotes an endearment while maintaining due respect and reverence), his bright gleaming eyes swept the hall, from one side to the other, commanding a view over the heads of the squatting congregation. His presence was majestic; he was clearly a man of power and compassionate energy. His wife, the potentate's Queen, sat beside him, serene and still, swathed in a blue-and-silver sari.

Goenka had grown up in Burma, born to wealthy parents. He had worked in the family business for several years before being introduced to a Vipassana teacher. After many years of study he had returned to his ancestral country, India, and it was there, twenty years ago, that he had begun to teach the technique. He and his wife had a large family, with several grandchildren. They led simple, peaceful lives, in spite of their travelling to centres throughout the world. He lived by those values and discipline he taught, and I believe he was a liberated, enlightened being, devoted to the service of others.

Goenka's discourse was a mix of profound insights and impish humour, jokes which lovingly highlighted some of the more crass aspects of human frailty. They were all the more amusing for his peculiarly Indian pronunciation of the English language and the use of phrases and idioms that had disappeared from common usage at least seventy years ago.

The discourse ended with another short meditation and by 9.30pm the dormitory lights were out. Unfortunately my first night was disturbed by heavy snorers in the two beds opposite. Happily though, during that first night, the management team of 'old' students cruised through the dormitories, and the next morning they corralled all the snorers together, relocating them in single tents under the trees where they could bellow and snort all night long.

The Tibetan bell chimed us awake at four o'clock in the morning. It was cold, dark and raining. By half past four, everyone had settled in the Meditation Hall, cushions and padding plumped up, head and body wrapped in a warm blanket, spine erect and eyes closed. We sat in silent repose for two hours until Goenka's chanting brought the session to an end.

In the chilly dawn light we lined up for a breakfast of muesli, yoghurt, fruit, porridge, bread and jam; drinks were ordinary or herbal teas, or chocolate. Coffee was not on the menu. We had just an hour and a half to eat, shave and shower, wash clothes and get ready for the next session at 8.00am, where we stayed in the Meditation Hall until eleven o'clock, taking two five-minute breaks, before two hours for lunch and rest. All the food was vegetarian, much of it picked from the gardens then prepared and cooked with loving care. Each day there were salads, vegetables with pasta, rice or potatoes, and a sweet dessert.

After lunch, the meditations continued until 5pm, then an hour's break for something to drink and two pieces of fruit. This was the last food of the day for the new students. I found that I needed less food each day and it was no surprise that the 'old' students followed the Buddhist practice of not eating after noon at all, drinking only lemon tea. At 6pm there was another hour of meditation, then Goenka's evening discourse. At 8.30pm the non-English-speaking students returned from their translated sessions to the main hall for the last half-hour of meditation before retiring to bed at 9.30pm.

This was the regular rhythmic routine for ten days. Each day, the still silence of the twelve hours spent in deep meditation was broken only by the farmyard cocks crowing or the cows moaning to be milked.

Occasionally a French air force jet buzzed low over the countryside, jolting some of us out of our reverie. It was a blitzing reminder that beyond the boundary hedges there was an exoteric world spinning round in life, death, war and peace. We were in isolation, totally unaware of what was going on. The solitude was so intense that only occasionally was I conscious of the others around me.

Vipassana meditation demands diligence, determination and hard work. The first three days were spent concentrating the mind on the natural breath flowing through the nostrils. By the fourth day, through the increase and sharpening of awareness, I could focus on the changing nature of my body and mind. Gradually, when in deep concentration, consciousness of the outward sensations became refined into hardly discernable subtle ripples. Although we experienced these transformations at varying times, by the eighth day my body felt as though it was an empty amorphous sheath, gently pulsating to a flow of energy from head to toe and back again, as if I could glimpse the unconscious mind reacting on my body. There was no past, no future; only the continual present: the here and now of existence.

Intellectually, we *understand* that the universe, the planet, and our own cells and genes are in a constant state of change. The Vipassana technique teaches us to *know*: to actually experience the natural truths of impermanence. Through such direct cognizance and insight, it may be possible to be liberated from craving, aversion and ignorance: three things that possibly form the root cause of all unhappiness.

Ten days of intensive meditation is considered to be the absolute minimum period needed to penetrate the deeper levels. With continued meditation practice, the tensions and miseries (generally self-created) in everyday life can be released, simply by not reacting to neither pleasant nor unpleasant situations but merely observing them with equanimity. Many people equate equanimity and 'balanced observation' with impassive stoicism. It is a fear that life could become a cold, ascetic non-event, but equanimity of mind avoids drowning or becoming overwhelmed in a storm of emotion. Equanimity intensifies tears of joy and compassion and removes those meretricious tears of self-pity and despair. The awareness of suffering and pleasure is heightened and observed without blind reaction or a need to cling to the sensation. (Counting to ten or taking a deep breath before reacting to a traumatic or irritating situation, taking a moment to first observe one's feelings, is a simplistic form of practising equanimity.)

Perhaps the archetypal model is the ancient warrior. He is a man in service to humanity, always in repose and yet totally alert and aware of everything around him. He has a vision of 360 degrees. He would never rattle his sword to threaten or react to provocation. Only when ready to take action on his own terms would he draw his sword and prepare to kill and more importantly, he is prepared to be killed. Vipassana teaches the lesson of the ancient warrior to demonstrate how one can avoid reaction; how action should be taken only with a clear equanimity of mind.

At the discourse on the evening of the ninth day, Goenka announced that our state of 'divine silence' would end at ten o'clock the following morning. This would allow a full day to begin our rehabilitation into the external world.

The next morning, most of the students filed out of the Meditation Hall, leaving just a few of us still trying to enjoy the quietness of the room. However, the chatter of those who had left became obtrusive so I emerged reluctantly, keeping well away from everyone for an hour or two (silence is indeed 'divine'). Couples and friends regrouped, now that the ropes separating the men from the women had been removed, and they busily recounted events along their own heroic journey.

I was invited to meet Goenka and his wife in private for about ten minutes. He was interested to know if I had followed the technique, whether I had got the 'flow', and we talked of my associations with India. It was like meeting up with long-lost well-loved relatives.

There was no discernable end-of-term euphoria. Several people came up to me and shared their impressions of me, ranging from a Catholic priest to someone in *Star Wars*. This was quietly amusing, but more interestingly I realised the extent to which we are affected and controlled by non-verbal communication. It confirmed the view that our other senses and prejudices impinge upon the subconscious mind to a far greater extent than we would imagine.

The transition to the exoteric world was easier than expected. I sat on the bed to write up my vivid dreams and the blessed messages that had come to me almost every other night. After breakfast, we cleared the dormitory and helped to restore the centre for the next intake of students who would be arriving in four weeks. I paused in my car before re-entering planet Earth. Later, as I drove, everything was much as I remembered but even the hazards of the Paris peripherique were relatively undaunting.

Back home, it was well after midnight when I suddenly realised that I had not slept for twenty-four hours. I'd had a long drive and had attended to personal and business matters on my return, but I still felt abundantly energised. I called my friend to thank him for telling me about Vipassana: it was a precious gift.

Vipassana has been described as a guide to the art of living. It is neither religious nor sectarian, but simply a technique to gain insight into the psyche. It is not necessary to be an experienced meditator to join the course. And while we and the world at large will continue to suffer and change constantly, equanimity of mind can replace misery with love and compassion.

Maybe there will be another time in my life when I will go on another ten-day Vipassana retreat. Until then, I will continue to meditate.

Mystery Schools

The Mystery School teachings of ancient Egypt and Greece and the initiation rituals of so-called archaic primitive societies, with their legends, myths and fairy tales, all encompass complex human conditions, expressed through the ubiquitous archetypes of heroes, heroines, wise men, monsters and evil witches. Some of these archetypal characters represent the deep, dark twins that are ever-present in the netherworld shadows of our inner selves, often the sole source of our pain, suffering and unhappiness.

Can our modern techniques of psychoanalysis and group therapies ever be superior to a profound study of any of the major religions or spiritual traditions, such as Kabbalah or the Bible? When interpreted as Mystery School teachings, their arcane knowledge and wisdom reveals an exquisite treatise on human psychology.

How is it, though, that when strongly religious people speak of joyousness, ecstasy, enlightenment, and the kingdom of Heaven on Earth, they can still find themselves stuck in Hades, in an underworld of personal despair and lack of fulfilment? Perhaps their teachers/preachers have yet to understand the full importance of the teachings!

During my travels I took the opportunity to visit some of the Mystery School teaching and healing temples in Egypt and Kyoto, the ancient Asclepius centre on the Greek island of Kos (the birthplace of Hippocrates), the Ayurvedic centres in southern India, and the round lodges of the American Hopi Indians. Inspired by the memories of these extraordinary places, I wrote *What is my vision?* In the *Dawn Note* below:

Dawn Note, 1st November 1985:

As an architect, I want to produce a building to create the same vibrations for spiritual experiences as when entering a cathedral or healing temple. The building, like a Mystery School of architecture and life would be an initiation into the lost knowledge of the mesoteric and esoteric worlds.

It would be a cavernous structure similar to a dilapidated but once grand riding school I had visited in France where the slated roof and brick walls with stone dressings were covered in moss and overgrown with ivy. Many trees needed surgery to be released from the strangulating bindweed. Some cracks had appeared in the main fabric and the roof leaked in the right hand corner soaking the straw still strewn on the floor from when it was used as a barn.

The main building needed to be restored and treated with new timber-boarded floors and the tall round-headed windows reglazed in tinted glass to bathe the interior with a rose luminescence... A new series of private rooms for the students would surround a courtyard with a lecture hall at one end.

The gardens would be replanted with pathways meandering through the trees and shrubs; energy fields could be set up around the undergrowth and the large oak trunks; sunflowers could create a Mandala to express the spirals of life and the Fibonacci codes like a garden of Eden on Earth where the lush plantings reflect a love and devotion to the planet and to remind us that if we have the wit and humbleness to understand and recognise the knowledge that is ours, we could live in a paradise here and now. The students would wear robes to avoid distinguishing clothing style and background to experience and review the metaphors and meaning of the great mysteries and then return to their homes, offices, family and friends to live in the essence and wondrousness of life.

I believe there are many such decrepit, abandoned farm buildings throughout France and other parts of Europe. They could become refuges and centres for learning and restoring the soil where sacred architecture, music, dancing and the ethereal vibrations of sound and colour can be transformed into our everyday lives.

Four years later, in 1989, I met up with the BBC Panorama anchormen, Michael Barratt and Robert Rowland, who were interested to read my seven-part TV proposal, *Mystery School of the Air*. When Channel 4 knew that Bernard Levin, the well-known author and broadcaster, would be pleased to be the programme presenter, a revised version, shortened to five segments, was included in the new schedules for 1990. Most disappointingly, due to a mini financial crisis, the year's programming cash dried up and subsequently the programme series was cancelled. (Robert Rowland and his wife Nuala became our good friends.)

Undeterred, I submitted a TV proposal on modern-day shamans, as well as one that proposed to decode some of the ubiquitous myths and fairy tales that were the original form of psychological teachings. I also devised weekend seminars on myths and fairy tales, which gave particular emphasis to the story of Psyche and Amor.

This was to spark off further excursions into mysticism, meditation, Vipassana, and later, the Tarot. On many occasions I attended the Wrekin Trust's annual Mystics and Scientists weekend seminars in Winchester (now run by David Lorimer's Scientific and Medical Network). Perhaps the most memorable event was listening to Pir Vilayat Khan, the Sufi master and mystic, who sat in a lotus position for at least three hours without moving while delivering an unwavering discourse on his mystical teachings. These seminars led to my studying the ancient religions of India, the Kama Sutra, Tantra, and the traditions of the so-called 'primitive tribes'.

Another high point was when I, and about two hundred others, spent three incredible days filled with wisdom, joy and pleasure, listening to His Holiness the Dalai Lama who was giving a talk in London. Among the many memorable things he said, one especially springs to mind: it was about worry. His Holiness said that if you can take action and do something about it (whatever *it* is) there is no need to worry; if there is nothing you can do, then why worry?

Deepak Chopra, quoting Carol Lynn Pearson in *Consider the Butterfly*, said:

According to Vedanta, there are only two symptoms of enlightenment, just two indications that a transformation is taking place within you moving towards higher consciousness. The first symptom is that you stop worrying. Things don't bother you anymore and you become light-hearted and full of joy. The second symptom is that you encounter more and more meaningful coincidences in your life, more and more synchronicities. And this accelerates to the point where you actually experience the miraculous.

(The Vadanta ancient Indian scriptures' basic teaching is for the seeker to have direct experience of his or her true nature.)

All this is everlasting work in progress and I'm doing the best I can!

Having Something to Say

Early in the 1980s, at a 'posh' Sunday lunch in Chelsea, my host said he would like to introduce me to someone. The guest, who was standing alone, turned out to be an Argentinean publisher. After the introduction was made, I asked, "How do you become a writer?" He looked puzzled and sniffed, then took a sip of champagne. Then, before hurriedly walking away he said, "All you have to do is to have something to say!" The remark deserved to be dismissed but it stuck firmly in my mind.

Before leaving TTSP, in 1984, I had already set about drafting the outline for a novel about a modern-day Mystery School. Later, at a friend's supper party, I sat next to an American author who generously offered to read through an early draft. His five-page response was an extremely helpful guide. He suggested that the best way to exercise and flex my writing muscles was to get up early in the morning and, before doing anything else, sit down and write whatever came into my head. From October 1985 through to the following January I followed his advice. Below (and elsewhere in the book) are some edited extracts of those writings, called *Dawn Notes*.

One of the Notes indicated that I was trying too hard to express the feelings of the characters rather than letting action and dialogue express the underlying emotional state. I was opening the floodgates and letting all the dammed-up energy pour out. I had wanted the novel to be a blueprint for a real, modern-day Mystery School for initiation into spirituality and ancient perennial wisdom. I recognised that teaching self-awareness and development, sacred architecture, psychic healing, the way of the spiritual warrior, and how to tread lightly on the planet went on already, but in fragmented and separate ways: I wanted to bring these elements together. Perhaps I had over-researched the philosophy and the circumstances of the basic story which had caused the writing to be too restrictive and confined.

Dawn Note, 18th November 1985:

Writing is self-expression which does not rely on staff to carry out the work on my behalf. In the practice, I employed many people and worked with construction companies and other professional disciplines – all were virtually under my direction and control. I was the 'Field Marshal' intent on winning the war: the 'war' was mostly about designing a functional, beautiful building, fit for purpose, built to a price and on time.

While I do not underestimate the strategic influence I had on the work, it is only in hindsight that I realise there was no deep, personally satisfying self-expression. Certainly, it was less egotistical than laying down rules and rigid design concepts saying 'we will do it this way'. Now I want something else – a statement that expresses who I am, what I think and believe in, instead of it always being created by the collective WE.

This quest to be an acknowledged writer has become an imperative to express what I have to say, knowing I must say it with humility and service but where is TOM in all this? Where is the creative expression?

The message is clear from the people I trust and from my own guided imagery that my creative fire is subdued, suppressed and dampened down. If this is due to my feeble excuses that lock up the energy release, then the transition from the release from TTSP to having the freedom of choice to work again on my own will be lost.

Dawn Note, 5th November 1985:

Uppermost in my mind is the question of spirit – the fire within – relationships, ecology, the welfare of the planet, the power of self-healing, transformation and the preparation for death. These are of great concern for me and the majority of my friends, acquaintances and other people I meet who are on a similar quest. It appears I am seen as a man who has taken the plunge into the unknown and has given up a secure job to continue to discover the hidden secrets of the golden treasures we all seek!

My psyche tells me everything I need to know about releasing the creativity, and the symbolism is very clear and concise. Why do I ignore such valuable gems?

Over a period of several months, and probably the previous few years, I had been attending and giving parties, as well as going to group meetings, where esoteric subjects were discussed. It was at one of these supper parties that I met the well-known screenwriter and playwright, Wolf Mankowitz.

Dawn Note, 24th November 1985:

Mankowitz called to ask me to help him with certain details about Kabbalah, which was the subject of his next play he intended to discuss with Terry Hands. We met at my house when I set out a brief outline of the tradition:

Kabbalah is an aspect of the mystical and perennial teachings of Judaism, about the nature of the universe, spirituality and the destiny of man. The Tree of Life (Jacob's Ladder) is a diagram dividing existence into four worlds – the material world, the psychological world, the spiritual world, and the world of divine creation. Each world has an active and a passive aspect of life which indicates notions of harmony and balance and how we can instigate a change in our life when disharmony and unbalance prevails.

We are born into the material world of the ego, unconsciousness, power and self-seeking activities without ever knowing or having a connection with the other realms. However and for whatever reason – an external event or an inner longing – we are urged to venture into the unknown, which can lead us to break out of the eternal triangles of our life, going around in circles, and experience a connection with the other worlds.

The first step is to begin to deal with our psychological 'stuff'. The greater our self-understanding, so the greater the connections with the realms of the spirit, and ultimately, the Divine. A problem persists if we are attracted to leap straight into the world of spirit without dealing with our 'stuff' otherwise, as there is no secure and permanent anchor we can become adrift. This often leads to illness or personal crises. How many so-called healers only want to 'reside' in the world of spirit without first getting to grips with self-knowledge? These are the folk who do not experience balance and harmony in their own life. The game of snakes and ladders is reputedly based on the Kabbalah – you can arrive at the top of the ladder and then, the next throw of the dice lands you tumbling down a snake to the bottom again.

I studied Kabbalah under the extraordinary master and mystic, Warren Kenton, who writes under the name of Z'ev ben Shimon Halevi. He and Keith Critchlow were student friends and have had strong working and spiritual ties throughout their lives. It was Keith who introduced me to Warren and, from time to time, Warren and his wife Rebekkah came to my house in Cheyne Walk with some of his other students for a teaching and meditation.

I suggested to Wolf Mankowitz that if the project went ahead he should contact Warren Kenton and if he needed special stage sets he should engage Keith Critchlow. If appropriate, I would be pleased to contribute too. During our discussion I mentioned that I was currently working (struggling) on a draft novel. Wolf then gave me a tutorial as if I were one of his students. I scribbled down notes and a booklist, vowing I would finish his suggested reading by Christmas before moving ahead on the writing. After his invaluable lesson I decided the novel needed to be in the prose of a fairy tale or mythical work, or even in blank verse. Perhaps, what I had written so far tended to be too 'artistic' rather than factual. Even just two weeks earlier, I had thought about transforming the book into a screenplay for a film and then realised this was another ploy to avoid completing the work: I would be allowing film producers, directors and scriptwriters to take charge of the project, and this was not a good idea.

Dawn Note, 1st December 1985:

It was probably through meeting Wolf that I was invited to dinner at Lizzie Spender's house in Hampstead. She was married to the comedian and actor Barry Humphries and was the daughter of the famous author and poet, Sir Stephen Spender. All the other guests were literary people. It was most accommodating of the universe to connect me with these professionals and I felt boosted to know I was able to express myself in an articulate manner. It was also encouraging to know from Lizzie that Wolf Mankowitz thought I was 'very clever'. I enjoyed being in the company of writers and would dearly like to be one of them and be known for my work, my personal philosophy of life and living, which a published book gives one a certain 'authority' and stamp whereas, at the moment, I can only talk about my views to those who are interested to listen.

Published Work

During the next fifteen years I attempted two more rewrites of the novel, which was still not fit to present to a would-be publisher. Instead, I decided to write a non-fiction work that would embrace the perennial design principles of sacred architecture and the master builders that were taught in the ancient Mystery Schools, and how, through a lack of such knowledge, we architects create health hazards in the built environment. In 2002, my first book, *The Boiled Frog Syndrome*, was published by The Wiley Academy. RIBA past-president, Ruth Reed, used the book with her student architects, and Prince Charles kindly responded in a personal letter when he received the book:

> Dear Mr Saunders,
>
> I am so grateful to you for sending me your fascinating-sounding book... It is wonderful to know that you have been a student and trustee of dear Keith's for so long and I am absolutely *thrilled* you have written such a book which, I am sure, will contain so many of the arguments I have been *trying* to bring to people's attention for so many years, only to find that one is rubbished, ridiculed and pilloried... I've always believed there is safety in numbers, so that's another reason I am so pleased to see your book.
>
> I have been quoting the *Boiled Frog Syndrome* at people for years – hence my reluctant belief that only catastrophes in the human and environmental field can finally bring people to their senses about what we have done to de-sacrilise *every* aspect of our environment – both on an inner and outer plane.
>
> Yours most sincerely,
> Charles
>
> Letter dated 27th August 2002 on Birkhall-headed paper

Later, I lectured at Prince Charles's Princes' Trust Foundation and was appointed an associate lecturer at the Central St Martins School of Art and Design (now part of the University of the Arts London). Two years after the publication of *The Boiled Frog Syndrome*, I was commissioned by the international journal *Complimentary Therapies in Clinical Practice* to write a paper on hospital design, nursing and midwifery entitled *Health Hazards and Electromagnetic Fields*. This was peer-reviewed and published by Elsevier Limited (later I was appointed to sit on their international advisory board). In 2007, my second book, *The Authentic Tarot: Discovering Your Inner Self*, was published by Watkins.

As soon as I have completed this autobiography I will return, for the fourth time, to rewrite the novel – I hope!

PART V

The Return

14

Janet

Dawn Note, 2nd November 1985:
Aphrodite

Who is she? I have seen her in many visualisations, walking towards me wearing a long white shift: her hair soft and flowing. She is lover, mother, sister and friend who possesses all the human and archetypal virtues of the goddesses expressing love, forgiveness, mysticism and mystery and to have experienced children, their feelings of pleasure and guilt and how to nurture them to trust their own love and tolerance.

Together, our world views would lean towards the goal of wholeness, life and living, fun and the divine right to prosper and to be of service to others. We would nurture and care for each other to discover the inner core of our beings, walk lightly on earth as two separate human beings and be uplifted to the heights of eroticism and ecstasy without limits on how high we can fly.

We would live somewhere by the sea near trees and plants where nature and the spirit of the earth live together. We would live and work together in harmony and balance and in high states of energy, enterprise and laughter.

Our home will be a sanctuary where we can explore our inner selves and have the freedom to be who we are.

I know I can't go out searching for you – you are here within me... I continue to prepare myself to be aware of your presence when I meet you.

Walk towards me; show yourself; come into my orbit – I am getting ready to be with you to love and be loved and share my life with you.

Come soon.

Five years later, this plea from my heart was answered when Janet Edwards came into my life.

Janet's Family

Janet's great-great-grandmother, Mary Alexander, was the daughter of Sir Claud Alexander MP. She was recognised as one of the best amateur pianists of her day and was well-acquainted with the leaders of the world of music. She was reported to have had a 'close friendship' with her teacher Mendelssohn, who gave her the original manuscript of his *Midsummer Night's Dream*. Janet's grandfather, Robert Crompton, was the brother of Rookes Evelyn Bell Crompton (Colonel Crompton), her great-uncle who was the youngest son of Mary Alexander's five children. His remarkable life story was told in his autobiography *Reminiscences*, published by Constable and Co. Ltd. in 1928 when he was in his eighties. The frontispiece photograph bears a resemblance to the portraits of CG Jung when he was of a similar age.

REB Crompton was promoted to the rank of Colonel in the South-African War (1889–1902). In the First World War he designed special traction engines, portable searchlights, and was appointed by Winston Churchill, then First Sea Lord of the Admiralty, to design and engineer 'landships', later called tanks. (As a security measure, they were concealed as water tanks to hide their purpose before they were first used in the battle of the Somme in 1916 to break the deadlock of trench warfare.) In 1903, he was one of the founders of the Royal Automobile Club (RAC), and was twice president of the Institute of Electrical Engineers and a Fellow of the Royal Society. He died in 1940, aged ninety-four.

A few years ago, Janet and I were invited to dinner at a ground floor flat in a mansion block in Kensington Court, a narrow passage that leads on to Kensington High Street. We sat at the table, staring out through the wide bay window when, suddenly, Janet jumped up in surprise and disbelief. There, on the opposite side of the passage, she saw a blue plaque honouring her great-uncle, Colonel Rookes Evelyn Crompton, on the wall of number 48, the house he had lived in between 1891 and 1939. (London commemorates the link between notable figures of the past and where they lived with a blue plaque.)

Janet's paternal Wilson and maternal Alexander family traits, hard-wired into the strands of her DNA, reveal themselves in her love and talent for music and creativity. She grew up in a house in Leeds Road, near the Huddersfield Town football ground, backing on to a narrow alley behind a steelworks. This tough environment fostered in her an innate spirit of adventure and fortitude, and an indefatigable tenacity. She was 'one of the boys': climbing fences, racing bikes and, at the same time studying to play the piano. She began playing at six, and was the church organist for services, weddings and funerals by the time she was thirteen.

Janet's father Frank Wilson, a tall, elegant and gentle soul, came from pioneering Border Country stock. Through the family's strong military connections, which included army service in India, he had been born in York Castle. He went on to become the manager of exports at the Josiah France fine worsted mill.

Her mother, Mary, came from Dewsbury in Yorkshire, and Janet's happy childhood was shattered when she died of leukaemia. Janet was just seventeen years old. It was hard for her having to cope with bereavement, taking care of her father and running the household, as well as keeping up with her piano and violin studies at Huddersfield College of Music. Here, the inspired teaching of Michael Kruszynski led her, aged nineteen, to become an Associate of the Royal College of Music and Licentiate of Trinity College. She then qualified as a music teacher, and worked in schools in Yorkshire. Her training as a Chopin specialist moved her career on as a solo pianist and a sought-after piano accompanist to international opera stars.

Janet's fortitude and indefatigable spirit would be called upon later when she had to provide for her two sons, Robert and Alex, after the traumatic divorce from her husband, Nick Edwards. And once again, she would have to call on her inner reserves to battle her breast cancer, almost forty years after her mother died, taking heroic steps to overcome it.

When Janet's sons were born she had to adapt her working schedule to accommodate motherhood. Initially, she continued to give performances at UK festivals and concert halls in Europe, but after her divorce she had to stop travelling and worked as a voice coach instead. She worked hard to pay the mortgage on her three-bed flat in Northwood Hall, Highgate, and to provide for her sons, who became weekly boarders at Highgate School.

Over the following years, her brilliant musicianship and talent as a voice coach would be recognised in the worlds of classical music and

West End theatre, where directors and producers, such as Cameron Mackintosh and Andrew Lloyd Webber, employed her services. As well as coaching many world-class stars and celebrities, she developed her own one-woman concerts, which she performed on international stages.

1991

At this time, England was in the throes of a mini-recession – the usual cycle of boom and bust – and I was about to lose all that I owned to pay for a disastrous speculative development. These dark, inner personal struggles for survival were mirrored in the outer world by the Iraqi invasion of Kuwait and the Desert Storm war.

In the midst of this turmoil, Paul von Ringleheim, an internationally acclaimed American sculptor, unknowingly served as the catalyst that helped transform my life of gloom, doom and despair into one of absolute joy. Through Paul, I met Janet and could never have hoped or imagined such good fortune would ever come my way.

Paul visited Europe every couple of years to meet architects, developers and building owners: potential clients for his large-scale sculptures. In London, through a web of contacts, he contacted me, thinking that I was still the senior partner running TTSP. We met at my house in Cheyne Walk and I suggested a number of people who might be interested in his work.

A month or two later, when Paul returned to London from his travels to Europe, we discovered that we had a mutual interest in esoteric geometry and other 'occult' explorations. Paul was known to Hollywood society and, through his friendship with the actor James Coburn, he knew the singer Lynsey de Paul, Coburn's one-time girlfriend. Paul told me that Lynsey had similar interests in spiritual matters and suggested the three of us should have dinner at my house.

She arrived an hour late in a state of agitation and distress. Her face was scratched and bleeding, her hair and clothing streaked in blood. After her wounds had been seen to, and once she felt somewhat calmer, Lynsey told us what had happened. She had been driving her open-topped Mercedes around Hyde Park Corner when she had cut in front of another woman who was also driving an expensive car. The woman was furious, pulled up in front of Lynsey, leapt out of her car, and in the midst of the full flow of fast traffic, laid into her physically. So much for spiritual peace and tranquillity! (Sometime later, Lynsey made a TV programme about the incident, and how it had led her to take up martial arts).

During the evening at my house, Lynsey invited us to a lunch party she was giving in Highgate that Sunday. Among the guests – a few of them TV celebrities, including Spike Milligan and his wife – would be a 'guru' who Lynsey supported and helped to promote.

At the party, Lynsey ushered me into another room so that she and the guru could have a private conversation with me. The guru was booked to give a seminar, called The Meaning of Life, and she wondered if I would like to come. The plan was that if the seminar needed extra momentum at any point, I could feed her questions, and comment where appropriate.

Lynsey had hired a conference room at the Sherlock Holmes Hotel in Baker Street for the all-day Saturday seminar. She had invited a crowd of her friends in the music business, which included Ian Adam, the West End voice coach, who brought along his friend Janet Edwards, an elegant woman with long blonde hair, wearing a black wide-brimmed floppy hat.

As it turned out, the guru turned out to be unimpressive and my interjections did little to enhance the situation, but during the lunchbreak in the hotel coffee shop, I sat with Janet and her friends and later, when the seminar ended, she and a few others stayed on a while. We talked, and discovered that we shared the same birth date. We exchanged telephone numbers and later, I called to invite her to my house for supper with my neighbours, John and Jane Craven.

The next time Janet came to Cheyne Walk I cooked supper for just the two of us. We were both free, divorced and unattached, and we enjoyed spending the last few weekends and evenings in the house before it was sold. We would sit up in bed, looking out at the fairy-lighting of Albert Bridge and across the river to the trees and pagoda in Battersea Park. We have been together ever since.

Eventually, the entire proceeds from the sale of the house – over a million pounds – went to pay off the bank loan and I was left with almost nothing. A neighbour kindly rented me one of his flats nearby for a knock-down price where I stayed for several months until I moved in with Janet in Northwood Hall. Gradually, through Janet's support and the good help of client friends, I was able to rebuild my one-man practice. At first, earnings were meagre but then the government introduced Health and Safety laws for building works.

I took a month's course to qualify as a so-called Planning Supervisor, a role which virtually began a new career for me, and which led to other more profitable commissions.

At the age of sixty, this house move marked yet another ten-year cycle in my life. There were other remarkable coincidences: apart from Janet and I sharing the same birth date; we both have strong ties with India; and Crompton's company had been taken over by a firm called Cooper – the same name as my brother-in-law's!

Together in Highgate

One weekend we stayed in Glastonbury with Janet's long-standing friends, Rai and Astra Herincx, and it was then that I made a pair of bent wire coat hanger rods for Janet to try her hand at dowsing for the first time. At the Abbey, I asked her to find north, and to her excitement, the bent wires crossed, pointing to the precise compass point. Janet became a gifted dowser and has helped me check out farms and houses for geopathic stress on many a dowsing trip. She uses her dowsing rods for homoeopathy treatments and in many other aspects of daily life.

A year or so after I had moved in with Janet, my mother died. I sold her house for £43000 and used the cash to buy a repossessed flat on the floor above Janet's in Northwood Hall. The bank selling the flat invited sealed offers: we put three different amounts into separate envelopes then dowsed each one to choose the sum we should offer. Our bid was the highest by £200!

The interior of the flat had been neglected, but after renovation work we doubled our much needed joint living space. At the time, Robert and Alex were still at Highgate School, coming home at weekends. Then, after graduating from Bristol University, they came back to live with us until they bought their own flat nearby. Robert is now an economist in the City; Alex divides his time between working as a freelance financial modeller and developing a career in acting and film production.

Janet continued to teach in the sitting room of her flat, while the new flat became our main sitting room, dining room and kitchen, with my office in one of the bedrooms. Two years later, we decided to get married. We sold the two flats and together with Janet's life savings and proceeds from my pension fund we were able to buy a house.

In 1996, after Janet had returned from a three-week tour

performing her one-woman show on cruise liners, we searched for a property in the City, Docklands, Hatton Garden, and around Highgate. After several weeks we stopped looking, booked a holiday break in St Lucia and decided to resume the hunt later. The day before we left for the Caribbean, a recently built three-storey detached house in Dartmouth Park Avenue, near Hampstead Heath, came on the market. We went to see the property, feeling half-hearted and weary from house hunting, and in an unexpected turn of events, bought the house before flying off.

Feeling refreshed after two weeks in the sun, we set about organising redecoration and furnishings to put the house in order. Once in our new home, life settled into a more comfortable pattern. I continued to work as a one-man practice and began writing *The Boiled Frog Syndrome*. A little later, Janet took a three-week break from her teaching, song writing and one-woman shows to visit Landour, north India, to seek out the birthplace of her paternal grandmother in the foothills of the Himalayas. In preparation for the trek, she hiked around Hampstead Heath in boots and a backpack.

Russi helped with the arrangements for her lone journey from Delhi to Landour. It was a long, exhausting car ride, and she arrived in Landour on 9th April. She was surprised to discover that around the town there were five different churches and chapels of Christian denomination. She used her dowsing rods to choose which particular chapel she should investigate. A middle-aged woman who had lived in the neighbourhood all her life helped Janet locate the part-time curator who consulted the chapel records for the years 1890 and 1891. There, in faded ink, was Janet's grandmother's baptismal certificate from 9th April 1891.

After finding what she had set out for, Janet went on to take a fifteen-hour taxi ride via Chandigarh, the capital of the Punjab, to Dharam Sala, near Dhera Dun, in the foothills of the Himalayas, less than eighty miles from the Chinese border.

Marriage, 1997

On 18th July 1997, we packed a suitcase and drove to Haringay Registry Office with our secretary and a financial advisor friend who were to act as our witnesses. Our families knew we had marriage in mind but were told nothing until three weeks after the ceremony. It was a moving and emotional service. The four of us had lunch afterwards at the San Carlos, a restaurant in Highgate, and while the other two were finishing their pudding, the taxi arrived to take us to Heathrow. We arrived in Amsterdam in the most glorious weather.

The pattern of the next four years of our life came to an abrupt end in 2001. I was recuperating from a cartilage operation on my knee when Janet was diagnosed with breast cancer. It was a shattering thunderbolt: suddenly we were overtaken by the speed of events and the shocking news to the pressurised insistence that urgent treatment was necessary. Everything was now focused on her recovery. All I could do was to support her, take care of her needs, and do some healing and meditation to visualise eradicating the cancer from her body. Although at first I felt helpless, it never crossed my mind that the situation was hopeless.

Cancer

The ordeal of dealing with the aftermath of surgery was dominated by the moribund, politically correct medical practices. In the health service there is still a steadfast rejection of well-proven complementary treatments to supplement the healing process, but Janet set up her own regime of twice-daily juicing and changed her diet, eventually finding those few in the medical profession who understood holistic therapies and treatments. I gave her every encouragement to take control of her own recovery, and as soon as her tenacious spirit took control, my anxiety was dispelled.

Four months after surgery, Janet's research took her to Doctor Waltraut Fryda in Bavaria who prescribed an extensive treatment of injections to regenerate her depleted adrenalin to restore the body's natural self-healing processes. Janet decided at their first meeting to stay for the full eight weeks, and rented a small flat. She only had an overnight bag with her: the following weekend I brought her a suitcase of clothes.

Doctor Fryda repeated the treatment a few months later to complete a permanent cure, and to enable Janet to return to living life to the full and continue her career in music, song writing and voice coaching. Janet's experience of the breast cancer politics of allopathic medicine urged her to write *Choosing to Heal – Surviving the Breast Cancer System*, which was published by Watkins in 2007. She then studied with Garner Thomson to become a Medical NLP Master.

Living in France

Serious illnesses and other challenging experiences often lead to a reassessment of one's life and lifestyle. In our case, we decided that we needed to take more time for holidays and long weekends in Italy and France, and over the next couple years we toured around the Mediterranean, looking for possible apartment locations. We found our villa, in a domain of several Bauhaus-style houses on the edge of Biot, a village on the Côte d'Azur. Since 2008, we lived in idyllic surroundings, close to nature; all around us the trees, the sea and broad horizons, sunshine and bright clear skies. I gave weekend Tarot seminars and readings; our field and map dowsing training sessions were popular and local contractors used us to dowse for buried septic tanks, water and drainage pipes. Janet continued to write songs and give concerts, performed under her new name, Narin Gylman. (In her voice coaching work and online programme, *Power Through Voice*, she still uses the name Janet Edwards.)

In 2013 we sold the villa and moved back to a delightful flat in Highgate. We do miss our neighbours, the frustration and fun with the language, the swimming pool, the weather and everything about the Côte d'Azur but there are many compensations and pleasures, as well as being in closer contact with our family and friends.

Postscript

I had self-doubts and a degree of reluctance when it came to writing this final chapter. I knew that I could recount how Janet and I met and what we have done together over the past twenty-three years, but I feared that I did not have the skill to adequately convey my deep admiration of her spirit, her immense talents as a musician, composer, performer and voice coach, nor the ability to express the profound, ever-increasing love, passion and adoration I have for her.

Needless to say, no man could possibly want more from a woman. Hearing Janet sing and play is a constant pleasure and joy, and I cherish every moment of my life with her.

Epilogue

There is no doubt that I was extremely fortunate to have been born between the wars in London's East End in 1932. Had I been born two or three decades later, the comprehensive school state education system would not have provided me with the same nurturing opportunities I experienced at Mayfield School where I was able to flourish, and where, importantly, we were taught the basic three Rs – reading, 'riting and 'rithmatic. Now, teaching is geared to a different three Rs – resistance, resentment and revenge!

I have also been fortunate to have inherited my mother's good health genes and to have been the surrogate beneficiary of her unresolved ambitions and drive. On reflection, I have strived to make the most of what I have in the way of abilities and talents and it could be said in my father's idiomatic turn of phrase that "I boxed above my weight!"

Perhaps, where we find ourselves at any particular period in our life is because it serves us best at that time and is the result of the choices we have consciously, or subconsciously, taken. Everyone operates according to patterns – some more obscure than others – and with insight and perception it is possible to see that all our actions and reactions are predictable because they will conform to a previously established pattern. Although deeper self-realisation – mature self-understanding – may help to avoid pitfalls into which, previously, we may have fallen, there does seem to be a perversity to 'action', so that it becomes a collision course in those aspects of our lives in which we are most vulnerable. Even when we know a particular course of action would be suicidal to pursue, there seems to be a magnetic force drawing us to it. Can destiny be avoided? Can repeating patterns – not coincidences – be redirected so that we avoid being wounded or wounding others? Or is it that one's life is simply a progression of recurring, unavoidable events – from childhood patterns at school, to one's teenage choice of career, and on to one's thirties and forties, through to middle and old age – so that it is like seeing a repeat of exactly the same play and the same plot with different scenery and costumes? Or can self-understanding, introspection and trust in one's intuition predict and then circumnavigate undesirable, disruptive patterns?

Tracing back the events, twists and turns of fate and the recurring patterns of time intervals that mark the milestones in our life I realised that there were several people, including the detractors, who unknowingly and unexpectedly turned out to be beneficial 'patrons'.

Although I had been aware of the so-called seven year itch, the more I delved into my box files of diaries and letters, the more I discovered the remarkable repeating patterns of seven, as well as a significant ten-year milestone cycle whenever I moved house or office. I also discovered that the Sun's solar flares that peak every ten years coincided with those times.

When I began writing this book in 2011 and first discovered this ten-year cycle of events, I wondered what significant change may be in store for me in 2012, apart from celebrating my eightieth birthday. At the time, there was little or no expectation that it would have something to do with property. How wrong can one be? Less than a year later, we sold our villa in France and permanently returned to our roots in London. Again, as my father's used to say: "You never know your luck until you tread in it!"

Later, when I mentioned to my long-standing friend Tad Mann (AT Mann, the internationally acclaimed astrologer and author) that in 2012 I was celebrating my eightieth birthday, he reminded me of the significant influences of Saturn and Uranus. Saturn returns every 29½ years to the same position in the sky from the date of your birth: for me, then, born in 1932, the years 1961/62, when I started my own practice, were certainly significant. The Saturn returns are a wake-up call to help us realise that we might have made choices at the age of thirty before we knew much about ourselves and whether we felt on or off course. The Saturn return can also bring fated and lasting relationships, as indeed it did in 1991/92 when I met Janet at the age of sixty. Saturn instigates change at a point when you can reap what you have sown.

Uranus takes eighty-four years to return to the same position it had at one's birth. It heralds a new and lively interest in life – Verdi wrote Falstaff and Picasso painted some of his best work after they were eighty-four. (So maybe I will finish the novel.) However, when Uranus is at the mid-way point, when we are forty-two years of age, it marks a break away from life's routine. At the time, not having any idea about the influence of Uranus, I recorded in a letter to a friend the separation, acute awareness and feelings of regret that I had laser-beamed into my business affairs with a single-minded tenacity that left no time or energy to 'pick the daisies' along a more meandering path. Unknowingly, this longing set me on a quest to explore the occult worlds and spirituality.

I regret not visiting the twelfth-century Ankor Wat complex of temples in Cambodia; sailing from the mainland of Ecuador to the Galapagos Islands; and seeing the giant stone statues on Easter Island. It is never too late but the long-haul flights are daunting...but one never knows! I would have liked to have developed my voice to sing opera, to have spent more time with the Saunders family in Essex and the Cooper family in India, to have had a closer relationship with Mark and Christopher, and to have kept my friendships in better repair. Now that we are back in London, some of these wishes, as well as completing the rewrite of my novel, may still come to pass.

Sharing my life with Janet is my greatest blessing and long may it continue for the next twenty years. I wish I had met her much earlier in my life but, at the same time, I know I would not have been ready to meet her any sooner.

My life's experiences and the patterns and arcane synchronicities I have discovered in writing these memoirs have most certainly revealed many things I needed to know. It is clear to me that on the occasions when I have not made good choices, had I listened to my intuition's quiet inner voice, there would have been more positive outcomes. I am still learning to understand how the psyche and spirit transcend matter and the material world.

Appendices

I

Moments of Music

Inspiration

Ever since June took me to the Royal Albert Hall to hear Beniamino Gigli sing, I have been passionate about opera. During my early schooldays, without being consciously aware of my being so, I was transported from the world of Chadwell Heath to another planet, and was enthralled by the experience of 'suffering' mild cultural shock.

When I first started my practice, I worked from home in a little bedroom and continually played Beethoven, Mozart and other classical works on a portable gramophone while designing, drawing or rendering coloured perspectives. The symphonies and piano concertos became 'pop' for me – the familiarity was comforting and anticipating the climactic endings were moments to relish, which tended to interrupt my drawing work because my pen became a conductor's baton. Whenever the telephone rang I resented the intrusion.

At one time during these early days working at home, Mark and Christopher, then about four and two years old, were both in bed with measles in the next room. They had no choice but to listen to the music. Later, sometime after they had recovered, Mark asked if he could hear the 'panio' music again. (At that time he was slightly dyslectic and got all his words, written and spoken, back to front, such as wanting to visit Keytor [Torquay] again and loving his grandparents' 'god' because Mark liked to make him bark!) Within a year or so, though, the UK music scene – The Beatles, Top of the Pops, and pirate radio stations – swamped any desire in the boys for alternative listening.

To rekindle their interest in music other than 'pop', to celebrate his seventeenth birthday I took Mark to the Royal Opera House in Covent Garden to see Margot Fonteyn and Rudolf Nureyev dancing *Romeo and Juliet*. At the time, he had a very catholic taste in music and saw no difference between Beethoven and Pink Floyd – to him it was all 'serious' music. After Fonteyn and Nureyev's memorable performance, one of the last times they danced together, I put my arm around Mark's shoulder and told him that one day he would be able to tell his grandchildren that he had seen Fonteyn and Nureyev dance.

A year later, sixteen-year-old Christopher said he too would like to see a ballet. It was such a pleasure to know he was interested when I took him to a performance at the Royal Opera House.

Opera

Opera is a gut sensation of raw emotion, as exhilarating as any football match, whereas ballet is more cerebral. I find the latter enormously enjoyable too, but opera is like sailing a boat on a broad reach at speed or some other physical experience that ends with the climax of winning.

I enjoy the sheer sensuousness of opera yet still find it difficult and teasing when I try to hum or whistle particular pieces. At one stage, I thought I could whistle all the main arias of the first two acts of *La Boheme* (how wrong can you be?). The more I played the recordings, the more I realised that I still did not know the music well enough other than to sing a few bars. I mentioned this to Dr Joscelyn Godwin, the musicologist I had met at one of the Kairos lectures (whose favourite opera is *Don Carlos*), citing the duet in *Madam Butterfly*, which I think is possibly the best duet ever written. Perhaps, I said, it is difficult to repeat because the music is so complex in construction, and yet it is so melodic. Despite listening many times, I could never memorise the whole piece, but when it was being played I could recognise each note as it was being sung.

Joscelyn's response was surprising: Puccini was the master and mentor of Shostakovich, Stravinsky, Schoenberg and other great modern (some people may think unmelodic and far too trendy) composers, whose music, although melodic, is highly complex and not easy to grasp.

Ethel

Most mornings, when living in Old Ford Road, Bethnal Green, I loaded up the opera long-playing reel tape while pottering about dressing and before walking to my office across the courtyard. Usually, I'd let the reel play itself out so that Mercedes, my housekeeper, and Ethel, the cleaning lady, could enjoy the music. Ethel, a local fifty-something born-and-bred East Ender, came in every day to clean and polish. Sometimes, when

I popped back to the house, I noticed her waving the duster, beating time with the music.

One morning she asked, "'ave a nice time last night, then?"

I said I had been to Covent Garden to see *Madam Butterfly*, the very piece she was listening to.

"Ooh, really? It's beautiful. I really love it."

"I didn't know you liked opera. What have you seen?"

"What, me? No, I've never been. I mean, I don't understand it, do I?"

"Ethel, there's nothing to understand. If you like the music, the programme gives you the story and it doesn't matter whether it's sung in Italian or English."

"No…I just don't understand it."

"It's very simple. You just listen to the music. Knowing the storyline adds to the enjoyment."

"What's this one about then?"

"It's based on a true story. Pinkerton, a US Navy officer falls in lust with a young Japanese girl called Butterfly and a broker arranges a sort of marriage ceremony. Her family object and ostracise her." (The long duet was just starting to play.)

"After the 'marriage', he sails away unknowingly leaving her pregnant. Butterfly patiently waits for him to come back to her and her child. When he returns a few years later with his American wife, she is devastated and kills herself." (Lots of 'Aahs' and 'Shames' from Ethel.)

"What's happening now with the clapping?"

"Well, Pinkerton has just married Butterfly and they've sent away the maid, Susuki, so that they can be alone."

"Go on," said Ethel, trying to look busy.

By now, I'm collecting a few things together and have put on my jacket, pausing now and then to take gulps of coffee. Each time I passed the kitchen Ethel called out, "So what's 'appening now then?"

"Butterfly is very shy and virginal, and although she loves him, she is timid about lovemaking and is full of remorse over the family. Pinkerton's trying to comfort and reassure her."

"So what's 'appening now?"

"Ah, well, he is convincing her that all will be well, edging her towards the bedroom."

The duet approached the climax. I needed to leave.

"So what's 'appening now then?"

"Well, he has her in his arms and they disappear behind the screens."

We wait for the final crescendo.

"So what's 'appening now?"

"He has just got her knickers off... Must dash!"

"Ooh, Mr Saunders," (nervous laughter) "I didn't think it was as simple as all that."

Aida

I'd met some business friends on my first trip to Egypt who told me there was an Egyptian Opera and Ballet Company production of *Aida* showing. Where else to see *Aida* than Egypt?

"Tickets? No problem," said my friend, picking up the telephone to call the wife of the principal tenor. The next evening I collected a ticket at the Sayed Darwish Theatre box office. (Darwish, a singer and composer working in the early part of the twentieth century, was considered the father of modern Egyptian music. When his satirical material became unacceptable to the Royal family and politicians of the day he was ostracised and blacklisted until King Farouk was exiled and the Nasser revolution built the concert hall in his honour.)

A few minutes before the eight o'clock start, I discovered the performance would end sometime after midnight. I wondered if the Egyptians were heavy drinkers, as clearly, they must be stretching the intervals beyond normal European standards. Then I realised, on reading my programme, that we would be watching *Cavalleria Rusticana*, with excerpts from *Aida*.

The concert hall auditorium was comparatively small and the balcony almost overhung the stage. The orchestra tuned up, then the conductor arrived, took his bow, and tried to bring the players to order. I sensed a power struggle between him and the musicians. He kept tapping his baton to no avail, grimacing as he half turned towards the audience. Ultimately, he won, and the overture to *Cavelleria* began. Each note seemed to be on elastic; the conductor's loving care, as he attempted to draw out every note of emotion, made the overture last twice as long as I had ever heard it played before.

Suddenly and startlingly, powerful floodlights mounted on the front of the balcony burst into full glare. The dazzle they made on the shiny gold lamé curtains was blinding, until the curtains rose to reveal the six principal singers standing at the front of the stage, each attired in various styles of evening dress, ranging from trendy midnight blue to sedate black. Behind them, the chorus were also attired in sombre colours: black tie for the men and grey skirts and white shirts for the women.

Although the quality of the singing was a pleasant surprise, there were various distracting elements to the evening. I became concerned for the performers who were desperately trying to see the conductor through the piercing spotlights that blazed directly into their line of vision. The audience, too, were a little disruptive: some members were so enthusiastic that they clapped and called 'bravo' in the middle of the arias while others sauntered in and out of the hall, treating the whole performance as if it were a cocktail party. All this time, a photographer took photographs, the flash from his camera less noticeable (due to the intensity of light already present) than the buzz of the time exposure. He moved around the auditorium without any awareness of the disruption he was causing.

All these distractions were relatively minor, however, when compared to the actions of the prompter whose rich baritone voice was audible by several decibels whenever he had to prompt one particular contralto, who needed help with almost every line. I'd always thought that prompters were supposed to be unheard and unseen but this one, in his enthusiasm, also gave into the desire to 'conduct'. Everyone in the audience could see his hands and cuffed wrists waving about above his hide. It didn't help that his 'conducting' was completely out of synch with the conductor's baton and the orchestra's music. It wouldn't have mattered so much if the blinding spotlights had not prevented the singers from seeing the conductor so that they followed the prompter instead. The orchestra, who could not see his dismembered hands, followed the conductor, and although the singers and orchestra were not together, at least they each had their own leader.

At last the first interval finally arrived. I could not endure another moment and walked out.

Ballet

By chance, in my student days, I came across ballet at the Regent's Park open air theatre and thought it would be a good way of reciprocating for the Gigli experience if I took June to see the Molly Lake Ballet Company's performance of classical ballet excerpts at the People's Palace in the Mile End Road, in London's East End.

The 1930s building, which no longer exists, was intended to be a political icon to provide culture to the poor masses at cheap rates. Unfortunately, it was built over London Underground's fairly shallow Central Line, which caused our seats and the whole building to shake as the frequent trains speeded through the tunnel. A good simulation would be 'Vibrasound', used in the screening of the film *Earthquake*.

Sadly, during the delicate passages of the dying swan, the noise of the trains below blanked out the music. Another drawback was the width of the stage: it was never designed for ballet and the fault was exaggerated when the principal ballerina, Molly Lake herself (who was much taller than the average dancer), came on to dance. Her giant steps across the hollow-sounding boards as she danced from one side to the other – strides that resembled those of a triple jump athlete – brought her up short before colliding into the proscenium arch pilaster. However, her performance should not be criticised solely because her heavy footfalls, as she pranced around the stage, were not synchronised with the sound of the arrival and departure of the trains running below the foundations.

June was unimpressed and, as far as I know, she never went to the ballet again.

Despite the Molly Lake experience, I continued to see most of the ballets staged in London. In the 1970s, I could afford to indulge my passion for opera and ballet and enrolled my practice as a corporate member of the Royal Opera House. Here I saw some exciting modern ballets, such as the Harlem Dance Theatre's *The Prodigal Son*, Scott Joplin's *Elite Syncopations*, dance set to the Elgar *Variations*, and so many other marvellous, so-called modern ballets. But my first love has always been opera. So much so that I always had to restrain myself, in the stalls at Covent Garden, from joining in the chorus or helping the tenor out during his best arias. This may be partly due to a nostalgia for my youth when I had the notion that I might want to sing opera professionally. I had the physique for it, and a natural ear for music. The problem was that the idea of becoming a singer first came to my mind at a time when I was also committed to finishing my studies.

Tokyo Concert

I went to a bizarre concert – a grand orchestral piece by Schoenberg, which was played in a geodesic dome. The 'conductor' stood at a consul sound desk controlling the electronic output while a violinist played in a clear plastic bubble, suspended about six metres above the ground. Two or three other musicians were similarly suspended in various strategic areas of the dome, presumably to achieve special acoustic effects.

The method of listening to the performance was also unusual: the producers insisted that the only way to appreciate the sensational sounds was for the audience to lie full length on long Dunlopillo pallets that were laid out on the floor of the dome. I found the sounds remarkable and uncanny, and thought that perhaps, after a few repeats, it would be possible to have a closer relationship with this type of music.

Paul Tortelier

The search for a reasonably priced marina somewhere on the Côte d'Azur to berth my boat Azulea was complete. Waiting in a queue at Nice Airport to board the plane to Paris, I found myself standing next to Paul Tortelier, the world-famous cellist. In my best French I plucked up the courage to talk to him about the time I had heard him play at the Royal Festival Hall. I'd been invited by Don Foskett, the manager of one of our clients, the National Bank of North Carolina. Don and his Japanese wife, both music lovers, had booked a balcony box on the left of the stage so that we could have a clear view of Tortelier's fingering and bowing.

The audience was enthralled with the music. After two encores, amid rapturous applause, an old man, raincoat neatly folded over his arm, came through the door facing our box and shuffled along the aisle between the stage and the first row of seats. He stopped in front of Tortelier who knelt down and kissed him on both cheeks. Tortelier hushed the applause, pointed to the man as he walked away through the door below us, and said, "That man taught me fingering."

Now reminding him of this poignant story brought gentle tears to our eyes. (No – my French was not that bad!) We sat together on the plane and shared a taxi from the airport to the centre of Paris when he confessed that before each performance he suffered from serious stage fright. Both his son Yan Pascal, an accomplished conductor, and his daughter Maria de la Pau, a talented concert pianist, also suffered from the same anxieties. So, in the back of the taxi, I taught Tortelier some basic meditation techniques that he and his children could practise in the green room before going on stage.

II

Random Writings

Thoughts on Architecture

Happiness: what is the relationship between design and happiness?

> The notion of happiness is so indefinite that although every man
> wishes to attain it yet he can never say definitely and consistently
> what it is that he really wishes and wills.
>
> Emmanuel Kant (1724 –1804),
> *Fundamental Principles of the Metaphysics of Morals*

Happiness is an expression of the full spectrum of feelings ranging
from being in a state of serene contentment (the Zen Zone) to high
elation, euphoria and bliss. Within each of us is a longing for happiness,
something which can come in the guise of good fortune, mental
and physical pleasures, personal attainment, satisfaction with one's
circumstances and what Dr Johnson described as "felicities which
cannot be produced at will by wit and labour". (It seems unlikely that
material wealth alone will ever lead to human happiness.)

According to Dr Candace Pert, we are all hard-wired for bliss
and all experiences and lifestyle emotions affect altered states of
mind. Located throughout our body are *receptors* (memory buttons)
which are stored in the molecules/peptides that stimulate energies and
are especially concentrated in the heart and pancreas. In her book
Molecules of Emotion she unifies the body, mind, spirit and emotions
into one intelligent system. Clearly, the processes and content of our
thinking can change the molecules in the body that in turn will affect
our emotions at any point, thus confirming that our emotional state
is a key to health.

In the foreword to Pert's book, Deepak Chopra MD says:

> ...our internal chemicals, the neuropeptides and their receptors, are the actual biological underpinnings of our awareness, manifesting themselves as our emotions, beliefs and expectations, and profoundly influencing how we respond to and experience our world... This information transfer takes place over a network linking all of our systems and organs, engaging all of our molecules of emotion... What we see is an image of a "mobile brain" that moves throughout our entire body...not just in the head.
>
> Dr Candace B Pert, *Molecules of Emotion*

In other words, the mind is 'non-local': we can experience this when a piece of music – vibrations – can send shivers and a tingling down our spine. In this way, every stimulant to the five senses – visual, audio, kinaesthetic, olfactory and gustatory – whether it is tobacco, chocolate, caffeine, prescription and illegal drugs, sex, deep breathing, skiing, and so on, will be filtered through our emotional receptors in the body and react on the subconscious mind.

All created work, whatever the medium, will invoke an emotional response whether the designer's motives are intentional or unwitting. Renoir tells us that as the purpose of painting is to decorate walls, so paintings should be as rich as possible, stimulating pleasure and happiness (although the viewer's response is rather short-lived and superficial). Contrast this with Karl Marx's dour view that all art forms should be based on ideological themes to express humanity's political and social struggles.

More recently, the American architect Rafael Vinoly, who has created the design for the thirty-seven-storey so-called Walkie Talkie building (also known as the Hunchback) at 20 Fenchurch Street in London, has stated that his consciously declared aim is to make us feel uncomfortable and disorientated. (Having seen the design, there is little doubt his mission will be achieved!) The building, a product of the designer's own arrogance, would be nothing less than a personal assault on the senses and sensibilities of both occupants and passers-by.

Unfortunately, we already have too many architects who have *unconsciously* created such buildings in abundance all over the UK. You only have to look at some of our relatively new schools and hospitals where first-time users of the building feel agitated, uncomfortable and disorientated simply because they must hunt around to find where the architect has deliberately concealed the entrance!

Throughout history, buildings are a material testament to the spirit and social mores of the age in which they were built. It is not surprising that today we have new, iconic buildings that express our celebrity culture and intimidate their neighbours.

It is a pity we currently ignore Sir Henry Wotton's seventeenth-century principles of design:

> In architecture as well in all other operative arts, the end must direct the operation. The end is to build well. Well building [and well-being] hath three conditions: Commodity, firmness and delight.
>
> Sir Henry Wotton (1568–1639), *Elements of Architecture*

These three tenets can be translated as being symbolic of Mind (*Commodity*), Body (*Firmness*), and Spirit (*Delight*), all of which have the same fundamental effect on our emotions.

This follows Professor Keith Critchlow's analysis of the word 'architecture':

Archi (the archetypal nature of the Cosmos – Spirit)
tech (the technical ability to build – Mind)
ure (Earthiness – Body)

Again, in Plato's *Seven Liberal Arts*, the Trivium deals with language:

Grammar (Goodness or Body)
Rhetoric (Beauty or Spirit)
Logic (Truth or Mind)
Plato (429–347 BC), *Timaeus and Critias*

According to Clive Bell:

> There is a particular kind of emotion provoked by works of visual art, and that this emotion is provoked by every kind of visual art, by pictures, sculptures, buildings, pots, carvings, textiles, [industrial design] etc., is not disputed, I think, by anyone capable of feeling it. This emotion is called the aesthetic emotion; and if we can discover some quality common and peculiar to all the objects that provoke it, we shall have solved what I take to be the central problem of aesthetics.
>
> Clive Bell (1881–1964), *Art*

Johann Goethe described geometry [architecture] as *frozen music*: we could say that industrial design is *mobile architecture* and similarly demands the same three components: it must be usable and fit for purpose (Body); be a technically workable dynamic balance that integrates and expresses the three components related to our Body, Mind and Spirit (Mind); and have aesthetic appeal (Spirit). This concurs with Candace Pert's view that there is a relationship between happiness and design when the designer has created a positive aesthetic emotion.

Living Daylight

A roofing manufacturer claimed that roof lights installed in school classrooms to supplement the daylight penetration from the façade windows would enhance the vitality, energy levels and academic achievements of the children. Can such a claim be substantiated?

The planet Earth and every living organism depend on the Sun's therapeutic light and energy radiations. Light, personifying spiritual enlightenment, is a fundamental tenet of every religion, from ancient Paganism to Christianity and Buddhism. Sound, colour and light are ascending vibrational frequencies on the cosmic electromagnetic spectrum; our genes communicate with each other by means of light and light sensors. When deprived of natural light, living organisms fall into decline, wither, and die prematurely.

Vitamin D, that owes its synthesis to the sun, is vital to our health and well-being. Through our eyes, daylight penetrates the retinas to the pineal, pituitary and hypothalamus glands that regulate the body's life processes and hormonal production: these govern our emotions, energy levels, stress responses, the autonomic nervous system and metabolic functions. The pineal gland, super-sensitive to extremely weak electromagnetic fields, produces hormonal secretions, including the release of serotonin and melatonin; all are controlled by *light*.

Throughout history, the healing power of light and the quality of colour vibrations have been used in medicine since the ancient Egyptians through to Hippocrates and on to the nineteenth century, when Nobel Prize winners Dr Robert Koch and Dr Niels Finsen used early morning sunlight and fresh air to cure many thousands suffering from rickets and tuberculosis.

Florence Nightingale, another nineteenth-century pioneer, campaigned to improve the design of Victorian hospitals. In the Crimea War, the unsanitary, dark, unlighted wards caused the death of 16000 soldiers from disease while fewer than 4000 died of their wounds or in battle.

Penicillin and antibiotics in the 1950s led the medical profession to believe the Holy Grail of allopathic medicine was in their grasp and that all other natural and proven therapies could now be discarded and treated as anachronistic. At the same time, the perennial wisdom established 2000 years ago stated that it was fundamentally important for architects to have an understanding and knowledge of medicine. This has also been discarded. If architects understood the holistic nature of human beings – our mind, spirit and body – their buildings would be free of sick-building-syndrome, and if the design of flagship hospitals could only dispense with tinted glazing and fixed windows the incidence of MRSA would be significantly reduced.

Why do we perpetually ignore perennial wisdom? Without light we can neither thrive nor survive.

City of the Future

Extracts from a 1981 article commissioned by *Chimo Magazine*, Toronto, Canada:

Preface

Civitas is a Greek word for 'city' meaning a self-governed state. Other definitions of a city include:

> A town incorporating the seat of a bishop
> Where a cathedral is located
> In the USA, any town that has self-governing powers
> Great conurbations – large urban sprawls of joined-up towns and
>   villages – have become classified as 'cities'

The choice of location may be attributed to:

> Beneficial climatic conditions or having certain therapeutic
>   properties (Bath)
> Housing for population overspill (Welwyn Garden City)
> Growth as a centre for trade and commerce (Dubai)
> Strategic defence or communal security (Brasilia)
> Expression of temporal power (Fatehpur Sikri)
> A spiritual homage (Angkor Wat)

Magnesia was Plato's model for an ideal city. New Jerusalem was the

Bible's concept of a city paradise on Earth. 2000 years ago, Vitruvius set out precise information on where to locate and how to build a new city and practical design details for the layout of the streets according to the prevailing winds as well as the fortifications and location of the temples and shrines to safeguard the physical well-being and morals of the inhabitants. Covertly, he also specified the geometric patterns and dimensions to ensure the plan conformed to cosmic laws.

Cities such as Angkor Wat, Washington DC, certain Aztec and Inca cities in Mexico and elsewhere were conceived and designed by a priesthood according to the esoteric patterns of the universe to create a 'Heaven on Earth'. Similar examples, such as the Great Pyramids of Giza and the location of cathedrals around Chartres, were planned to reflect a specific heavenly constellation. The 'architects' understood the numbers (dimensions), geometry and music (harmonic ratios) that govern the cosmos.

Whatever the overt appearance of the built environment may be, certain cities do appear to have been conceived to express a tradition of esoteric/spiritual principles found in architecture, painting, music and theatre that symbolically express a covert philosophical concept or ideology that was the source and essence of its inspiration. Using an analogy in graphic art: on the one hand, a traffic sign is a mundane statement of fact, whereas a symbol such as a Mandela or the Chinese emblem for Yin (female) and Yang (male) principles will register intuitively to the psyche and reach beyond the rational mind.

Political Utopias

The question is whether the architectural environment can have a more profound influence on the physical, mental and spiritual health and well-being of a society's quality of life than the political governance of city's community. Plato's *Republic* was an idealistic political system controlled by philosopher-statesmen. His philosophers were not concerned with the design, planning and architecture of a city but were primarily engaged in reshaping the spirit and character of the society as it then existed. *Utopia*, a word coined by Sir Thomas More, was a state of society, a political ideal of law and order and the pursuit of happiness which consisted in 'every motion and state of the body or mind wherein man hath naturally delectation'. Both More and Plato imagined how a restructuring could make a 'better', more enlightened and intellectually conceived city or state.

However, More's *Utopia*, was a communistic, ordered regime that failed to reconcile social justice with an individual's democratic freedom. As ever, the dilemma is striking a balance between everybody and everything – including all art forms – having to be subjugated to the good of the community and allowing human nature to freely express itself. The anti-Utopia of Aldous Huxley's *Brave New World* or George Orwell's *1984* are fierce warnings of the dangers of such intellectual moulding. There have been some 200 'Utopias' actually created in America, such as Owen's New Harmony, Oneida, and Brook Farm, many of which have failed because of the rigidity and joylessness of the conformity demanded by such organisations of state.

Rudolf Steiner (1861–1925) predicted that the twentieth century would be a time when old forms of civilisation would have to be discarded, suggesting that wherever old social forms were perpetuated, unhealthy social conditions would ensue. He also stressed that people working in modern institutions and communities who were striving to realise such new social forms would be greatly hampered in their work if they were surrounded by architectural forms incompatible with their strivings.

Perhaps, the freedom of self-expression currently enjoyed might benefit if it were tempered by values, such as a sense of permanence where traditional culture and customs are respected, which produce a social order and quality of physical and spiritual nourishment. These qualities are not found in our modern cities; however, attitudes may change as we enter the era of *New Urbanism* which heralds the planning of new towns based upon humanism and sustainability.

Architectural Utopias

One's own outer world is a manifestation of one's inner self, so cities and buildings are manifestations of the collective consciousness of the society or social groups created and demanded by them. Similarly, the architectural design of a building is determined by and an expression of the inner activity for which it was created.

The 'Utopia' architects, such as Le Corbusier, omitted dealing with social/political aspects of new societies. Instead they believed their new cities and buildings would create an environment so harmonious that the city dwellers could lead nothing but good and balanced lives. Unfortunately, the architecture seems to be as rigid and joyless as the literary Utopias. Many new towns have been conceived with the sole idea of relocating the overspill populations of the larger cities slowly dying through the implosion of overloaded services and facilities. These new satellite cities tend to repeat the same technology, energy sources, forms of transportation and interdependence on the State for food and goods. This repeats the original cause of decay and recreates the same philosophical, moral and spiritual poverty. Chandigarh is one such 'brave new city'. This newly built conurbation in north-west India looks just like any other poor, old city of that continent. The grand Secretariat buildings designed by Le Corbusier are brave statements in concrete, except the interiors remained unfinished and had to be furnished with tea chests due to lack of money. An example of the ego of the State leading to literal and metaphorical bankruptcy!

Brazil is virtually as large as the USA. Its new capital Brasilia, which was conceived in the nineteenth century and eventually executed in the twentieth, was a strategic 'Utopia', the plan being to site the political centre equidistantly from its boundaries. (A few lines drawn on the map readily plotted the location of Brasilia in a desert!). Modern twentieth-century technology made it possible to build a huge lake and reservoir, modern chemistry eliminated mosquitoes, and modern transport then allowed vast distances to be covered by the men and materials to build the buildings. Ironically, twentieth-century technology also created the intercontinental ballistic missile, making Brasilia as vulnerable as Rio de Janeiro!

Brasilia's social engineering failed due to the lack of insight by the planners and architects who devised a fast, efficient and safe network of roads for cars which segregated and isolated each separate 'village' community from the next. This, in turn, prevented the major and important social event for all Latin peoples: promenading or cruising – how else can a young Latin boy or girl find and choose their mate? This grand Utopian design gave the motor car a higher priority than the promenade, a simple and necessary human activity. No doubt, the young people now living in Brasilia do find their mates and perhaps, as the Latin societies tend towards a greater freedom and permissiveness, so the need to promenade may be reduced. Here, 'planning' certainly had an impact on social behaviour.

The Twenty-First-Century Utopia
What would be our ideal Utopia city of the future and could we create a modern Heaven on Earth? Much would depend on new technology,

which could either be in the realms of far-out science fiction or, through global catastrophe, a return to the simplicity of the early Bronze Age. Will we have cars and aeroplanes? Will each city have to be self-sufficient in food production? What will be the sources of energy?

Certain technological changes would have an effect upon the planning and architecture of a new city: even now a 'factory' is more like an office building designed to house high technology, machinery and computer robots where the 'workers' sit at consoles in white overalls. Pollution would be reduced, if not eliminated, to allow residential areas to be built next to the workplaces where employees could enjoy the walk rather than spending hours commuting.

Energy conservation would be a social, economic necessity and low rise buildings would encourage the use of stairs rather than a lift. Low rise also means one could open a window for fresh air rather than rely on air conditioning, as well as negating the fear of being sucked out of a skyscraper building on a windy day! Façades with more wall than window area would reduce heat loss and gain through large glass areas.

Private household computers are part of present day technology which allows shopping to be ordered from the home. Online shopping and global communication systems reduce travelling on a day-to-day basis. Although the location and planning of shops and office buildings may change, it is unlikely to influence our need and desire to go out to meet other human beings, to be stimulated and to generate that creative energy on the basis that $1 + 1 =$ more than 2.

A greater awareness and collective maturity would automatically change our current attitudes concerning status, power and money. The work ethic could transform into a leisure ethic. Changing our present attitudes and understanding abundance, prosperity and the sense of inner security could start a healing process. The insecurities of the present day workaholic or those who allow themselves to be dependent on the welfare of the state might gradually melt away and transform into a positive and more imaginative use of time and energy.

The planning and design of hospitals will need to provide facilities for both medical science and so-called unorthodox healing methods, so that they could be utilised to the full. Healing rooms, constructed to form therapeutic spaces, shapes and volumes, and treated with colours and textures giving off various beneficial vibrations and energy, will be as important as the standard, high technology of the operating theatre.

The present architectural concept of school classrooms and playing fields may change as progress is made in more enlightened attitudes towards teaching. The curricula will be expanded to assist the awakening and spiritual development of a child. The root of the word 'education' is *educari*, meaning 'to draw out': Plato's view was that we are all gifted with wisdom and knowledge; the true teacher helps us to *remember* that which we already know! Such fundamental changes would emanate from a state of higher collective consciousness and a return to the elementary application of the principles of universal laws where the city allowed the freedom of expression and human nature, and provide the space for the mind, body and spirit to expand to release our natural genius and creativity, and to progress towards psychological maturity.

Frank Lloyd Wright's View:

The principles of architecture are simply the principles of life. Just as a house built on makeshift foundations cannot stand, so life set on makeshift character in a makeshift country cannot endure. Good and lasting architecture gives or concedes the right to all of us to live abundantly in the exuberance that is beauty – in the sense that William Blake defined exuberance. He did not mean excess. He meant according to nature, without stint.

A good and lasting life must yield that right to all of us. And the only secure foundation for such a life is enlightened human character, which will understandingly accept and not merely ape the organic relation between the welfare of one and the welfare of the whole. Only that sort of character is fit for and able to create a permanent and universal well-being.

To put it concretely again, architectural values are human values or they are not valuable. Human values are life giving, not life taking. When a man is content to build for himself alone, taking the natural rights of life, breath, light and space away from his neighbour, the result is a monstrosity like the pretentious skyscraper. It stands for a while in the business slum formed by its own greed, selfishly casting its shadow on its neighbours, only to find that it too is dependent upon their success and must fail with their failure.

Trained imagination and true thought are our human divinity. These alone may distinguish the human herd and save it from the fate that has overtaken all other herds, human or animal. All this leads to the realisation of a new civilisation with an architecture of its own, which will make the machine its slave and create nobler longings for mankind.

Source unknown

More Thoughts on Architecture

The following quote from my book *The Boiled Frog Syndrome* (page 246) encapsulates my views on architecture and design:

> According to the 5000-year-old Hindu tradition, the souls of both the architect and the client were inseparably involved in the success of the final form of a building. The form had to be sufficiently geometrically accurate (sacred) for the gods to be compelled to be present. Whether a private dwelling or a commercial or public building, the architect alone cannot produce a sacred vehicle for the expression of a "spiritual presence and a space for the heart" without the client and users of the building understanding and sharing that same vision. Whenever we approach and enter a building designed according to the universal laws or canon, all the vibrations created by the earth energies, the geometry, the colour and sound will resonate with the whole of our being. Subliminally, our senses and every part of our body will see, hear and feel these vibrations and at the most subtle level, our psyche will respond to the occult wave patterns. Physically, biologically, intellectually, emotionally, spiritually and joyfully we will be reminded of our 'common bond' with nature. We will feel healed and the building, whether it be humble or grand, will be a temple of the soul.

Head

Jack McCarthy

In the early 1970s, when I persuaded Jack to join the practice to develop our own graphics art department and workshop, it was suggested that he might like to do a sculpture of my head. Although I was concerned that it might be interpreted as conceit or a touch of narcissism, we decided to get on with it. He took photographs to study my bone structure, shadows and other technicalities to arrange a particular pose, and a date was set for the first sitting. In his studio, I propped myself up on a high stool in a direct line facing a wooden stand with the basic formwork armature piece – a sawn-off broomstick and two thick pear-shaped wires crossing each other at right angles.

Jack told me to relax and slightly tilt my head. I focused on a small crack in the ceiling while he prowled around a few times, then pounced on the open sack of damp clay on the floor, plunged his hands into it and, as if he were kneading dough, stuffed the sticky, elastic mud between the wire pieces until they were buried. (Throughout the five or six subsequent sittings, Jack was dressed as if he were ready to go out to dinner and, apart from his hands, there was not a trace of clay elsewhere: this was indeed the sign of a real craftsman.)

The first two sessions were light-hearted: while Jack worked the clay we told jokes and chatted in our North Country-type accent party pieces. Then, as each significant stage progressed the banter dried up. I knew where to sit, where to find the crack in the ceiling and when to take a break from the pose and glance at the work. Jack worked with feverish speed and intensity. Towards the end it was so tense and taut that not a word was spoken except for a fleeting word to help Jack through moments when he needed an uplift. After each session he was quite emotionally drained.

When delicate finishing touches were made to the characteristic features such as the lips and eyes, the studio felt charged with energy. The tension was only relieved when he wrapped the damp cloth around the clay at the end of each session; it looked like the head of an Egyptian mummy. I too felt drained. Molly, having lived and worked with Jack for so many years, could sense the moment when he needed to rest or look at the work to offer a fresh view of the piece. Occasionally, she would point out a minute detail which was not quite right because he was literally too close and too tired to see.

Memories of all the weekly sessions merge into one continuous moment of staring at the little crack in the ceiling and recollecting the changing moods as each progressive moulding emerged from the sack of clay on the floor to become transmogrified from the shape of a pear to the appearance of a skull with two craters for the eyes, a barely protruding blob for a nose and a rough outline of the flesh of a jaw.

Perhaps the most profound and lasting memories I have of the later sessions were of watching the uncanny and almost supernatural transformations from amorphous clay to a recognisable head – it was like witnessing death in reverse: is this how a corpse looked before the muscle and skin had decayed? Each session progressed from decay to the point of death, then becoming living flesh and a reunion with the Earth. Miraculously, the clay moulding became alive – I had been reincarnated.

All the fine subtleties and details were revealed when it was finally cast in bronze, ready for the unveiling. At first glance I saw this image of myself – not as a mirror-like reflection but the portrait of some other person. In time I was able to recognise my own mannerisms: my seriousness coupled with the ability to smile at myself and treat life as a joke; there was also a sadness – 'pathos' would be too self-indulgent – and a sense of long-term loneliness. A tear trickled down my cheek: it was nothing to do with self-pity or relief that the work had been completed, and, certainly, I did not feel alone. Perhaps the whole experience had been like witnessing my own rebirth and the first viewing of the casting had revealed a part of my past life which was now exorcised by the very sense of self-realisation.

Wherever the head has been located, I treat its presence as if it were a guest in the house: currently, it stands on the worktop in my office. Few people are aware of the piece because it is rarely placed in a prominent position. Those who do spot it are curious to know if it is of anyone famous. I tell them it is someone who is my hero and leave it at that. Maybe, it simply fits in well and requires no comment.

Date about 1977

Pity, Letter to a Friend 1985

As promised, I am writing to you about *Pity* and *Compassion*, which arose when you were telling me about how you felt such pity and sadness for a certain talented person who had designed the credit titles and graphics for the early Bond films until he got hooked on heroin. He had just come out of hospital following treatment to get him off drugs and was still suffering from severe withdrawal symptoms when his girlfriend decided to give him a celebratory birthday party. At the party he spent the whole time sitting alone in a corner of the room, ignored by all the guests except you. After talking to him you went over to one of the several well-known film star guests, who apparently meant a lot to the druggy, to suggest – even pleaded – that he might spare a little time to talk to him. You said the celebrity turned abusive to you, pointedly ignored the druggy and immediately left the party. All the other guests studiously ignored the druggy and soon they too walked out of the party without even bidding him 'Goodnight'.

Understandably, you felt pity for the druggy and were naturally upset by the rude abuse. When you told me this story, my view was that your feeling of pity expressed arrogance – even a sense of superiority – on your part; on the other hand, having *compassion* for the man was not arrogance. Your assertion that pity and compassion were synonymous and that I was playing with semantics have led me to write to you about the differences.

The dictionary's definitions of pity and compassion are indeed synonymous and the same words are used and transposed to define the meaning except that *compassion* indicates a desire to do something to alleviate the suffering. To my mind, the word suggests something softer and more humane than *pity*. It meant an asexual love of varying degrees depending upon one's personal and deep involvement. The degree of love for humanity usually increases as one's involvement becomes more intimate and such variations range between close personal connections – parents, children, wife, husband, lover and friends, through to 'fellow countrymen' and then humanity at large. With this form of love – agape – action is necessary to devote time, effort and energy to help someone in need and the extent of the devotion is often conditioned by the intimacy or closeness of the connection.

Pity, often expressed in terms of 'feeling sorry for...' someone or something, is a passing emotion when no action is taken but one is 'sparing a thought' for someone or something considered to be 'unfortunate'. Expressions of pity may well be vacuous, meaningless statements imploring some spiritual entity or person to intervene and help: it also suggests to others that you recognise a certain defect or problem and 'thank God it is not mine'. In other words, you are above having such particular problems. When someone says, "...pity those poor bastards who can't afford a morsel of food, a bed, a TV, a Rolls Royce...whatever," are they expressing a genuine concern for 'those poor bastards' or are they covertly telling us that they can afford food, drink, a Rolls Royce, and so on? Often there is no intention to give a second thought to these 'poor bastards' or take any positive action to overcome the deprivation which has made them 'poor'. Should one feel pity for anyone? Perhaps not if there is a choice or choices open to the person for whom one feels pity.

Those who do take action by voluntarily working in hospitals, schools and charity organisations come under my meaning of *compassion*. If, for example, a nurse feels pity for the aged, infirm or defective, or if they did take on their patients' pain, they would be far less effective and professional in their caring work. Instead, compassion empowers us to positively contribute to the well-being of others which, in turn, supports them to help to lift themselves above self-pity and enjoy life and living, whatever the constraints and misfortunes.

The Dubliner Christy Brown's first book, *Down all the Days*, was hailed as a fine piece of literature and yet he was born seriously crippled by cerebral palsy – almost dumb – and spent most of his life in a crumpled heap in the corner of the room, ignored by his family and everyone who came to the house. He typed the book with his big toe, writing the most sensitive, poetic work. It is an exceptional case to highlight the power of the spirit of one human being. On the other hand, there may be many articulate people who are crippled by arthritis whose physical handicaps are relatively minor compared to Christy Brown's. No doubt, they too may feel and want to say something but are reluctant to use a tape recorder, or dictate to a friend, because they feel inadequate or shy...or whatever. I could feel sad for them but they do have alternative ways and means open to them. I suggest that instead of thinking 'What a pity' it would be more useful if we took positive action to help them with solutions, provide them with a tape recorder or give time to sit and write for them, provided always that they want our help in the first place! (What feelings should we have for those people who possess all their faculties and yet believe they have got nothing to say?)

To return to the question of choice and how it may be related to your friend the druggy: at this moment, I am writing this letter on an aeroplane bound for Riyadh and have little opportunity to exercise free will. I can decide whether to have orange juice, tomato juice or Coca Cola but if I had wanted to drink alcohol I should have chosen to travel to Riyadh by a different carrier other than Saudi Arabian Airlines. While I can choose whether or not to see a film, listen to music or when to sleep, in fact I have very little control over my life for the next few hours. Additionally, due to my decision to travel to Saudi Arabia, I have been in the airport lounge for about eight hours, waiting for the fog to lift. Restricted movement in an airport lounge is like being in an open prison. And so, for today and most of tomorrow, I have very little choice in anything except peripheral and unimportant matters. My destiny, my direction, the speed at which I go is decided for me. I can't even decide to jump off the plane. Further back in time, I could say that my decision on which date to go to Saudi was determined by my availability and how soon the client needed me to be there. I had the choice, of course, to send someone else in my organisation to go instead of me.

The reason for my being asked to go to Riyadh is the result of a chain of decisions taken in the distant past such as: that I wanted to be an architect; that I wanted to do international work; that I met a Saudi entrepreneur who asked me to travel to Riyadh, and so on... Today somebody might 'spare a thought' and feel sorry (pity) for me having to be in the airport lounge for eight hours but it was not all that bad. All the passengers were taken to an airport hotel for lunch, I made a few phone calls, read a book, slept a bit, and although I would rather have been on my way to Saudi, I wasn't going to let external factors make me angry or waste my time. However, destiny – fate if you will – has led me to be in this aeroplane, which is the result standing at a crossroad and choosing which path to take – will it be left or right? One can never know where either road will lead, and sometimes there will be a way to get back to the other road if the choice was wrong: there may even be a shortcut to a better track. The problem is not when you become aware that you have taken a wrong turning, it is when you pretend to yourself and others that you want to change direction yet continually refuse to do so.

Your druggy friend had talent, ability and a keen mind. He could also choose many options, some of which resulted in a collision course with disaster, wasted abilities and squandered talent. Is it surprising that he was tucked away in a corner at the party with no one except you to talk to? Does he need or deserve your pity? Certainly he needed compassion; he needed love because that is the only thing anyone could give him. It could be said that his girlfriend showed him love – she gave him a birthday party – but was the party given for his benefit or was it an opportunity for his girlfriend to receive pity from all the guests when they could see the burden she is carrying, and what she is going through, having to look after this wreck of a man. Did she set him up?

From your description, the man should have remained under intensive care rather being out at a party. When you were the only one spending a long time talking to the druggy, how many of the guests were feeling pity for you? And what about the 'friends' who came to celebrate his birthday – what were their motives? If they came 'out of pity' for him, then ignoring him and not even saying 'Goodbye' indicated that they too were indulging in self-pity.

Could it be that the druggy was seriously affected by his feeling of pity for the guests!? After all, he was there, having gone through agonies of mind and body and in the same room were these jet setters, needing to be seen, small talking about people and possessions, sipping their cocktails, worrying about being criticised, their bank overdrafts or trying to stretch out what might be their comparatively meagre talents. Who will be arrogant enough to say who pities whom? The blind man in the street does not want our pity – that is a well-known killer – he may need our help to across the road or catch a bus. He is likely to reject any feelings of sorrow or 'pity' for him because he may already have bonus compensations such as being able to hear much better than sighted folk like us.

If, as you said, he had already rejected positive rehabilitation to wean him off heroin, it seems a bizarre and macabre way, on the part of his girlfriend and so-called intimate friends and colleagues, to spend an evening with him. Instead, it would have been an act of compassion if you had joined the others to complete his total ostracism, eliminating him from the guests and hostess. This might have encouraged him to accept that he was a stupid shit for getting himself into his present state. Maybe that would have had a better chance to help him to help himself on the road to recovery.

Perhaps he sensed the overwhelming pity and this led him to despair and eventually commit suicide!

My purpose in writing has been an attempt to clarify my own thoughts. Unfortunately, I don't think it has helped to clarify a thing!

Easter Holiday, 1976

A week before the Bank Holiday, I yearned to be somewhere in the country or by the sea and called my friends Raymond Maggar and Mimi for ideas. They said they were going to Scotland to a place called Inverlocky Castle where they had reserved a suite for themselves and Mimi's thirteen-year-old son Christopher. They invited me to join them, and a phone call to the hotel confirmed I could be 'squeezed in'.

The following Friday afternoon, we set off to Heathrow. I couldn't believe it would take one hour fifty minutes to fly from London to Inverness until we walked along the concourse and all became apparent: our plane on the tarmac was the small one with propellers. Two hours later we landed at Inverness, collected a Godfrey Davis car and drove the seventy-odd miles along Loch Ness to Fort William. The evening light was still bright enough to enjoy the serene, beautiful scenery until a young stag suddenly leapt out of the hedgerows and collided with our car, leaving it slightly grazed.

We arrived at 9.15pm. Inverlocky is not a castle with fortified battlements – the ruins of the original castle rested close by. The hotel was built by a Lord Abinger about 100 years ago in the gaunt mock-Tudor Gothic style well-favoured in the Victorian era. (Queen Victoria did actually stay there and a short footpath is named Queen Victoria's Walk.)

A team comprising a husband and wife, their son and his wife, together with thirty staff, ran the hotel for a maximum of just twenty guests (a nice ratio). The son apologetically explained, in a liltingly soft Scottish accent, that as dinner had already been served, perhaps we would like a snack in our rooms. He suggested a smoked salmon omelette and a bottle of his special Chablis. Our disappointment at having missed dinner evaporated when they brought the 'snack' to the suite: it was a private banquet.

Relaxed after such a delicious supper, we studied the breakfast order form. The choice was extraordinary. Next morning, four waiters (one for each of us) wheeled in trays of hot fresh food served on white bone china. After breakfast, we discreetly explored the library and lounges, each of which had magnificent views over Ben Nevis, the lake, the fawns leisurely grazing in the fields, and the more formal gardens of pink, copper-green and blue rhododendron bushes. A tame peacock continually displayed a fan of feathers as if trained to pose for the guests.

The owner's son greeted us with, "Good Morning, I hope you had a pleasant night. Now, if you don't mind, because we don't have a menu as such, I would like to tell you what the cook has suggested for dinner tonight. We can start with a salmon mousse and caviar, and then a beef Wellington. Of course, if you want something else we can arrange other choices."

We looked at each other and couldn't think of anything better than the cook's suggestions.

"Now, Sir, perhaps you'd like to choose some wines and we can open them an hour or so beforehand."

He added that lunch was not a set meal but we could order sandwiches or whatever, to take with us for the day's trip.

We returned from the easy drive through the remote countryside in good time to be dressed and ready for the eight o'clock dinner. We sat at one of the six richly polished mahogany tables with silver cutlery, candles and the usual hunting lodge decoration of silver partridge and pheasants. Dinner was delicious and immaculately served. After coffee, the son suggested that for tomorrow's dinner there was Scotch poached salmon or fillet steak, home-grown fruit and vegetables, and other delectable delights. Even the desserts were the sort only found in the best French restaurants. We ventured to ask where the cook had come from.

"Ah, well, she's from the Outer Hebrides. We really don't know what we'd do without Annie."

This fine-quality, simple cooking demanded long walks through the glens and gorges around the Castle and Fort William to prepare for the next feast.

On the Saturday, after a tiring day in the glens (plus the champagne and claret), the subject of pills did not spring to mind, but on Sunday, both Raymond and I felt a mild anxiety about the return journey. I had packed three sleeping pills to ensure I would sleep well each night in a strange bed. (It is odd now to think back to a time forty years ago when taking sleeping pills was considered to be a normal and usual occurrence.) Raymond, thinking he would be relaxed away from the pressures of London, had purposely left his pills at home. I'd popped one of mine on the first night, and Raymond had 'borrowed' the second. Sunday afternoon's thoughts turned to the next day's long drive back to Inverness and the flight back to London. I told Raymond I had just the one pill left. We agreed to play a sort of triathlon of three games – tennis, backgammon and snooker – the winner of which would get the pill as prize.

We quickly changed into tennis kit in order to catch the last of the evening light and dashed down Queen Victoria's Walk to the court. I was losing when mosquitoes stopped play. Before dinner, the best of five games of backgammon began. Two or three American guests, witnessing the vicious slamming down of counters and the heavy breathing into the dice for luck, sipped their aperitifs and politely asked how big were the cash stakes? They looked distinctly puzzled when we told them the prize was my last sleeping pill.

After dinner, the final score would be decided on the snooker table. Our audience, having to watch such poor play, soon lost interest and the game dragged on towards a tedious end. I tried to summon up my inner strength and the Zen Buddhist bit about willing the arrow to the last black ball target. Eventually, the last ball was potted. I had won.

Exhausted, we waved to the night porter and climbed the dimly lit stairs. I stumbled into bed and forgot to take the pill. I slept so well that I didn't wake up in time for breakfast. The son told us that some of the guests were curious to know the result: perhaps some had made a wager on the winner?

At our point of departure, the son discreetly handed us our list of wines and services in a small envelope, which we could check against the invoice once we'd received it in the post. Everything, even the presentation of the bill, was gracious, cool and smooth at Inverlocky Castle.

III

Blank Verse

Butterfly

I was sixteen years old when I read Clive Bell's *Civilisation*. In essence, his view was that a truly 'civilised' person would never be shocked, particularly by someone else's – or indeed their own – sexual or moral behaviour. Its impact led me to scrutinise strangers in the street or on the trolley bus and pigeonhole them into categories: *civilised* possibles, probables, or non-starters. I thought that making these classifications according to Clive Bell's ideas was perfectly acceptable, without having any understanding that what I was doing was so *uncivilised*.

Either consciously or subconsciously we categorise people into those we either 'like' or 'don't like', leaving the 'don't knows' open to question. We may be persuaded to give them the benefit of the doubt if a 'don't know' person is liked by a certain group or if they have achieved something particular, or if a mutual friend suggests that 'once you get to know him...' To be generous and open-minded is, apparently, a very civilised thing to be, and so our judgement is held in abeyance temporarily while we continue to look for the smallest signs, until the point where we are convinced that our original view is confirmed, and then a 'don't know' becomes a 'don't like'. It is like being introduced to someone who is 'very funny and amusing'. The first thing you want to say is: "Go on then, make me laugh," staring at him all the while with a menacing look, having predetermined that absolutely nothing this chap could say would ever make me laugh.

A degree of maturity has moved me on to acknowledging 'butterfly' people instead of looking out for 'civilised' persons. Also, I am beginning to understand the extreme difficulties of classifying any species, especially 'butterfly people'. My interest in butterflies really began in the Amazon jungle where the birds, animals, insects and vegetation are equipped for attack and defence. The exception is the butterfly: with its brightly coloured, non-camouflaged wingspans of up to twenty-five centimetres, it simply adorns the foliage, flitting through the air in broad sunlight without armour or protection. A butterfly's distinction and definition is unique because it is not a creature which has been born from an embryo or hatched direct from an egg: it evolves through a metamorphosis – a reincarnation or rebirth – from the caterpillar larva. Once a butterfly, it is totally different to how it started out. Can we become 'butterfly people'?

This analogy between the life cycle of the butterfly and 'becoming' a human being seemed extremely pertinent. First, the butterfly searches the underside of leaves where it lays eggs, thus providing protection for the embryos and foliage for food when the larvae emerge. Nature and the natural habitat determine when the caterpillar emerges from its egg. It is born with a soft skin and organs that swirl within its body, and it proceeds to devour the vegetation within its limited range. No other plant will do, and it will continue to look for it, to the point of starvation and death, rather than eat an alternative, equally edible foodstuff. To satisfy its voracious eating habits, a caterpillar will hang tenaciously on to a leaf with its front claspers, leaving its hind legs holding on firmly to another piece of foliage, grasping to the extent that it will pull itself apart rather than 'live and let go'.

Caterpillars' slow pace leaves them vulnerable to predators and parasite insects. The horsefly injects its eggs into the body of a caterpillar and as they mature the larvae gradually eat away their host's innards leaving the vital organs until last. The caterpillar stays 'alive' until only the head and outer skin remains. Other parasites burrow through the skin and devour the larvae in the same way. It seems that the only 'good' parasites are ants which feed off a caterpillar's secreted nectar and fight off other predators.

The caterpillar depends on its hairy body emitting pungent smells, as well as its camouflage, to stay alive in its struggle for survival. As it grows bigger it must make ever more strenuous efforts to stretch out of its old skin to continue its life cycle until, after the fifth shedding, it spins a silk-like secretion that seals its mouth and anus, and weaves a chrysalis cocoon around itself that ultimately causes its own 'death'.

Again, nature and the natural environment determine when the next metamorphosis will transform the body of this destructive, crawling, grasping, squelching tube of matter into a butterfly with its beautiful patterns of colour, flying and floating on the eddies of a breeze in the sunlight, in and around the trees, never nocturnally elusive. It neither bites, stings, carries disease, nor destroys crops. It simply feeds on nectar, tasting with its proboscis and the tips of its feet to enhance sensitivity. Its brilliant colour is a defence mechanism (the big eye-like patterns frighten away enemies); it can also emit a smell which is obnoxious or poisonous to predators. Weaker species of butterfly that do not possess defences such as smell or poison, strangely, can mimic the colours and characteristics of their predators. All the variations of colour on butterflies come from the structure of the minute diaphanous scales on the wings that reflect light; the colour is integral to their being and not a pigmentation of a coloured powder. Entomologists often find it difficult with many species to distinguish between males and females because of the similarity of behaviour and characteristics. Some migrate prodigious distances to other continents.

Are there butterfly people who give pleasure simply by 'being': who have no fear of displaying their natural and beautiful nature; who can fly and float in the sunlight without destroying or polluting; who use every sensitivity they have in their bodies to 'taste' what is offered and, like butterflies, are able to 'see' the colour of flowers in ultraviolet light? Perhaps a butterfly's relatively short lifespan might discourage a person in their desire for transformation to become a 'butterfly person'. Would it be worth the effort to try to emulate such a metamorphosis? The lifespan of a butterfly is about twenty-five or thirty days, which can be thought of as either the twinkling of a moment or an eternal eon – it is all relative.

Butterfly people have no need to celebrate – already they just 'are' and exist simply 'to be'. The previous 'caterpillar' existence is of little consequence once they have recognised an inner core that wants to become a butterfly. The opportunity exists for us all, but in order to emerge from such a traumatic transformation the caterpillar has to fight and struggle to be free, and discover from within itself the mystical thread of fine silk that is the beginning of its own evolution.

Lepidoptera: The Life Cycle of a Butterfly

And so...
Bursting brimming full, still searching...
Anxious and breathing shortly to placate pressure
Not to be forced to lay under a lesser leaf
She, at last exudes with relief, this is where she will release the seed.
Here is the finest to touch, smell and feel
And, still laden, she balances firmly and bends under
The precipice and with compassion and love, carefully plants her egg.

And now...
She can make her last flight and as she floats up
The depth of her being knows all is well chosen
And senses that her close demise will have meaning
For here, under this leaf, has been left her extension into eternity.

And so...
I emerge.
But this undulating boneless tube is heavy
It cannot manoeuvre.
There are only shades of darkness
My being is centred in my brain,
Slowly I grasp and search for food without
The coordination, to connect with my jaws.
Hiding in fear, too slow to turn to resist even one attack
Lurking and merging into the shades and shadows
And for ever dragging up this sack of matter, stuffing and stuffing.

And so...
I sense a constriction, my skin is a tightening band...
Stop... Stop...
I must burst out...I can feel a lower layer...
I must push and break out
I am emerging again – the brittle carcass is broken.

And so...
What has emerged?
A new body?

A new mind?
A deeper consciousness?
Or just the sameness enlarged?

And so...
It seemed endless.
I devour, burst and devour again
But each bursting out strips more than a layer of dead flesh.
Somewhere in my depths stirred my real being
Not a mythical parasite but ME...
My purpose, my knowing, my reason for survival,
The release from casting off those skins,
Almost expending my total life force to exude...
This was with purpose.

And so...
A gradual awareness of the trace of my being
Could be found from the silken thread within me,
Finely linking me to my deepest recesses,
Which had to be extruded and expelled
To wrap myself with my own essence to understand
That, although this may seem like death
There will still be the gentle breathing out of the gasses of this existence
And project me to the next.

And so...
Spinning out the last threads of this cocoon
Can there be an alternative?
I know that to span this silken shroud
To my real being, the past will be beyond memory,
Life will be for each moment,
Consciousness will not contemplate the past nor the beyond,
And that all is inevitable.

And so...
I pause before the final encapsulating seals.
Is there, within me, a capability to live again?
To be beautiful?
To fly and float in a new warm light?

To see all in multi-dimensions?
To feel and sense with every part of my existence
And drink from the sweetest blooms?

And so...
Each breath is shorter...
Will there be strength to pull that last length of thread
To complete the envelopment of my whole being.
The drawing from the deepest and full length of silk
Is vital to my metamorphosis.
Yes... Now, I am within myself.

And so...
Breathing...has almost...ceased.

And so...
What...of these imaginings?
...As the darkness becomes darker
...I am becoming...can be...
...It is elusive...but, a fleeting glimpse...
...My own compulsion has forced this moment...
...This is not death...

And so...
All is slower.
...I gradually desist and end this existence...

And...so...
Waking...I pause...I am.
I have tensile sinews
I float within the sunlight, fragrance and colour.

I am

I Am

I AM

IMAGO

Reflections

Reflections reverse reality
They blind our sense to see and so...
Why stare into the mirror?
It is not even as others see you
And you obscure them from seeing me.
You peer and admire in wonder
At the reflections of a mountain seen
In the glass lake of inland waters
But the blinding glistening glitter
Obscures the essence of the depths
And optical tricks diminish
The inner mound of the mountain.
That mass of slabbed strata
Logging layers of timelessness,
The untouched seams of riches
And the uncovered caverns within
Need a different light to be seen.
Enjoy the mirrored reflections
But see the reality and
The separateness of being
Which is integrated only by the single simplicity of the universe.

And now, through that mirror
You stare at me again,
Hoping to perceive your soul in perspective
And then move near to scrutinise
But the image is not imprinted and beware,
Too close and the surface will shatter
And like Narcissus you will be devoured
By an illusion which resembles not that which you seek.
Stop searching in reflections
But stand still, where you are and
Now, will me closer to you and through that mirror pass
Effacing all my reflections from that deceptive glass.
And as you draw me through, turn me full about
Making my left eye see through your left
And make my right eye see likewise.

Body and soul have vision only through
The same sided eyes.
Merging is our reality of oneness
Reversed illusions are gone.
Now, one body and soul, floating in eternal consciousness.

23rd June, 1976

Soul Mates

The essence of the thoughts, textures and colours of my being
Are like the thread of a helix holding the ranging, rhythmic wave bands
Like the unseen undulating core of the cosmos
The pitches of peaks and troughs are pulled together
Moving through time and space
Nudging and touching the orbit of others,
Connecting where outer wave lengths coincide.
But that spiritual specialty occurs only when the separate threads of
    another
Become entwined to form a helical twin,
Pulsating together in a rhythm triggered by telepathic prompting
Is such a possibility even beyond romantic fancy?
Can such conjunctions occur or is it only the deep inner self balance
And readiness which permits such uniqueness to be conjoined?
Without receptivity one could meander through a lifetime
And never, still meet a soul mate.
Aggressive anxious searching will not suffice.
'Twould be tragic to meander, meet a mate but lack the perception
To recognise that such an eternal moment had passed
Then how can one interlace with this elusive separate being
And how will this harmonious helical structure
Herald its presence?
Perhaps the waves will not immediately spiral upwards
But first lie on a more level plane
Like the long gentleness of an oncoming tide over washing
Then seeping through the sand.
So one may sense the gathering pulsations of that other being
Flowing over the mind
Gradually the in-time rhythms of wave bands
Join two threads and become entwined.

Date unknown

Man

Men...from teenage to eighty
Spend most of their adult life
Choosing girls from the screen or a blue magazine
In search for a perfect wife.

Men...long for the *ideal* woman
With poise and serenity
With grace wit and charms – no hair under arms
Who never get PMT.

Men...want a whore but a princess
One who's artistic, psychic and bright
Who dresses to kill – undresses to thrill
Who's dying to screw morning 'til night.

Men...want a sexual gold medallist
Who's extremely athletic in bed
So their sex life could be like a porno movie
Then turn over asleep – as if dead.

Men...feel terribly cheated
They think it's grossly unfair
When they finally find – they're not even blind
That we're blond yet brunette down there.

Men...don't want real, live women
Who occasionally scream and fight
Who sometimes get broody and cry when they're moody
When thighs hang with cellulite.

Men...we must always be ready and willing
To swoon with a baby doll pout
To be sensual, erotic – but never neurotic
And headaches are definitely out.

Men...want to be cared for,
A nurse – tender hearted and kind

A muse, lover, tomboy brother – a mother
Who comforts and says "Ah, never mind."

Men...we must always be even tempered
To smile and laugh at their jokes
If they say something lewd – we must never be prude
But swear back like one of the blokes.

Men...don't want a normal woman
They want someone made up of bits:
Claudia's legs, Lisa's thighs, Sheila's lips and Gina's eyes,
A tight bum and very large tits.

Men...crave for our protection
From being classed as a wimp
Because they dress up in our frocks or stand nude 'cept for their socks
And it's not just their wrist that goes limp.

Men...we must be romantic and female
With a passion for sex and sex toys
Be a wine connoisseur, gourmet cook á flambé
And drink booze like one of the boys.

Men...when you plough through our perfumed garden
And almost finished before you've begun
Hanging in limbo, we're supposed to be grateful
And thank you for what you've just done.

Men...who search for the angelic woman
A young virgin who's beautiful, rich
Beware – she could turn out to be rigid, probably frigid
...A spoilt untouchable bitch.

Date unknown

Conversations

Introduction

He is on a long business trip. He calls his wife every night and they
have the same conversation. Neither can express their innermost
feelings. He longs to be with her, to hold, stroke, touch and feel her,
to see her, talk and walk with her. Why does he not say how he feels?

Conventional conversations... Unexpressed

> They have passed through, that traumatic pain of
> parting
> When at some moment before the second of severance
> They suppress to sub-consciousness their life as lovers
> And then are able to separate as almost strangers
> They continue these conventions to ease the ache of
> absence.

Hello darling...and how are you?
They've taken hours to put me through

> But when time and distance creates this crevasse
> What mode of speech has been established to
> conceal thoughts which are real?

The weather? Very hot today.
This line is bad...what did you say?

> The sun is not an adversary to lovers
> The warmth ripens their skin with a sweet smelling
> fragrance
> Which bears whispered thoughts, inaudible to
> others,
> As, together, they only want to speak with intimate
> quietness.

I'm taking too much food, too much wine
Otherwise I'm feeling fine
But exercising to compensate –
Afraid of getting overweight.

Only the taste of sips between parted lips can satisfy
their thirst
When they can retune the tone of passionate love-
rhythms.

Me? Tonight – nothing stunning
Ran a bath – Christ, it's still running.
Just a minute, don't go away
Hello: hello. What did you say?

And then, while bathing in the innermost essence of
each other,
Anointing themselves with the fluid fragrance of
love
needed to glide in that integrated penetration of one
being.

You're feeling what?…tired and low
The time I'm when?… I'll let you know.

Thus vibrate and energise when fatigue
is melted away by nature's soothing balm.
But immediately they must remain suspended in an
eternal stop.

As soon as all is finished here
(At this rate it will be next year).
Hell, hello...I thought you'd gone
Next month I'll know which flight I'm on.

Love you, darling – are you all right?
Do take care – big kiss – goodnight.

> And now they can only muse upon the moments of
> last lingering
> Memories to avert loneliness by soliciting solitude.
>
> Date unknown (probably 1980s).[3]

---

3 When making transatlantic sea crossings, in the days before international mobile
phone calls and internet emails, you had to make a radio-telephone call to Portishead, in
the UK, to book a place in the queue. You then had to keep the radiophone's loudspeaker
on all the time until Portishead told you that your line was connected. While waiting
your turn, you could not avoid having to listen in on other people's conversations. Other
than a merchant ship's captain's business calls requesting instructions, there were the
weekly calls allowed to the officers to talk to their family onshore, as well as calls made
by 'yachties' like me.
Most of the conversations between an officer and his wife were rather strained and often
repeated what had been said only a few moments before because, it seemed, neither party
wanted to be the one to end the call.
The expansion of satellite communications forced Portishead radio-telephone services to
close in 2001.

IV

Additional Notes

Chapter 1

Father's Family

My grandparents, Tom and Charlotte, had five sons and two daughters. In peace time, when he was not in the Boar War and the First World War, Granddad Tom stoked the boilers at Ilford Films Limited. With the exception of their eldest son Tom and daughter Nancy, all their other sons, as well as their eldest daughter Cissy and most of their male grandchildren, worked in either the Borough, Spitalfields or Covent Garden markets. My parents, and all Father's siblings with their families, lived within a couple of miles of my grandparents' home in Ilford until my then widowed grandma died soon after the end of the war. The Saunders family then dispersed to other parts of East London and the Thames estuary.

My father's eldest brother Tom, a well-built man like my grandfather, was married to Flo (Florence), who was thin, poorly, unkempt, and in a permanent state of agitation and unhappiness. They had one daughter, Doreen. Apart from serving in the First World War, all his working life was spent as a packer at Ilford Films Limited. On Doreen's wedding day, immediately after the formal reception, he picked up a packed suitcase, said goodbye to everyone and walked out to live happily with a very homely woman he had worked with for many years.

Albert – always known as 'Sid' – was married to another Florence, called Florrie, who had nicotine-stained fingers and a smoke-tinged upper lip. Their children were Phyllis, twins Lenny and Queeny, and a younger daughter, Marie. I loved going to Sid's house – it was always filled with laughter and fun. Lenny's marriage to Vera was a fraught affair that eventually ended in divorce. Queeny married Leonard-

Henry, who was as fun-loving as Sid, and Marie married Victor, her second cousin. My sister June had a crush on his elder brother Ronnie, a RAF pilot who was killed in the war. Phyllis and her husband emigrated to Australia.

Cissy, Father's eldest sister, was a sporty type: she and her husband Oswald frequently rode their tandem bike from London to Canvey Island in the Thames estuary to their boat. They had one son, Peter.

Nancy, Father's younger sister, married George Martin – a hairdresser. My mother insisted my hair was cut every fortnight by Uncle George, whose hand-clippers painfully tugged the hairs on the back of my neck. They had one son, Colin.

Billy, Father's younger brother, was nicknamed Bertie, after the song *Burlington Bertie*, because he was a smart dresser in sharp suits and spats, and carried a black Fred Astaire walking cane. He and his wife Daisy had a daughter, Jean. Billy was the ambitious one of the family who became a director of the wholesale firm W Bruce in Spitalfields market. Just as the war ended he took me in his Rover car to Grimsby to see the fish cold-store warehouses which led to his starting up a frozen food business in London.

Teddy, Father's youngest sibling, married Flossy. They had four children: Pat, Kenny, Malcolm and Janice. After the war, Teddy and Flossy moved out to Essex where their immediate family followed a similar East End pattern in which all their children, grandchildren and great-grandchildren still live in close proximity to each other. There are about thirty in the immediate family, all of whom remain a close unit, even after the demise of Teddy, Flossy, Kenny and Malcolm. These are the only members of the Saunders family I have stayed in contact with over the years and love being in their company.

My father Josiah (Joe) married my mother Frances (another Cissy).

My sister June married Russi.

June and Russi's daughter Dinaz married Hoshang. They have two sons, Eruch and Rustum.

I was Joe and Cissy's only son. I married Betty: we had two sons, Mark and Christopher. Mark married Ilga and they have two sons, Leon and Teo. Christopher married Christa who has two daughters from previous relationships.

Betty and I divorced and I am now married to Janet who has two sons, Robert and Alex, from her previous marriage.

Chapter 4

Mark

In 1992, Janet and I had lived together for about ten years in Northwood Hall in Highgate. We rarely saw Mark and his live-in girlfriend Siobhan because they were in a state of constant unpleasant conflict. Their 'relationship' came to an end a year or two later, then along came Natallia who transformed the household. Peace and calm prevailed for a while until their son Leon was born in 1996.

Before he was born, we already knew he would have a cleft palate and would need a series of operations that would continue until his mid-teens. This knowledge compounded Mark and Natallia's distraught despondency.

After their relationship had gone sour, Mark's arguments with Natallia over access and money continued for many years. Leon suffered the operations with great courage and is a 'knowing' boy who will benefit from his ordeals.

Janet could not have given Mark and Natallia more care and comfort, nor could she have given more love and tenderness to Leon. Two years later, for the baby's benefit and the sanity of both parents, all Janet and I could do was to help the pair come to terms with an inevitable split. With great sadness, we went with Natallia and Leon to a park to say goodbye before they left to go back to her home in Greece. We took turns to cuddle him for as long as we could, knowing we would not see him again for many years. I am sure Natalia's extended family in Greece gave Leon the love and kindness he needed and deserved.

Mark then met Ilga from Montreal, who was born in Latvia and became a naturalised Canadian. They married in Chelsea Registry Office and their son Teo was born in 2008. Ilga is a gifted artist and supplements their joint income with her life drawing classes at various architects' offices (including my ex-practice). In 2011, they rented out Mark's two-bed flat in Battersea and bought a large four-storey house in Peckham. The extensive renovation works to rectify the derelict state of the building added to the seemingly continuous sense of conflict in Mark's life but once they began living in the house things settled down, and it is pleasing and comforting to know that Mark, Ilga and Teo are leading a happy and enjoyable family life with good neighbours.

Christopher

About the time when Natalia and Leon had departed for Greece, Christopher introduced us to Christa, a British national of Caribbean parentage, who was totally unlike his previous girlfriends: she was elegant, well-dressed, made-up and clearly knew how to look after herself. She had a regular job and lived in a council house in Wembley. Although she had never married, she had two daughters, one of whom was fathered by a fellow Caribbean, the other by an Anglo-Chinese.

They were married in 1998. Christopher's idea was to arrange a ceremony at the Roll Right Stones in Oxfordshire – a special Pagan sacred site – and get 'a spiritual person' to give a blessing and pronounce them husband and wife. I told him it was a nice idea which should take place *after* he had been legally married. On their wedding day, Janet drove to Wembley to cook an English breakfast for Christa's kids, her sister and other house guests, before dashing back to Highgate to get ready herself. We dressed the car with white ribbons, and stacked glasses and a couple of bottles of champagne in the boot for after the ceremony and arrived back at Wembley to pick up the bride.

While they were on honeymoon in India, Janet and I took care of her two daughters, the eldest of whom became ill in the three weeks they were away, needing Janet to take her to hospital and various visits to the local doctor. When the couple returned to London we saw very little of them and their visits became even less frequent. Then, one afternoon three years after their wedding, when Janet was ill with cancer and I was recovering from having a cartilage operation, the doorbell rang. Janet was teaching in the sitting room and I was upstairs asleep. She opened the door and was surprised to see Christopher and Christa. She invited them in, and told them she would be with them in ten minutes, as soon as she had finished teaching. She suggested that they go into the kitchen and make themselves a drink; she could hear that I had woken up and no doubt would be downstairs shortly. But in the short time before I came downstairs and Janet finished teaching they had left.

Without any indication or prior warning, they severed all links with the family – Janet and myself, Christopher's mother Betty, Mark, and all the relatives in India. Even Christopher's friends were cut off. Apparently, Christa had a habit of cutting off all communication with her friends and family for long periods and, clearly, it suited Christopher to do likewise. Undoubtedly, Betty has suffered the greatest distress of all. We still have no idea why they suddenly disappeared from our lives. Their whereabouts remained a mystery until 2009 when, by chance, we discovered where Christopher and Christa were living, which was about two miles from where Janet and I used to live in Highgate. It was comforting for all of us to know that he appeared to be in good health, happy and contented, and that, at last, he had a 'proper job'.

Christopher's absence has caused sadness, stress and anxiety to everyone in the family, including those in India. In hindsight, I suppose we should not be surprised that both he and Christa have severed all communication with us – it is history repeating itself.

Chapter 7

Venezuela
Venezuela has immense natural resources – petroleum, gas, iron, gold, diamonds and other minerals which attracted foreign investors. Caracas Airport is at sea level and the City of Caracas, on a plateau about 800 metres above, is thirty-two kilometres (twenty miles) away. All traffic had to use the main route through a long tunnel. Accidents and breakdowns often caused chaos and delays. A giant American civil engineering firm made an offer to the Venezuelan government to build a second tunnel at zero cost provided they could keep whatever minerals they excavated during the construction. The government declined the offer!

Venezuela was also blessed with two other great natural resources, the Rio Orinoco and its main tributary, the Rio Caroni. In 1980, one of our American bank clients introduced us to a Venezuelan property developer they were funding to build a new town satellite to the city of Ciudad Bolivar close to the Rio Caroni. This river already had a number of hydroelectric dams and the intention was to build yet another further downriver where the government wanted the new town and were offering to sell the huge site for the equivalent of peanuts per hectare.

Prospecting in the Middle East
During the several years of prospecting, I made friends and connections with business people who helped to take the struggle out of 'local difficulties', but taxi life was always a strain, especially the ceaseless and senseless hooting of horns, which was done in much the same way as the drivers fingered worry beads. It was impossible to take a quiet stroll at any time of day along the main streets of Beirut: the

taxi drivers cruised alongside every pedestrian, tooting their horn for business. It was beyond their understanding that anyone would want to go for a walk. In Iran, taxi rides were frightening: everyone drove their Mercedes like fairground dodgem cars and at any time of the day, along any two-kilometre stretch of road in Teheran, there would be at least five major accidents.

In Cairo there was no real public transport and, as with most of the Middle East, the taxi is the only form of transport for non-car owners. As there was always a shortage, taxis would take any passengers who were going in their general direction. Standing off the curb on a busy street yelling out my own destination (most times finding pronunciations somewhat difficult) could be hazardous, and was most unbecoming to an English gentleman architect. Forty-five minutes had to be added to the journey time to allow for the driver and everyone else in the vicinity to run around making frantic enquiries with shopkeepers and passers-by, attempting to find a particular business address. The street names were frequently changed, mainly because they honoured the groups of government officials of the day who were in favour at that moment. Each district liked to pay similar homage and sometimes, the driver found the right street name in the wrong area. Meetings and appointments were often missed.

At least in Egypt the taxis do have meters, the fares are cheap and the driver expects a tip. Elsewhere, it can be guaranteed that at the end of each journey, especially in Saudi and the Gulf States, there will be an argument over the price. The rule is to get the luggage out first, then ask the price and offer a third. You will end up paying two-thirds, provided you look big and can shout.

In Saudi Arabia, there was no liquor officially (neither public nor private), no cinemas, discos or theatres, and on TV, sixty per cent was devoted to religious matters, thirty per cent to news, and the rest seemed to be British soccer and bad American 'B' movies. Unofficially, of course, some of the wealthy (the majority) and the influential people, such as princes, did have caches of booze, as well as a vast collection of video tapes (*Deep Throat* and the like were quite popular at the time). Out in the desert, their secluded houses had a swimming pool and a few non-Saudi women for their further entertainment.

Their own women were, and still are, kept completely out of sight. Occasionally, they could be seen, covered from head to toe in a black veil, being driven around (they are still not allowed to drive themselves). Underneath the opaque *niqab* (so I am told) they wear the latest Ted Lapidus, Yves St Laurent, Valentino, and so on, bought from London and Paris.

Are all Arabs inherently indecisive? Were they all born under the sun sign of Libra? I have sweated days before departure, and right up to the last few hours before my flight time, fretting about whether my confirmed booking would hold good, only to find the plane was less than half full. Maybe the ticket agents created an artificial shortage so that they could take 'fix-it' money for getting you aboard, but most likely, the reason must have been that travellers who wanted to go from A to B for business but because they couldn't make up their mind which day of the week to go, they would instruct their menservants (slaves) to book a ticket for every day for that week!

(While I was writing this diary note at the airport at 11.30pm, a prince – there are so many members of the Royal Household – still hadn't turned up. The flight was overdue by one hour already, and I would not be in Riyadh before morning.)

Flight delays were often due to other local dignitaries needing to commandeer planes, usually to nip off to see their girlfriends at short notice. These are the lands of privilege.

Attempting to make telephone calls was also a test of endurance particularly if contact was actually made. At that point, when they said that they would call you back, it was impossible to give them a number because although the dials had numbers in Arabic and English there was no information on the handset that indicated the actual number of your phone. In Egypt there was always a very short length of cord leading from the handset to the telephone which meant that if you were sitting down at a desk, you had to prop up the phone on directories or risk breaking your neck leaning over. Once, having waited for hours for a hoped-for response, I dashed to grab the telephone, yanked up the receiver and the other part swung wildly off the desk and dropped to the floor, leaving me with a telephone to my ear with a short length of wire connected to fresh air.

Saudi telephone systems were rarely automatic. One would have to wait until it pleased the telephone operator to answer. I learned never to express urgency or remonstrate with an operator for fear there would be a reprisal when he would say either that all his lines were busy or that the number I wanted was busy. 'Wait five minutes' was the most dreaded response.

The poor travel and other arrangements I encountered on arrival in Teheran left me in such despair that I unleashed a scathing report to the partners and senior staff:

Our expanding practice in the UK has, so far, come to us from repeat bank and development clients which represent nearly ninety per cent of our workload. As with any business, there is a need to develop new clients to increase that last ten per cent of turnover. I have confidence in prospecting for work abroad but to succeed we must escalate our approach and understand the problems and adapt our business efficiency and quality to be competitive.

Prospecting abroad alone means being one's own secretary, telephone operator, and confidante to combat fierce competition from the locals and foreigners who are backed by their organisations with international reputations and often work in a two or three man team.

Travelling abroad on business is trying and difficult enough in itself. There is the fatigue of actual flying and the time spent getting to and from airports plus the delays usually encountered: the problems of using unfamiliar currency, foreign languages, dealing with taxi drivers and others who are continually trying to screw everything they can out of you. The usual frustrations over communications and the sense of isolation, trying to make the right contacts, learning local customs and regulations for doing business as well as a change of diet, lack of familiar faces, long hours waiting for appointments, time changes and different hotels. In future, travel arrangements and hotel bookings must be done by experienced, responsible people who have ventured further afield than the Isle of Wight.

The hotel bookings were a fiasco. Necessary changes to my dates for arrival in Beirut and Teheran were finalised more than a week before departure: these were not co-ordinated with the bookings at the hotels. I arrived at the Teheran Hilton, where they were overbooked already due to the foreign conferences, when I was told they expected me the following day. Reception suggested an alternative hotel for the one night. I took a taxi there, saw the rooms and walked out in disgust at the appalling dirt and general appearance. I returned to the Hilton and tried to sleep on a hard seat in the reception lounge until 4.30am when they had a room available. I did not need to pay for two expensive taxi fares and an almost sleepless night after an already fatiguing flight from Beirut.

These frustrations were caused through a lack of competence by our own staff who may have had the impression that I had been going to Bognor Regis and Torquay rather than Beirut and Teheran. It was sloppy, inconsiderate and totally out of touch with the realities of being such distances from home with primitive communications and even an attitude that they could not care less.

I cannot express my feelings of anger, frustration and totally unnecessary waste of hours of time and money due to yet another fiasco over the essential documents I needed Tahranchi to sign. The reason the papers had to be sent to me by special air delivery was because they had not been completed in our office before my departure date. Firstly, there are always telex difficulties due to a lack of machines; secondly, the telephone system is also overloaded and it took twelve hours for a free line to London. I eventually received a telex message four days after transmission from London. Urgent cables may only take five hours from time of transmission plus the time it takes the operator to decode the message. Eventually I had the parcel tracking number. (The time difference of three and a half hours only adds to the problem).

Later that afternoon, Iran Airways telephoned me at the hotel (pure chance that I was in my room at the time) to tell me that they had transported the parcel and gave me another code number which was for their records and to collect their authorisation note from their cargo section in the Teheran offices. The following morning (Saturday), I was given a piece of paper to be taken to the airport for customs clearance and collection. At the customs office I had to pass a number of security checks showing passport and documents. In the customs hall, a clerk passed me on to a young man who snatched the piece of paper from my hand and hurried over to another clerk for processing with more pieces of paper with signatures. He then ran out of the Hall to another building to search a cupboard for my parcel. I ran with him as I had no idea who he was or where I would find him again. I discovered the reason for the great rush was that, at 1.30pm everything would close down in the main hall and the clerks would not return until 3.30, which was the time of my meeting with Teheranchi to sign the papers. It will be too lengthy to describe every step I had to take, nor shall I describe the pleading to get, in all, the thirteen people involved in writing down the information in their separate ledgers and then producing counterfoils and carbon copies. I ran from one building to the other, no less than five times, and just before 1.30, the parcel was in my hands and then having to pass through three other checks and signatures before I was allowed through the gate. Without these papers one of my main purposes for visiting Teheran would have been lost.

Now, to return to the Teheranchi presentation: the model, design drawings and perspective were a great success that have enhanced our name and reputation. I was proud and delighted to present the work and I feel confident that good things will flow from this in the future. Also, more positive aspects were that I made inroads with other contacts in Beirut and Teheran.

Having said that, I hope the work on this project will create a fresh appreciation of the priorities and urgency of such projects abroad. There has been an inhibited reluctance to produce concepts for projects due to lack of understanding of the nature of such work, a feeling that it may not be 'real' and a (often justified) sense of inferiority in tackling such projects. Is this due to a lack of experience, talent and ability or a generally pedestrian and insular approach to all things beyond the boundaries of Essex?

Hitherto, the business in the UK has come to us without having to put in too much prospecting effort because we have established reputation for producing efficient work which runs fairly smoothly and is technically and professionally correct and proper. But this is not enough in itself. I get the feeling that our design work becomes routine and lacks direction, flair and innovation. Colour schemes and the use of certain materials are without grammar and many adventurous design opportunities are missed. Often we may be delegating important design concepts to second-rate designers through mediocre leadership.

The oil-rich countries wanting to build prestigious projects will only consider architects with internationally recognised status. Perversely enough, they even boast about the exorbitant costs of engaging the big names and insist the quality design work must be good, adventurous and different without being simply fashionable at any one time.

To compete we must nurture imaginative and creative design concepts especially in the world where they are only after prestigious people and designs which satisfy their egos. There must be an encouragement of design 'flair' and imagination and a division between the design strategists and the technicians. While no organisation needs many strategists, we have too few. Quality and uncomplicated presentations are prestigious and even though the project may not hit the right formula the first time, it is the client's initial reaction which engenders confidence in the ability of the practice.

The method of approach learned on this trip has been invaluable. But now we must return to a speed of reaction and regain the thrusting activities.

On a personal basis I have learned a great deal.

Chapter 9

Parsis

Parsis, who form the mainstay of India's professions and commerce, are outside the so-called caste system, a system often hotly criticised by Westerners. Ubiquitous myths, fairy tales, astrology, the Tarot and the perennial teachings of most, if not all, cultures and traditions relate the human condition to the four archetypal elements of Earth, Water, Air and Fire.

These archetypes correspond to the four types in the caste system: manual labourers, farmers and artisans are the Earth people (*Shudras*); the Water people (*Vaishyas*) are the commercial traders and bankers; the Air people (*Brahmins*) are the priests, philosophers, poets and artists; and the Fire people (*Kshatriyas*) are the kings, warriors and protectors. There is a fifth group, representing the quintessential element of ether: the *Dalits*, otherwise known as the Untouchables or *Harijans* ('children of God'). These people, who do the most menial, dirty jobs, including disposing of the dead, are considered to be outside the caste system, along with foreigners and tribal folk.

Some form of caste segregation or social discrimination is practised in most, if not all, cultures: it is a universal trait. The difference between a rigid caste system and, say, the British class system is that in Britain, someone from a so-called 'lower class' can have aspirations and be able to transfer to a higher class. It is also possible to descend from an upper class to a lower one! While the caste system remains strong in rural parts of India, in more recent times upward social mobility has become more common, and was achieved by a *Dalit* who was elected a chief minister in the government of Uttar Pradesh.

Before criticising the caste system, or indeed the British class system, people from other parts of the world should view their own racial and cultural standards, where they will find strong similarities with those practised elsewhere.

After dark, street people bed down for the night along roads: narrow stretches of pavement lined with a blanket or piece of carpet covering the footpath with little personal things, such as a broken mirror, hung on the railings behind. Whole families stake out a few paving slabs that mark their living and cooking areas, and where they sleep. Here they live, die, make love, give birth and face each new dawn, which may bring torrential rain, fierce heat or extreme cold to challenge their daily lives. I felt an embarrassed intruder whenever I had to walk or drive past these 'homes'.

When Indira Gandhi was in power, every cinema performance showed her giving a twenty-minute talk on birth control. Lining the streets were cartoon posters illustrating a mum, dad and their three kids saying in Hindi that three were enough. Ironically, the only people who could afford to go to the cinema practised some form of contraception and rarely had more than two children in any case.

The rich people's kids around the swimming pools at the exclusive clubs in Bombay were encouraged to be podgy – almost obese – to show off their parents' wealth, in contrast with the malnutrition suffered by the vast majority of the population. Being skinny was not considered to be sexually attractive.

Visitors, or those too afraid to travel to India, tend to focus on the poverty, but once seen, I believe no one escapes having their Western attitudes rewired when they experience first-hand the extraordinary dignity and resilience of the locals, their fortitude and resolve, as well as seeing some of the most beautiful and exquisite art and architecture.

Of course, every visitor to the country flocks to see the Taj Mahal in Agra; Fatehpur Sikri, the deserted 'ghost city', once capital of the Empire, in the state of Uttar Pradesh; and Jaipur, an important thriving city in Rajasthan. The palace hotels are conversions; some were like fairyland buildings which Hollywood and Walt Disney could never have emulated. Such was the Lake Palace Hotel in Udaipur, originally built in the middle of a lake in the early eighteenth century by the ruler to house his harem. The palace was built of white marble inlaid with black and coloured stones; three musicians gently played evening Raga music, and in the various fountain courtyards, gardenias and other exotic, fragrant flowers scented the night air, secluded behind lace-like screens, each pierced from huge slabs of white marble as if they were carefully worked ivories.

Chapter 14

Janet's Family Background

The family seat was Sion Hill, near Thirsk, which was later demolished. The current, rebuilt, Sion Hill was designed in 1913 by the York architect Walter H Brierley, known as 'the Lutyens of the North'.

Colonel Crompton was born at Sion Hill in 1845. At the age of eleven, he became a cadet in the Royal Navy and saw action in the Crimean War (1853–1856), after which he was awarded the Crimean War Medal and Sebastopol Clasp. He later became a scientist and engineer in the mould of the great Victorian and Edwardian industrial pioneers, inventors and explorers. Colonel Fawcett (see Amazon chapter) was one of his contemporaries.

When Crompton was thirty-three years old he set up a lighting business which became Crompton and Company in Chelmsford. He was invited to install the electric lighting in the new State Opera House in Vienna, making it the first theatre in the world to be lit by electricity. He also installed the 'three wire system' in Le Mans, and street lighting in the UK, including Kings Cross railway station, Mansion House in the City, and Windsor Castle. He built power stations in India where he also pioneered steam railway systems in the mainline station in Mumbai where Crompton lighting is still advertised. By 1887, Crompton was supplying electrical goods and installations across the British Empire. (The company was eventually taken over by Cooper Lighting and Security Ltd in 1999.)

V

Relevant Dates

Date	Age	Event
1932	**0**	**Born East End then moved to Ilford**
1939	7	Evacuation to Wales, War declared

The Seven Year *TITCH* – (Adolescence)

1942	**10**	**Moved to Chadwell Heath**
1944	12	Mayfield Secondary Modern School
1946	*14*	*Met Betty, decided to be an architect*

The Seven Year *ITCH* – (Puberty)

1949	17	First year student architect
1951	19	Festival of Britain
1952	**20**	**Moved out of family home**
1953	*21*	*Qualified Intermediate RIBA*

The Seven Year *SWITCH* – (Light up career)

1954	22	Qualified Finals RIBA, Married Betty, Start work Biltons
1955	23	Start work Ley Colbeck & Partners
1956	24	Mark born
1957	25	Qualified Professional Practice exam, Associate RIBA
1957	25	Dad died

1958	26	Christopher born, Start work Sydney Kaye & Partners
1960	*28*	*Start own practice*

The Seven Year *NICHE* – (Start my own practice)

1962	30	*Saturn Return* (Wake-up call and making choices)
1962	**30**	**Moved office to Cranbrook Road**
1967	*35*	*Business expansion, Moved to large house*

The Seven Year *RICH* – (Good business)

1968	36	Elected Fellow RIBA, Moved to Devonshire Row
1972	**40**	**Moved to Old Ford Road**
1972	40	Divorced Betty
1972	40	Set up Paris office
1974	42	*Half Uranus Return* (Rethinking one's life and spiritual work)
1974	*42*	*Trip to the Amazon, Occult explorations*

The Seven Year *WITCH* – (Craft – occult explorations)

1975	43	Sold OFR and TTSP lease back
1976	44	Set up Dubai office
1978	46	Married Mary
1980	48	Bought sailing boat
1981	*49*	*Bought Cheyne Walk, Atlantic crossings*

The Seven Year *DITCH* – (Otherwise known as the Atlantic)

1982	**50**	**Moved to Cheyne Walk**
1982	50	Notice to quit TTSP
1982	50	Divorced Mary
1984	52	Retired TTSP
1985	53	June died
1986	54	Board member City Merchant Developers

1988	**56**	*Hubris, disasterous speculative development*

The Seven Year **GLITCH** – (Bad business)

1991	59	*Saturn Return* (Out of synch with destiny)
1991	58	Met Janet, Leave Cheyne Walk penniless
1992	**60**	**Moved to Highgate with Janet**
1992	60	Started to rebuild practice
1995	*63*	*Mother died, CDM qualification*

The Seven Year *TWITCH* – (Mother died)

1997	65	Married Janet
2002	**70**	*Published The Boiled Frog Syndrome*

The Seven Year *PITCH* – (To publishers for my book)

2002	70	Advanced Certificate in Crime Prevention
2004	72	Elected RIBA Client Design Advisor
2005	73	Associate lecturer University of the Arts London
2006	74	Published EMF paper
2007	75	Published *The Authentic Tarot*
2008	76	Move to France
2009	*77*	*Established in France*

The Seven Year *WHICH* – (Country to live in?)

2011	79	TTSP fifty year anniversary
2012	**80**	**Plan to move back to London**
2013	81	Sold villa in France
2014	82	Moved to Highgate
2015		
2016	**84**	*Uranus Return* (New lifestyle)

NOTES:

Bold dates and text = Ten-year cycles of location moves
Italic dates and text = Seven-year cycles

Lightning Source UK Ltd.
Milton Keynes UK
UKOW04f0051011015

259590UK00001B/16/P